# The Cocktail Seminars

# The Cocktail Seminars

**Brian D. Hoefling**

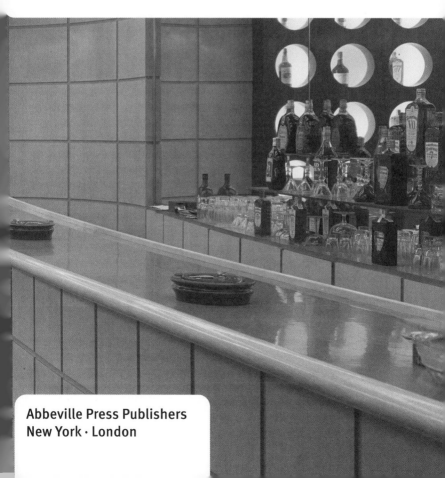

Abbeville Press Publishers
New York · London

# Contents

## A FOURTH COURSE IN COCKTAILS

## Tropical and Tiki

## A FIFTH COURSE IN COCKTAILS

## Topics in Contemporary Mixology

# Introduction

**This** book has been a long time coming. Everything I've ever done in hospitality has, in a way, grown out of a moment during my senior year of college—the kind of life event that feels significant even as it's occurring, but the true, far-reaching importance of which becomes clear only in retrospect.

In the autumn of 2011, several of my friends approached me with a concern: they didn't know how to drink like adults. Graduation loomed, and in a few short months they would be out in the real world, trying to navigate grown-up drinking situations that called for more savvy than they possessed. They knew I had an interest in classic drinks and asked me to help ensure they received this essential component of their education before departing campus for adult life.

They did not know what they were getting into. Rather than give them a page of recipes and send them on their way, I wrote up a syllabus of thirty drinks I felt we all should be able to identify in the wild after graduation. Weekly meetings were scheduled in my suite at which two or three recipes with some common elements could be attempted, tweaked, discussed, and understood. We would talk about their history, read modern commentary, and come to the best recipe we could collectively muster. This was my first cocktail seminar, styled "Mixology 110b" in keeping with Yale's course-numbering practices.

I did not know what I was getting into. Granted, I had a more comprehensive education in classic drinks than the average college senior, but I was ambitious for all of us to learn even more. Many of the drinks on our list were ones I had never made but felt were important to know; the course was a learning exercise for me as well. One of my roommates took to the material particularly strongly, and since the class's "resources" lived with us, we had many opportunities to experiment and practice. He ended up effectively co-teaching the class, which gradually diverged from the syllabus but still provided my friends the mixological crash course they'd been looking for. They would remain on the patrons' side of the bar after graduation, but for me that first cocktail seminar was the spark that began the transformation of my cocktail hobby into something more substantial.

In a sense, I have been chasing the high of Mixology 110b ever since. After graduation, I took my act on the road, offering abbreviated cocktail lessons in homes and businesses for special occasions. This was the beginning of the Herzog Cocktail School. I attended Tales of the Cocktail, the largest of the annual cocktail conferences, for the first time in 2012. After a week in New Orleans immersed in the Cocktail Renaissance at its peak, I was even more hooked than I had been before.

With the aid of some good luck and a talented editor, my nascent writing career and mixological practice coalesced into my first book in 2016: *Distilled Knowledge*, a guide to common scientific questions and misconceptions about alcohol and drinking. Its publication brought me fully into the hospitality industry for the first time. I began giving lectures at conferences instead of just attending them. I found a career in spirits marketing and distribution. I felt as though I had arrived.

Even so, I never lost interest in finding a place to develop a course in cocktails. I had been refining the syllabus for Mixology 110b since the seminar ended, and began to contemplate what 200- and 300-level sequels might look like. Somewhere along the way, it occurred to me that such a class sequence presented in person could still be done by other means: What if all this work on cocktail curricula could be collected for publication? What if I could write a book, rooted in the principles at the heart of my first cocktail course and its imagined successors, with no less a stated aim than to provide the reader with a comprehensive education in the art of mixing drinks, firmly grounding them in the techniques, ingredients, and most essential recipes that constitute the cocktail canon?

This is that book. The culmination of years of education, effort, and contemplation, all with the goal of elevating the popular consciousness about cocktails and bringing the fruits of the Cocktail Renaissance beyond the realm of bartenders and hard-core enthusiasts to the wider world of curious drinkers.

What does that look like in practice? First, this book is geared specifically to nonprofessionals. You will learn how to outfit and use a home bar. You'll get 150 recipes for major and valuable minor classics. And you will gain a theoretical understanding that enables you to make far more drinks than that on your own time.* I am hopeful that many people in the hospitality industry will also find it useful, but that is not its purpose; you will learn nothing in these pages about wash lines, drink pricing, or the management of resources on a commercial scale. Other books do that better than I ever could.†

This book is divided into five seminars, each a self-contained course covering thirty cocktails. I proceed from the assumption that my reader knows nothing about cocktails at the outset and chart a course from there to becoming a respectable generalist; more advanced readers are welcome to skip ahead to the later seminars if they wish. To overextend a metaphor, each of the five seminars can be thought of as corresponding to a stage in a college class sequence, beginning with an introductory 100-level survey and concluding with a 500-level course dealing with advanced current topics.

Each seminar will introduce the reader to new techniques as well as a slate of new ingredients to explore; each will be used at least twice—usually more—to prevent the accumulation of dead weight in your home bar. Of the thirty drinks in each seminar, twenty-seven draw exclusively on that set of ingredients and ones introduced in previous chapters. The remaining three will function as tests of your understanding: two **exercises** will ask you to apply lessons from previous recipes in novel situations, using at least one ingredient that doesn't occur elsewhere in that chapter. Each course will conclude with an **examination**, which takes a similar approach but presents more difficult problems. In later seminars, examinations will look more like **final projects**, requiring the preparation of homemade ingredients before the cocktails can be attempted. While it's possible to use this book as a recipe reference text, you will get the most out of it if you treat it as a curriculum, making and drinking each cocktail as you read about it in

---

* I tested recipes for this book and my previous one, *Classic Cocktails*, until I came to versions I was content to put my name on. There is considerable overlap between the two, but *Classic Cocktails* presents its recipes without theoretical context and most of its simplest ones have been replaced in this book with more advanced drinks.

† If this is your area of interest, start with *Meehan's Bartender Manual*, by Jim Meehan of PDT. It would be my nominee for the Cocktail Renaissance's magnum opus.

succession—and using the assessments to make sure the lessons are sinking in.

Each seminar is also gathered around a theme, representing an aspect of the Cocktail Renaissance that began in the late 1980s and concluded in the mid-2010s. The first seminar focuses on the drinks that survived the Cocktail Dark Ages of the mid-twentieth century and formed the foundation for the later revival. The second highlights ingredients that remained available during that period but were seldom used, and those recipes which have brought them back into circulation. In the third, we encounter ingredients that had ceased to be imported or made, and the cocktails for which a generation of newly educated drinkers yearned until their proper components could be had again. In the fourth, we cover the history and ingredients of tiki cocktails, which could not be revived seriously until hospitality had reestablished itself as a legitimate art form and a respectable profession. Finally, in the fifth, we contemplate the new inventions of the Renaissance era itself and the ingredients they incorporate. Completion of all five seminars will give the cocktail novice some sense of the grand sweep of that Renaissance, although it is worth noting that these themes overlapped considerably in practice.

More to the point, though, completion of all five seminars will provide an extensive understanding of a wide variety of ingredients, preparation techniques, and ways of thinking about cocktails. The historical framing is convenient for breaking this list into manageable chunks—and as a historian, it is to my personal taste—but it is far from the only way of conceiving of these recipes.

Many writers have, for example, theorized that all cocktails can be thought of as variations on some number of essential templates. If that appeals to you, I recommend *Cocktail Codex*, *Regarding Cocktails*, *The Joy of Mixology*, or *The Fine Art of Mixing Drinks*—the original suggested reading for Mixology 110b—for further study.

I happen not to agree with that framing. At its core, the art of making cocktails is the art of augmentation: we begin with a base—normally but not necessarily a distilled spirit—and we incorporate other ingredients to enhance, complicate, or otherwise modify the flavor of that foundation. One can think of it like painting, with a shot of gin or whiskey as the canvas. If we can understand each brushstroke, each discrete elaboration on the base and how they interact, we can understand how the recipe works and why.

In this book I favor this kind of incremental analysis. Each recipe will be accompanied by an eight-spoked wheel representing the ways in which the base is modified by the other ingredients. Each section will correspond to a particular kind of modification and will be shaded to reflect its degree. In particular, I will use this to indicate when the following levers are pulled:

- Sweetening
- Souring
- Aromatizing
- Bittering

- Lengthening
- Aerating
- Thickening
- *Other Techniques*

Each of these first seven metrics affects the drink's balance of smells, tastes, and textural characteristics. The eighth will vary by cocktail as it is called for. Many other things can be done to drinks, most commonly serving them at or above room temperature rather than chilling them, making them salty or savory, or drying them. These are not common enough to get their own octants, but they do happen and will be discussed when relevant.

I will note in passing before we proceed that experienced makers of cocktails may take issue with my notion that every cocktail is an elaboration on a base, on the grounds that there are many cocktails out there that are equal-parts mixtures of assorted things. This is fair to a certain degree: I have presented both the Last Word and the Negroni as gin drinks, for example, even though they contain more of the modifiers than they do of the base. It strikes me as more true to say that in the Negroni, the gin is the thing having its flavor amended with the addition of vermouth and Campari than to try to make a similar claim about either of the other two ingredients. Nevertheless, I recognize that if this is a sticking point for you, my system for analyzing cocktails will not be satisfactory.

To that, I say good. Cocktails *ought* to defy classification. I have set up my method in the belief that most attempts to understand cocktails systematically are overly reductionist, failing to capture either the variety or the specificity of the canon. And I hold to that position far more strongly than I hold to the system presented in this book. If anything,

I am relieved to find imperfections in the latter. It is meant to provide an architecture for understanding, particularly for those who are new to the art or encountering a theoretical approach to the cocktail for the first time. It can be useful without promising absolute clarity.

And I should say in all sincerity, that every rule ever purported about cocktails has been or will be broken—indeed *should* be broken, *must* be broken. We owe David Embury a great debt for publishing the first serious work of mixological theory, but his classification system, under which all cocktails are either "sour" or "aromatic" (and never both!), is one we can safely set aside.* The canon, the art form, and the medium are too vital for such blanket designations.

As we move ahead into the first of these five cocktail seminars, please bear in mind that we will proceed in a manner akin to an introductory physics class, which neglects friction, air resistance, and other obvious everyday phenomena in order to teach the basics in a way that can be understood. We will begin with a set of premises that we will treat as fundamental, and over time we will graduate from this first-order approximation to a more thorough understanding of the art.

This approach is one of several idiosyncrasies particular to the author which have informed this book. While it is inevitable that books reflect the personalities of those who write them—and it is particularly apparent in the case of cocktail guides—it is nevertheless advisable to make the reader aware of them at the outset. A few others that you may wish to keep in mind . . .

I do not use brand names in recipes, except where a particular brand is synonymous with a category (e.g., Bénédictine). Many bartender's guides specify which brand of gin or triple sec to use in a given preparation to enable you to make the drink precisely as it is compounded in that bar. Bully for them. I am approaching this with the expectation that you will use whichever gin or triple sec you happen to already own until the bottle is empty, after which you might—but only *might*— consider trying another brand. To be a classic, a cocktail's recipe must permit such things; a drink which cannot be made to work with spirit brands other than those used at the time of its invention can have no

* Embury is in some respects the Thales of Miletus of the cocktail. He was the first serious theorist in the tradition, and his analyses are invaluable even if we would no longer accept his conclusions. (Thales is best known for the theory that everything in the universe is made of water, Embury for his sour/aromatic dichotomy and the eye-watering dryness of his cocktail recipes.)

hope of surviving for the long term. You can find some brand recommendations on my website (www.herzogcocktailschool.com).

I have also long believed that the essence of a classic drink is not any particular recipe so much as a list of ingredients and characteristics. I regard the recipes here as good, reliable *benchmarks*, but not the only solutions to the problem of making these cocktails well. If, for instance, you would like to mix your Manhattan to be more or less whiskey-forward than I recommend, I have no problem with that. You should always tailor your drinks to the ingredients you have on hand, and to your own tastes or the tastes of the people you're mixing for. Very little is appreciated more than knowing your guests' preferences and mixing drinks to suit them. This is true for professional bartenders and their domestic counterparts alike.

Certainly, there are idiosyncrasies of ingredient selection. I regard raspberry syrup and crème de violette more highly than some others do, while I haven't gone out of my way to find extra recipes for amaretto or blanc vermouth. I am a rum drinker by first preference, I consider apple brandy as woefully underrated, and a quick glance at the list of recipes will tell you how I feel about Bénédictine. I am also biased in favor of cocktails that originated in Boston, which, in addition to being the Hub of the Universe, has been the North Star of my own life. And certainly I have chosen to elevate certain cocktails and exclude others on the basis of my personal preferences—as do all who take on this surprisingly challenging task. But you have my word that I have included each drink in this book in the service of the education I aim to provide, that I have excluded nothing that is essential and included the nonessential only when I felt it had a legitimate place, and that I consider every recipe herein to be a good expression of a cocktail worth knowing and worth drinking.

The sad and beautiful truth is that I could write about cocktails forever. Consideration of the subject raises endless new thoughts and questions, inspires innumerable ideas. But you have come here to learn the concrete art of cocktailery, and I am here to help you do just that. So let us proceed to the foundations of the discipline, and thence to the first lesson.

# Summer Reading
## BASIC EQUIPMENT AND TECHNIQUES

Just as we had to know the alphabet before we learned to write, we need some grasp of the tools and techniques of mixology before we make cocktails. These items will be indispensable to your studies:

- A **jigger measure,** or simply a **jigger,** is a device for measuring the volume of liquids, generally consisting of two small metal cups of different volumes attached to one another at their bases. This device, or another tool for measuring liquid volumes on the order of an ounce, is essential for the preparation of cocktails.

- A **cocktail shaker,** or simply a **shaker,** consists of glass or metal vessels that form a seal for shaking cocktails. The most popular option consists of two metal cups—called **tins**—which fit together and contract when cold to form the seal. This is sometimes called a French or Parisian shaker. A Boston shaker, by contrast, consists of one metal cup and one glass one, often with a rubber gasket connecting them. A cobbler shaker consists of three pieces and includes an integrated cocktail strainer as well as a cap. Cobbler shakers' caps get lost easily and Boston shakers' glass components can break, so I advise the tin-on-tin model. Although, anything that seals can be used as a substitute in a pinch.

- A **barspoon** is a long, slender spoon used for stirring drinks. Most of the time there will be a series of twists in the handle, to make it easier to rotate the spoon between the fingers while stirring and avoid unnecessary turbulence. The bowl of the spoon may measure 1 tsp. (⅙ oz.) or ⅛ oz. depending on the model. Be sure to check before using it to measure.

- A **cocktail strainer,** usually just called a **strainer** in this context, is a perforated piece of metal with a handle, suitable to let liquid ingredients out of a shaker tin or a mixing glass while trapping the ice behind. I recommend the **Hawthorne strainer,** the business end of which is a flat plate with a spring around its perimeter to snare small bits of other solids and form a snug fit with tins of various sizes. The **Julep strainer** uses a scalloped plate with no spring; it looks a touch more elegant and is slightly easier to clean, but it is less practical overall. Certain recipes may also call for a **fine mesh strainer,** to be used in conjunction with the above to catch tiny ice shards, pulp, or particularly small solids.

- A **muddler** is a cylindrical tool used for bruising, pressing, or smashing solid ingredients. It resembles a large pestle and is used the same way. Wooden ones do a nice job, just don't get one that has been *painted*, lest you end up with paint chips in your Old Fashioned. (Best not to ask how I know that.)

- For cocktails requiring the use of citrus, you will want a **juicer** and a **peeler** or **knife.** You have some options here. Electric juicers do a fine job of extracting the juice from the fruit, provided that you can avoid getting too much of the white pith, which can be unpleasantly bitter. The common manual citrus press works just as well and is less of a hassle unless a lot of juicing is to be done. Bartenders are fans of the **Y-peeler** for drinks that use citrus peels, but a decent-quality knife of appropriate size (i.e., no bread knives, cleavers, big chef's knives, etc.) will do the job. It can also do double duty cutting your citrus in half for juicing.

- For cocktails involving crushed ice, you can get an electric ice crusher or use the crushed ice setting on your refrigerator if it has one. The traditional and more enjoyable option is a **mallet** and a **Lewis bag.** The latter is a canvas bag that can be filled with ice and folded over to keep any from escaping. The former is a wooden hammer you use to smash the contents of the bag to the desired consistency. The canvas absorbs any water that melts off the ice in the process to ensure that you end up with crushed ice rather than wet slush.

- A **rocks glass,** sometimes called an **Old Fashioned glass,** is a short, flat-bottomed glass that holds about 10 oz. of liquid, or less with room for ice. A similar glass that holds a few extra ounces may be called a **double Old Fashioned glass.**

■ A **cocktail glass** is a stemmed glass, holding about 5–7 oz. of liquid in a bowl that is more broad than tall. Rounded ones are **coupes,** angular ones are **Martini glasses,** and small ones with an in-between shape are **Nick and Nora glasses.**

■ A **highball glass** is a tall glass with a flat bottom that holds about 8–10 oz., or less with room for ice.

■ A **Collins glass** is a very tall glass with a flat bottom, holding 10–14 oz. in principle but not generally used for any mixed drinks unless they will be served with ice.

The first seminar in this book will cover the basics in some detail, including the following standard preparation techniques:

■ A **built** drink is prepared in the same glass in which it will be served. Ordinarily they are not chilled during preparation, but are served with ice, which melts into the drink over time, chilling and diluting it. Built drinks are usually ones the drinker is meant to sit with for a while, either because of their spirituousness (if they are short) or their volume (if long).

■ A **stirred** drink is prepared in a mixing glass or one piece of a cocktail shaker, by combining its ingredients with ice and stirring with a barspoon for about 10 seconds. The mixture is then strained into the glass in which the drink will be served. Stirred drinks arrive cold but gradually warm to the temperature of their surroundings. As Harry Craddock famously said, a stirred drink is "meant to be drunk quickly, while it's laughing at you."

■ A **shaken** drink is prepared by combining its ingredients in a cocktail shaker with ice, sealing the shaker, and shaking it for 10–12 seconds. The mixture is then strained into the glass in which the drink will be served. Shaken drinks are like stirred drinks in how they're meant to be consumed. The difference in preparation serves to more evenly distribute heavy or granular ingredients that may not dissolve easily; to aerate the mixture, introducing an element of texture; and to chill and dilute the cocktail more than stirring does, because shaking is more efficient at both.

- **Muddling** is breaking down a solid ingredient using a muddler. Put the thing to be muddled into the glass or mixing tin, grip the muddler and press one end of it firmly into the muddlee, twist to grind the ingredient a little bit, then pull up the muddler. Repeat until the desired amount of crushing—or, in the case of sugar, dissolving—is achieved. **Bruising** is a gentler version of this technique, used to break open herbs' or fruits' aromatic glands without actually pulverizing them.

- **Expressing** is a method for extracting a small amount of citrus oil from a peel and adding it to the drink. Cut a piece of the citrus peel a bit larger than a quarter, hold it between two fingers over the drink with the outside pointed at the glass, and then give it a pinch. A fine spray of citrus oil should be released onto the surface of the drink. The peel can then be rubbed around the rim of the glass or dropped in as garnish.

# A Note on Ice

Most cocktails have been served chilled for nearly two hundred years, ever since Frederic Tudor started harvesting lake ice commercially. As this component transforms temperature, it could be considered another playful manipulation of the base ingredient. It counteracts the burning sensation that can come with drinking straight spirits: the cocktail is thus an expression of creativity and a more forgiving drink.

Similarly, cocktails are ordinarily much weaker than their base spirits, due to the addition of nonalcoholic or less alcoholic ingredients—but also due to the ice, which served with the drink or used in its preparation will result in some amount of dilution by melting into it. This is in fact *how* cocktails are chilled: cold meltwater coming off the ice cubes and commingling with the other ingredients cools them down faster than the presence of cold ice alone could do—to the point that a drink can get 10° colder than the ice itself in about 10 seconds.

This brings us to the Fundamental Law of Traditional Cocktails, as defined by contemporary cocktail scientist Dave Arnold: "There is no chilling without dilution, and no dilution without chilling." All drinks prepared or served with ice are subject to Arnold's principle. And our tastes are acclimated to it—we expect cocktails to be colder and less alcoholic than straight spirits, with all the enhancements and suppressions of flavor that go along with that. Cocktail recipes in the post-ice tradition are written with this in mind.

# The Survivors

Allow me to paint a picture for you. The cocktail, a nascent culinary art form being cultivated principally in the United States, has undergone a century or so of growth, experimentation, and evolution. A mixological golden age has arrived, abetted by the development or importation of new ingredients, the popularity of the medium, and the increasing enthusiasm of talented practitioners for writing down their secrets. Cocktails are modern. Cocktails are exciting. Cocktails are progress. Cocktails are America. This is the view from the world inhabited by the bibulous in the cocktail's mother country around the time of World War I.

Simultaneously, though, there was another trend, at least as pervasive and no less American: the temperance movement. For those in the "Dry" community, it was sobriety—voluntary if possible, legislated if necessary—that equaled progress, along with women's rights, the abolition of slavery, and occasionally eugenics, depending on the year. While the cocktailians of the day, to borrow a term from Gary Regan, were busy whipping up elaborate potations and sharing fanciful stories with the press, a social revolution was creeping across the country. State by state, county by county, town by town, laws against alcohol would find their way onto the books of enough jurisdictions to cover most of the land. The "Wets" had lost so slowly and quietly that they hadn't even noticed it until nationwide Prohibition took hold, and they didn't fully believe it even after that—until the arrests began.

In the long arc of American drinking, Prohibition may have ultimately been beneficial by driving out of business the many unscrupulous household chemists who made a living tending bar in the nineteenth century and replacing the proliferate unwholesome saloons of the day with establishments modeled on their upstanding competitors, opening bars to women en masse, and accelerating the global spread of that mixological marvel of the United States: the cocktail. Even so, in the short term it kicked us off a cultural precipice, and it would take decades for American cocktail culture to really recover.

Prohibition was followed by the lean years of the Great Depression and the patriotic rationing of World War II, with the result that a full generation of American drinkers had little exposure to good spirits or well-made cocktails. In any event, the culture of the bar continued to be disrupted. Innovation in the belly of the twentieth century occurred most commonly in the tiki style of drinks, a parallel tradition originating in 1930s California at the height of the nation's desire for escapism. Tiki drinks appeared at tiki bars and gradually followed at assorted tropical resorts; few made the leap into mainstream mixology alongside the Martinis and Sidecars of yesteryear. That canon—the truly classic drinks, that is—ceased to grow in this period. Instead, in the face of a dearth of raw materials and demand, it shrank. It is telling that the most significant cocktail guide of the era was written by a financial attorney rather than a bartender.

There will be more on this in future chapters. For now, suffice it to say that this calcification of the art form also gave us a period of remarkable stability in the canon, filtering out the dross—and some of the gold—but laying the foundations of what would come to be regarded as truly classic. This canon provided the core of the inspiration for the modern Cocktail Renaissance. Any latter-day student of the art must begin here, with the drinks that survived the postwar Cocktail Dark Ages and kick-started the revival. These will be the chief concern of this first lesson, augmented with other drinks that employ the same ingredients and techniques in different combinations. Completion of this course will give you a more rounded and comprehensive understanding of the mixological arts than many—and will be more than sufficient to outfit and make good use of a respectable home bar. Remember, though, that it will not confer mastery. This is only lesson one.

# Ingredients for This Course

## GROCERY

| | |
|---|---|
| Angostura bitters | **2, 6, 12, 13** |
| cocktail onions | **5** |
| ginger syrup/soda | **22, 27** |
| grenadine | **9, 14** |
| honey/honey syrup | **7, 17** |
| lemons | **3, 7–9, 11, 12, 14, 17, 25, 26, 29, 30** |
| light cream/half-and-half | **18, 19** |
| lime cordial | **20** |
| limes | **4, 10, 24, 27, 28** |
| mint | **1, 28** |
| oranges | **13, 14, 16, 23** |
| seltzer | **21, 24–26, 28** |
| sugar/simple syrup | **1–4, 8, 10, 12, 17, 25, 26, 28–30** |
| tomato juice | **30** |
| Worcestershire Sauce | **30** |

## ALCOHOL

| | |
|---|---|
| apple brandy | **9, 15** |
| blended Scotch | **13, 17, 21** |
| bourbon | **1–3, 17, 22** |
| brandy | **8, 11, 15, 19** |
| crème de cacao | **18, 19** |
| crème de menthe | **11, 18** |
| curaçao/triple sec | **8, 10** |
| dry vermouth | **5, 16** |
| filtered lightly aged rum | **4, 28** |
| high-proof rye whiskey | **14** |
| London dry gin | **5, 7, 16, 20, 24–26, 29** |
| rye whiskey | **2, 6, 17** |
| sparkling wine/Champagne | **12, 29** |
| sweet vermouth | **6, 13, 15, 16** |
| tequila | **10** |
| vodka | **23, 27, 30** |

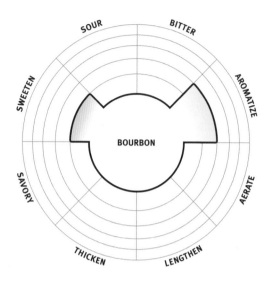

**The origins** of the Mint Julep are lost to time. As is often the case with venerable drinks, its preparation is so simple and harmonious that it has probably existed under one name or another since the first time a single person had access to all its components and has almost certainly been derived independently many times. We do know that it's a creature of the American South, that its name derives in a roundabout way from the Persian word for rose water, and that brandies were favored in the earliest recipes we have before bourbon supplanted them. I lead off with the Mint Julep not only because it is a sort of ur- or proto-cocktail in the historical sense—attested earlier than anything called a *cocktail*—but also because it is fundamental in its construction, being simply a spirit that has been iced, sweetened, and aromatized. These characteristics are common to the vast majority of mixed alcoholic drinks.

Cocktails are after all an art form dedicated to the proposition that nothing is finished just because it comes in a bottle. The maker of cocktails treats the spirit as a starting point, a base upon which to construct some grander edifice of flavor. It is nearly always the case that sweetening is a component of this process. Our palates are primed to respond to sugar, likely for the simple evolutionary reason that it means the food is dense in energy-providing calories; its presence suppresses our perception of sour and bitter tastes, while enhancing

# Mint Julep

2 oz. bourbon

2 tsp. sugar

2 tsp. water

3–4 sprigs of mint

Combine sugar and water in a rocks glass, and stir or crush until they form a syrup (alternatively, replace both with ½ oz. 1:1 simple syrup). Add bourbon and stir to combine. Fill to the brim with ice. Insert a straw and surround it with the sprigs of mint, so that they must be smelled while drinking. If available, use crushed rather than cubed ice and a silver cup rather than a rocks glass; however, neither is required.

our awareness of the aromas of whatever we're consuming. This is an important factor, because "flavor" incorporates both taste and smell, the former enabling us to discriminate among sweet, salty, sour, bitter, and savory, while the latter tells us whether a thing is minty or floral or reminds us of spring rains or Thanksgiving at our grandparents' house. The Mint Julep incorporates the aromas of its eponymous herb, to which the sugar makes us more attentive, into the whiskey. It is a form of ornamentation, or play, an expression of the deep human desire to rearrange the world around us. Because mint is a smell and not a taste, it can become part of the drink's flavor even when it is only used as a garnish, as is the case here. Smack the mint leaves a few times against the back of your hand to release their aromatic oils and arrange them so that they must be smelled with each sip.

The Mint Julep could be found in bars decades before ice could, but the two have formed a special bond. The archetypical Julep today is served with crushed ice in a silver cup. The crushed ice has a high surface area per unit of volume, facilitating quite a lot of chilling and dilution. Because of silver's thermal conductivity, the cup will get very cold very quickly, and will help keep the ice cold so it doesn't melt too fast and overdilute the drink. Neither step is necessary, but both are worth it to perfect the experience.

# 1.2

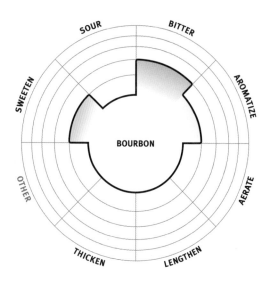

**Perhaps** the most repeated words in mixography belong to Harry Croswell, an Episcopal minister who in 1806 published the first known definition of a cocktail in *The Balance, and Columbian Repository*:

> Cock-tail is a stimulating liquor, composed of spirits of any kind, sugar, water, and bitters—it is vulgarly called bittered sling, and is supposed to be an excellent electioneering potion, in as much as it renders the heart stout and bold, at the same time that it fuddles the head.

In these early days of spiritous mixed drinks, one would order by naming a spirit and a preparation—e.g., a brandy sling, a gin sour, etc.* *Cocktail* dropped right in as one of the preparation options, and we must imagine that the whiskey cocktail was particularly popular, given its later evolution. As the *cocktail* moniker came to cover all manner of potations over the course of the nineteenth century, including novel inventions and drinks like the Mint Julep that antedated the designation, barflies nationwide must have found their thirsts frustrated by the same conversation: "I'll have a whiskey cocktail." "What kind of whiskey cocktail? Do you want an improved whiskey cocktail, or a fancy whiskey cocktail, or a Manhattan cocktail, or—" "No, [expletive] it, I want an *old fashioned whiskey cocktail*." We can deduce this progression because bartender's guides of the late 1800s

---

* Not unlike the modern practice of ordering Vodka Martinis and Vodka Gimlets.

# Old Fashioned

2 oz. bourbon or rye whiskey

2 tsp. sugar

3 dashes Angostura bitters

splash of water

In a rocks glass, muddle sugar with water and bitters until dissolved. Add ice and whiskey, and stir. Express an orange peel over the glass and drop it in.

list this drink as an Old Fashioned Whiskey Cocktail, a term coined only in opposition to new inventions (like *acoustic guitar*). In time, *Old Fashioned* became sufficient to identify the drink—without a doubt the best path any cocktail has taken to its name.

The Mint Julep may be older, but the Old Fashioned was technically the first cocktail—a spirit sweetened, bittered, and aromatized. Cocktail bitters, highly concentrated infusions of aromatic plants in an alcohol or occasionally glycerin base, are sufficient to accomplish the last two, even in very small quantities like a dash or a drop—though an expression of lemon or orange peel often enhances the result.

For dashes, turn the bottle until it is nearly upside down with its top pointed into the glass, and give it a good shake as many times as specified. For a drop, hold the bottle horizontally instead and gently wobble it; the amount released in this way should be noticeably smaller than a dash.

Like many solid ingredients, the sugar must be **muddled** to be fully incorporated. Combine it with water and bitters, then grind it with the muddler until the sugar is largely dissolved. We do this first because it's easier in a mostly empty glass and sugar dissolves more readily into a room-temperature liquid than an iced one.

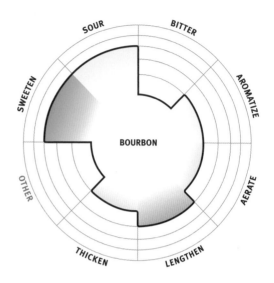

**Another** preparation that would have been available on early mixed-drink menus alongside cocktails—and juleps—was the *sour*, a spirit sweetened with sugar and soured with citrus juice. As we proceed through the canon of classic cocktails, you will find that this approach is extraordinarily common, if often elaborated upon. David Embury, in *The Fine Art of Mixing Drinks*, classified cocktails as sour or aromatic types based on the presence or absence of citrus juice. The latter category functioned as a kind of kitchen-sink designation in Embury's taxonomy, encompassing everything that wasn't soured in some way, and still the sour category was by far the larger of the two.

Like most drinks in this unit, it survived the Cocktail Dark Ages but emerged changed, made with spirits marketed for their blandness and bottled artificial sour mix. Do not make this mistake: always use fresh juice when mixing cocktails. Remember, *a drink can only be as good as its lowest-quality ingredient allows*. It takes very little effort to juice a lemon, and less to keep sugar in the house. The difference is enormous.

With rare exceptions, drinks containing citrus juice should be prepared by **shaking**—that is, the ingredients should be combined in a cocktail shaker with ice, after which the shaker should be sealed and shaken with both hands for 10–12 seconds. As the ice melts, cold water mixes

# Whiskey Sour

2 oz. bourbon

1 oz. simple syrup

¾ oz. lemon juice

Shake with ice. Strain into a chilled cocktail glass.

into the cocktail, chilling and diluting it. The shaking action ensures that viscous or solid ingredients are evenly distributed throughout the finished drink. Strain the drink into a stemmed glass after shaking. You may want to **double-strain** it, using both a cocktail strainer and a fine mesh strainer, to remove small chips of ice resulting from the shaking process and any seeds or other solids from the lemon juice.

It is advisable to serve the Whiskey Sour **up**, that is to say, in a stemmed cocktail glass. Shaken drinks are ordinarily served without ice because they have already been chilled and diluted in the shaker. That, however, means that they will warm up in the glass if given enough time. Because the hand is much warmer than the drink, stemmed glasses are used to keep the two separated so that this process is not needlessly accelerated.

While it is possible to prepare the Whiskey Sour with plain sugar, it is more convenient to make it with **simple syrup**, a preprepared combination of sugar dissolved in water. Combine equal volumes of sugar and water in any container that seals, and shake or swirl until the sugar dissolves. Strictly speaking, you've already made a 1:1 simple syrup while preparing the Mint Julep. One part sugar and one part water will yield roughly 1½ parts 1:1 syrup, so to keep the sugar content the same, you could substitute ⅔ oz. white sugar for the syrup in this recipe.

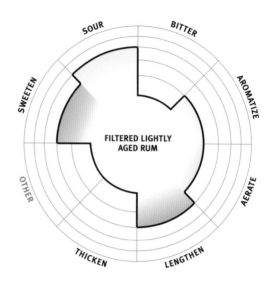

SOUR

BITTER

SWEETEN

AROMATIZE

**FILTERED LIGHTLY AGED RUM**

OTHER

AERATE

THICKEN

LENGTHEN

**Nonsense** is a recurring theme in cocktail origin stories. It is occasionally alleged that the Daiquiri was invented by a group of Americans in Cuba at some point in the early twentieth century, but it is hard to imagine that it took that long for three common Cuban ingredients to be combined—or that it was a non-Cuban who first had the idea to mix them. Like the Mint Julep, it was probably invented independently each time someone had all its components on hand.

The classification of rums is complicated. In most spirits, color is broadly indicative of time spent aging in an oak barrel, which imparts certain flavors and strips out others, while allowing the organic compounds to react with one another or break down and reach a durable equilibrium. Spirits that have an amber color acquire it from the oak during the aging process; clear spirits, by contrast, may have spent time resting in a container that imparts neither flavor nor color—usually a steel one—but have not been exposed to wood.

Rum is the exception to this rule: most clear rum has been aged in oak barrels for several years and then filtered to remove the color. Truly unaged rums exist, but they are relatively uncommon. Most "white" or "silver" rums follow this practice, including those of Cuba, long recognized for excellence in this style and much imitated as a result. The most traditional Daiquiri preparation would use a Cuban white

# Daiquiri

2 oz. filtered lightly aged rum

¾ oz. lime juice

¾ oz. simple syrup

Shake with ice. Double-strain into a chilled cocktail glass.

rum or something close to it if one is not available, e.g., a white rum from Puerto Rico or another place belonging to the Spanish Caribbean distilling tradition.

That said, there is no rum worth drinking that will make a bad Daiquiri. I enjoy them with the truly unaged rums being made by craft distillers in New England or with a combination of rums. As Martin Cate writes in *Smuggler's Cove*, the Daiquiri is a "perfect rum delivery system."

Certain ingredient pairings work famously well—apple and cinnamon, tomato and basil, rum and lime. Limes are about as sour as lemons, but have relatively more malic acid and less citric acid. Because malic acid lingers more on the tongue, a lime cocktail gives us a longer experience of sourness than a lemon one does. Citrus juice in general also contains dissolved organic solids that capture air bubbles during shaking and add texture to the finished cocktail.

According to experiments by Dave Arnold and Don Lee, American drinkers seem to prefer the flavor of lime juice after it's oxidized for a couple of hours, while in Europe the freshest juice is favored. This is in all likelihood due to divergent mixological practices on each side of the Atlantic giving people different perceptions of how a lime is *supposed* to taste. *De gustibus non est disputandum.*

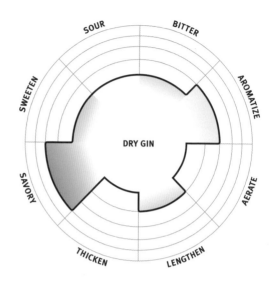

**1.5**

**Ironically**, the drink most commonly recognized as a Martini might be better described as a Gibson. While the Martini was originally made with sweeter stuff, the Gibson has always called for dry gin and dry vermouth specifically. When the Dry Martini evolved later on, it still included orange bitters, while the Gibson has always been served sans bitters with an aromatic garnish. That last point is recognized as the sole distinction between the two today: a cocktail onion for the Gibson, as opposed to an olive or a lemon twist for the Martini—but in truth, that is because in losing its bitters the Martini has largely *become* a Gibson. And so we will discuss the Gibson here, and save the traditional, bittered Martini for a later seminar.

Vermouth is a marvelous ingredient and a sensitive lever to pull in modifying a cocktail. Where sugar and lemon juice can be more or less completely reduced to *sweet* and *sour* in thinking about their roles in a cocktail's structure, vermouths do a bit of everything.* They are wine based, and carry with them the sweetness, acidity, and astringency of their parent liquid; they are flavored with spices, giving them aroma and bitterness; their sugar content richens their texture and that of the drinks they are mixed into. There is a reason that vermouth's

---

* In fact, sugar and lemon also do other things, particularly to the drink's texture, but this is a reasonable first-order approximation.

# Gibson

2 oz. London dry gin

½ oz. dry vermouth

Stir with ice and strain into a chilled cocktail glass. Garnish with a cocktail onion.

archetypal cocktails pair it with a spirit and a further aromatizer but nothing else: vermouth cannot be balanced against a one-note ingredient, but rather its complexity demands a complexity of counterpoints, whether in the form of a single spirit with a lot to it or a collection of simpler flavors acting in concert.

The Gibson—along with the Martini—calls for *dry* vermouth, which has less sugar than *sweet* vermouth. It has a certain savoriness to it, a crispness and a subtlety, for which reason it is more often paired with unaged spirits, rather than ones that have spent time in oak and picked up the bold, tannic flavors of the aging process. With its cocktail onion garnish, the Gibson doubles down on the savory notes the gin and vermouth share—a strategy evidently employed since its creation, given that its first recorded garnish was a pickled hazelnut. The olive garnish in a Martini does much the same, while the twist of lemon pulls it in the opposite direction, picking up the gin botanicals' bright citrus notes and the vermouth's fruity acidity.

There is a delicacy to this flavor balance, so the drink should be **stirred**, rather than shaken, which is to say the ingredients should be combined with ice and stirred briskly for about 10 seconds. Stirring is less efficient than shaking, so a stirred cocktail will be less diluted—and less chilled—than a shaken one that takes the same time to prepare.

**1.6**

The Manhattan predates both the Martini and the Gibson. It was the first spirit-and-vermouth drink to achieve wide popularity, which it has enjoyed from the 1880s straight through to the present. It also elaborates further on the vermouth cocktail template: where our recipes for the Gibson and the Martini relied on garnishes to aromatize them as the Mint Julep does, the Manhattan gets there using bitters, as the Old Fashioned does.

These distinctions are subtle, but essential to an understanding of what makes cocktails tick. The Manhattan is **bittered**; it is aromatized with the scents of spices rather than produce. Its usual garnish, a cherry, is visual rather than gustatory, not tasted until it is taken as a snack after the drink is consumed. These slight variations on a structurally similar base accrete, taking the drink in a distinct direction—and a complex one, due to the density of flavors in the bitters.

We often speak of a sip of a cocktail in spatial and temporal terms. As it moves from beginning to end, from front to back of mouth, our perception of it evolves: salivary enzymes break down certain flavors, our senses adjust to some and notice others for the first time, and aromas increasingly reach our olfactory bulb by wafting up from the back of the throat rather than through the nose. The most common place for a recipe to be weak is in the **middle**. The issue is usually one

# Manhattan

2 oz. rye whiskey

1 oz. sweet vermouth

2 dashes Angostura bitters

Stir with ice. Strain into a chilled cocktail glass and garnish with a brandied or maraschino cherry.

of insubstantiality: the drink's texture is too thin, or the flavors lack an adequate foundation, or a gap exists where everything should be coming together. This may be a problem with the recipe, in which case adding sugar may help to enhance aroma and increase viscosity. It can also indicate that the modifiers are being asked to do too much, and a more robust base is needed. The Manhattan provides a study of this last case.

Manhattans are traditionally made with rye whiskey. Rye and bourbon are by far the whiskies most called for in cocktails, but one consequence of the mixological doldrums in the mid-1900s was a gradual market shift away from rye, which eventually limited its availability. Bourbon became the standard Manhattan whiskey, and similar tricks were pulled with other recipes to keep them in circulation. For those who knew a little about what was lacking, Canadian whisky was often called for as a rye replacement, on the grounds that it was made with a relatively higher proportion of rye grain. In truth, these bottlings tended to be lighter-bodied blends of whiskey with neutral grain spirits, which used little more rye grain per ounce of distillate than the average bourbon does. They stand up poorly in recipes designed for a full-flavored rye and flourished as substitutes only as long as the real thing was hard to find. Mercifully, we have access to the good stuff again—and should accept nothing less.

# 1.7

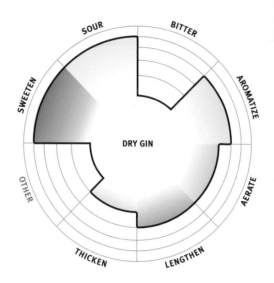

SOUR
BITTER
AROMATIZE
SWEETEN
DRY GIN
OTHER
AERATE
THICKEN
LENGTHEN

**As alluded** to in the introduction to this unit, Prohibition was an exceedingly bad time to be drinking in the United States. Worthwhile mixological work at the time was being done on other shores, and the Americans who could afford to drank their cocktails in London, Havana, or Paris rather than Chicago or Kansas City.

"Bee's knees" is the kind of 1920s slang one might hear around a speakeasy—meaning roughly, "the best."* But recent research suggests that this drink was invented in France by an American socialite and *Titanic* survivor named Margaret ("Molly") Brown, known among other things as the subject of the musical *The Unsinkable Molly Brown*.

Sugar is common in cocktails, but there are many other avenues to sweetening them. Honey is one of the simplest and most accessible alternatives, with a flavor that blends well with most spirit classes and citrus fruits. Maple syrup and agave nectar also appear in this book, as do various prepared syrups concentrating the flavors of fruits and spices. All these heavier-bodied sweeteners encourage shaking just as citrus juice does.

---

* See also, "the cat's pajamas."

# Bee's Knees

2 oz. London dry gin

1 oz. lemon juice

¾ oz. honey

Shake with ice. Strain into a chilled cocktail glass.

Honey's viscosity can make it uncooperative when you try to mix it into a cocktail, especially when the mixture is cold. If you find yourself having this problem, you can instead make a honey syrup, by warming three parts of honey and one part of water in a pot and stirring until they're combined. Because the flavor will be less concentrated, you should use a quarter ounce more syrup than you would honey when making substitutions to the recipes in this book. Less viscous boutique honeys can be found if you are interested.

Despite its virtues, the Bee's Knees remains underappreciated, rarely appearing in a book of cocktails with the prominence I've given it here. It was, however, a favorite of the late Sasha Petraske and the basis for several famous riffs from his bar Milk & Honey. We'll discuss these in later chapters, as well as another trick to address honey's viscosity and further elevate the Bee's Knees itself.

### FURTHER READING

The Gold Rush, essentially a Bee's Knees with a bourbon base, is one of the most successful recipes of the modern era. Its inventor, T. J. Siegal, was a childhood friend of Petraske's and an investor in Milk & Honey, where the recipe was introduced to the world. I recommend using a quarter ounce less of the honey and lemon in the Gold Rush than in the Bee's Knees, to make room for the bourbon.

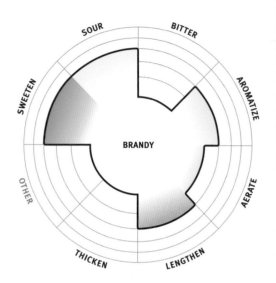

**Where** the Bee's Knees sweetens with honey, providing an additional kick of flavor per unit of sugar, the Sidecar makes use of a liqueur. This is a common technique in cocktails, but a tricky one: liqueurs add alcohol as well as sugar and can unbalance a cocktail along one axis even as they're being used to balance it on another.

The selection of an orange liqueur has a substantial impact upon the Sidecar's middle. Triple secs of decent quality can be too dry to hold the drink together. This is especially true of higher-proof expressions, like the 40% ABV Cointreau, with which the Sidecar was originally made: these add relatively little sweetness per unit of added spirit, making it difficult to bring the pieces into alignment unless one is working with a relatively rich brandy.

All aged spirits lose a certain volume of ethanol and water to the atmosphere each year. Distillers call this, rather poetically, the "angels' share." This also means that other things get more concentrated with time, whether those are sugars picked up from the wood of the barrel or aromatic chemicals that don't evaporate as quickly as the medium does. David Wondrich has sensibly pointed out that the first Sidecars would have been made with much older, richer Cognacs than the ones available at cocktail-mixing prices today.

# Sidecar

2 oz. brandy

¾ oz. curaçao or triple sec

¾ oz. lemon juice

¼ oz. simple syrup (optional)

Shake with ice and strain into a chilled cocktail glass. If not using simple syrup, sugar the rim of the glass first.

Mixing the Sidecar with a ten-or-so-year-old expression will make its balance far more forgiving. The bottle may set you back $100 or so, but if you can get past the initial outlay, your cost per cocktail will *still* be appreciably less than it would have been if you'd gotten a bottle's worth of Sidecars at bars—and the results probably more to your liking, given the economic realities of the brandy-slinging business.

One can fill out the Sidecar's middle by incorporating more sugar, enhancing both its texture and our awareness of its flavors. The simplest method is to add a bit of simple syrup to the shaker. More elegantly, Sidecars are often served with the rim of the glass sugared (or half-sugared, so the patron can modulate the sweetness to taste), and it can be just the thing for a young brandy or an orange liqueur that doesn't pack enough sweetness per degree of proof. While not original, it's been done long enough to be accepted as part of the Sidecar's canon.

To sugar a rim, pour some sugar into a small dish. Then, moisten the lip of the glass. You can do this by running an ice cube or a bit of lemon around the rim, but the most elegant solution is to chill it, either in the freezer or by filling it with ice for a little while, and let the resulting condensation provide all the moisture you need. Once the lip of the glass is slightly wet, press it into the sugar in the dish and turn it until it's sugared to your satisfaction.

# 1.9

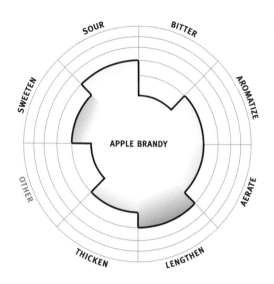

**SOUR** · **BITTER** · **AROMATIZE** · **AERATE** · **LENGTHEN** · **THICKEN** · **OTHER** · **SWEETEN**

**APPLE BRANDY**

**It would** not be unreasonable to imagine that half of the apple brandy cocktails consumed in the United States today are Jack Roses. A century-old drink that was a darling of midcentury cocktail menus, it became the spirit's standard-bearer as the other classic recipes in the apple brandy canon fell gradually out of circulation. The restoration of those drinks has been one of the great successes of the Cocktail Renaissance era, but the Jack Rose maintains a commanding lead in recognition and popularity.

Those, of course, are relative terms: it is quite likely that some readers will not be familiar with apple brandy at all. This is a shame, because it was the hometown favorite in the U.S. long before whiskey came along—the first federal distillation license ever issued went to Laird & Company, which started producing apple brandy in the ballpark of three hundred years ago and continues to do so today.*

To make the Jack Rose and other apple brandy cocktails, be sure you are using a spirit that is actually distilled from apples, and not an apple-*flavored* grape brandy, which are sometimes labeled "apple brandy," much as one might label a product "cinnamon whiskey."

* Laird & Company is the country's oldest independent distillery. George Washington even drank their apple brandy (and asked them for the recipe).

# Jack Rose

2 oz. apple brandy
½ oz. grenadine
½ oz. lemon juice

Shake with ice. Strain into a chilled cocktail glass.

Likewise, get yourself a real grenadine. The vaguely red-flavored corn syrup one sees in Shirley Temples will not do. Properly, grenadine is a pomegranate syrup—the term derives from *grenade*, the French name for that fruit—and you can make a very satisfying version at home with sugar and pomegranate juice. The wonderfully titled 1912 court case *U.S. v. Thirty Cases Purporting to be Grenadine Syrup* opened the doors to all manner of pomegranateless syrups bearing the name, but reputable commercial varieties are also available. (Flip to the appendix for recipes and brand recommendations.)

We have experience with simple syrup as a sweetener already, but grenadine is the first of many syrups we will encounter that add both sweetness and flavor. In practice, these ingredients work much like honey and other viscous natural sweeteners, but because they are made by human hands, they can be tinkered with, just like the cocktails in which they appear. Grenadine recipes may call for spices, a dusting of orange flower water, or a dollop of brandy as a tasty preservative. We will see various fruits, spices, and even nuts made into syrups before the end of this book. In many cases, they are more convenient to work with—and stay fresh longer—than the raw ingredients from which they're made.

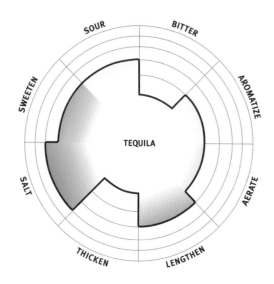

## SOLUTION

Unsurprisingly, the closest cousin to the Margarita that we've seen so far is the Sidecar. Both are sweetened using orange liqueur and soured with citrus juice. Drinks along these lines with a squirt of seltzer were sometimes called *daisies* in the nineteenth century, and since *margarita* is Spanish for "daisy," that seems the likeliest way for this drink to have gotten its name.

Tequila, more than most other spirits, appeals to salty and savory flavors—even its most famous highball, the Paloma, calls for a pinch of salt. Merely adding salt to the Sidecar template, though, would throw off the existing balance. The sweet and sour notes need to be slightly reduced, in order for the salt-tequila dynamic to have a space to fill in the flavor profile and ensure harmony among the ingredients. If you came to similar conclusions in your own contemplations, congratulations: your mixological instincts are developing well!

2 oz. blanco or reposado tequila

½ oz. curaçao or triple sec

½ oz. lime juice

1 tsp. simple syrup

Shake with ice. Strain into a chilled cocktail glass with a salted rim. Garnish with a lime wheel or a lime wedge.

# EXERCISE
# Margarita

blanco or reposado tequila

curaçao or triple sec

lime juice

simple syrup

*Using the given ingredients, determine the proportions of the Margarita and its method of preparation.*

**Several** of the major building blocks of cocktails are now in place, so it's time for an assessment. For our first exercise, I have selected the Margarita, a cocktail with which you are likely to be acquainted already. Any bar that serves spirits can prepare something that would at least pass for one. This was not always the case: tequila was a rare sight outside Mexico for many years, and its establishment as an essential spirit class is a relatively recent development. (Its next appearance after this will be in seminar five.)

For our present purposes, think of the Margarita as a recipe built on a familiar template, distinguished by the fact that it incorporates tequila and salt. These ingredients are novel to our study and occur nowhere else in this unit.

In approaching this cocktail, consider what makes it different from other ingredients we have seen, and what those distinctions might suggest about how the recipe will work. Try to determine what the Margarita's essential features are. Think about the drink(s) presented so far to which it bears the strongest resemblance. Gather and taste your ingredients, and see how they might fit together. The answers are on the facing page when you're ready to proceed.

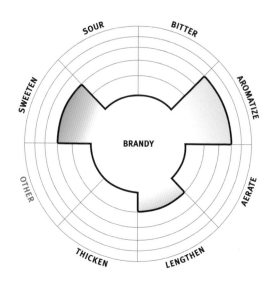

**In his seminal book,** *The Joy of Mixology,* Gary Regan coined the terms *duos* and *trios* to describe classes of liqueur-driven drinks. The Stinger is a duo in his system: a spirit mixed with a liqueur, with the balance usually tilted toward the former. (We will consider trios later on.)

Regan was right to recognize the commonalities across mixed drinks of this type—which encompasses the B&B, the Rusty Nail, and the Godfather, among many others. The liqueur is the sole modifier, so the direction the drink takes is determined entirely by its characteristics.

Let us begin with the general case: *liqueurs* are definitionally sweet and aromatic, and occasionally bitter as well. They are also spiritous. They cannot *just* add sweetness or aroma, because of their other features.

In the particular case of crème de menthe, the mint flavor can be overpowering if it is used injudiciously. Fortunately, it is also particularly sweet. Liqueurs which are called *crème de [X]* must have a minimum of 250 grams of sugar per liter; they are named not because they contain any actual dairy cream, but because this high sugar content increases their viscosity and gives them a rich, almost creamy texture, even relative to other liqueurs. (A sufficiently high alcohol content would undo this, but liqueurs of this type are normally bottled at 15%–25% ABV.)

# Stinger

3 oz. brandy

½ oz. crème de menthe

Stir with ice and strain into a chilled cocktail glass. Express a lemon peel over the glass and discard.

This is great news, insofar as it means we can mix a good Stinger with very little crème de menthe. A little goes a long way, and a lot is likely to be too much.

In a way, we've done the same things to brandy to make a Stinger that we did to bourbon to make the Mint Julep: it has been chilled, diluted, sweetened, and aromatized with mint. Certainly the particulars are different—and the standard presentations quite far apart—but the things that make the recipes tick are similar.

Having said that, I strongly advise expressing a lemon peel over the glass in the case of the Stinger to counterbalance the flavor of the crème de menthe, which can still be fairly potent even when it's just one-seventh of the drink. If you have access to a very high-quality expression, this step may not be necessary—and you may even wish to experiment with increasing its relative proportion in the recipe, as was popular for much of the last century.

A Stinger-like cocktail can be found in *The Flowing Bowl* by William Schmidt in 1892, while its present name first appears in *The Ideal Bartender* by Tom Bullock in 1917. The recipe given here is an aperitif, but for a dessert version, adjust the proportions to 3:1 or 2:1 and skip the lemon peel.

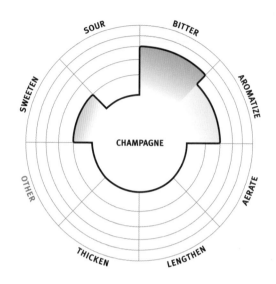

**1.12**

SOUR · BITTER · AROMATIZE · AERATE · LENGTHEN · THICKEN · OTHER · SWEETEN

CHAMPAGNE

**Let us** return for a moment to the cocktail in the nineteenth-century sense of the term: a combination of a spirit with sugar, water, and bitters. This template may have principally been applied to the popular hard liquors of the day, but it was by no means limited to them. The Vermouth Cocktail had been invented by 1869, not long after French and Italian vermouths began to arrive in quantity on American shores.* Other wines have likewise served as the base for this type of cocktail, the Champagne version being particularly enduring.

Properly, Champagne is a particular kind of sparkling wine, made in its namesake French region via a somewhat complicated traditional process involving multiple fermentations and natural carbonation. We should conclusively reject the designation "domestic Champagne" as an impossibility if we are not French, and a redundancy if we are.

This is not to say that we should accept no substitutes for Champagne in our cocktails. On the contrary, your preferred bottle of cava or California bubbly is perfectly sufficient for most cocktail purposes, to say nothing of its being appreciably less expensive, and for the most part in this book I call for *sparkling wine* generically. But when

* Noilly Prat was shipping dry vermouth to the U.S. by 1851. Sweet vermouth may have arrived as early as 1836 and was well established by the 1860s.

# Champagne Cocktail

5 oz. chilled Champagne

1 sugar cube

4 dashes Angostura bitters

Place sugar cube in a chilled flute and soak with bitters. Fill with Champagne. Stir gently with a barspoon to dissolve sugar. Express a twist of lemon over the glass, run it around the rim, and drop it in.

making something called a Champagne Cocktail, one really ought to use *Champagne*, and there is of course nothing wrong with doing likewise for every other sparkling recipe contained herein. That is, after all, how most of them were originally prepared.

Besides, Champagne is an ideal base for a cocktail of this type: its dry and delicate character is filled out by the sugar, its subtle flavors contrapuntally augmented by the bitters. It has the stature to work with either and the nuance to make it worth the effort to mix them.

Preparing the Champagne Cocktail is like preparing the Old Fashioned, but the differences are important. One cannot easily muddle sugar in a flute, for example. The addition of the Champagne is the principal action by which the sugar and bitters are mixed into the drink. Stirring with the barspoon helps to finish the job, but one must be careful not to introduce unnecessary turbulence. Sparkling wines are bubbly because they contain dissolved carbon dioxide gas. That gas can escape the solution and form bubbles most easily where it is in some way interrupted—consider the bubbles that collect on a straw in a glass of soda, for example. The barspoon will have a similar effect, with vigorous stirring only magnifying it; too much of this, and the effervescent quality of the drink can be lost to the atmosphere.

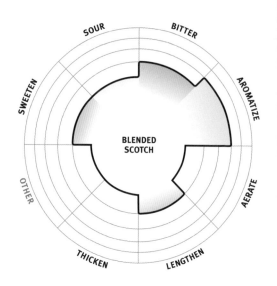

SOUR · BITTER · AROMATIZE · AERATE · LENGTHEN · THICKEN · OTHER · SWEETEN

**BLENDED SCOTCH**

**One** could be forgiven for regarding the Rob Roy as merely a Manhattan made with Scotch. The similarities are manifest, while the difference is subtle: where the Manhattan is aromatized using bitters and the Gibson employs an aromatic garnish instead, the Rob Roy does both.

This may seem like too fine a distinction to bother drawing, but remember, every component that contributes flavor to a drink affects its final balance. Expressed citrus peels are a common way of *finishing* a drink, not unlike the flourishy underline in John Hancock's signature. And they are often used in conjunction with bitters, as we've seen in the Old Fashioned and the Champagne Cocktail, although this is our first encounter with them in a drink that also gets considerable aroma from a fortified wine.

These sorts of combinations will proliferate in future chapters. While there are often practical constraints on the number of different aromatizing agents one can employ in a cocktail—including the law of diminishing returns—there is no theoretical limit, and a cocktail of arbitrary complexity could still conceivably be improved by a citrus twist.

The orange flavor is so important to the Rob Roy that some recipes call for orange bitters in lieu of Angostura, but I consider this a bridge too far. Bright, aromatic citrus oil is a better fit, in part because it matches

# Rob Roy

2 oz. blended Scotch

1 oz. sweet vermouth

2 dashes Angostura bitters

Stir with ice and strain into a chilled cocktail glass. Express an orange peel over the glass and discard.

particularly well with Scotch, which has something of the flavor of being in a log cabin in winter: the earthiness of the peat, the wisps of smoke in the background, the heartiness of barley malt and the warm woodiness of oaken barrels. Combine that with the herbal and spice notes from the vermouth and bitters, and the orange oil completes the tableau.

Another lesson the Rob Roy can provide: great cocktails are evocative, not just because their names are often mysterious and enticing but because they inspire stories and call memories to mind quite strongly. I am waxing scientific, not poetic: scent is a powerful, visceral memory trigger, unfiltered by the thalamus in contrast to all the other senses.* And speaking purely of its chemical properties, alcohol is a fabulous aroma-delivery system. Do not underestimate the capacity of aromatic ingredients to transform a cocktail.

* No, really. The thalamus filters out sensory information before it gets to the rest of the brain and you can become consciously aware of it—mostly things you prefer not to be aware of, like the sound of your blood pumping. It does this to all senses except smell, which instead is piped directly into the hippocampus and the amygdala, two regions of the brain involved in memory and emotion.

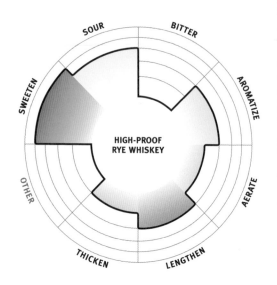

**1.14**

SOUR · BITTER · AROMATIZE · AERATE · LENGTHEN · THICKEN · OTHER · SWEETEN

HIGH-PROOF
RYE WHISKEY

**The Ward Eight** is a child of Boston, although there is significant dispute about the circumstances of its birth. An historic eatery called Locke-Ober has published an "official" version purporting that the drink was invented there in 1898, at a victory party for an election—one that would occur the next day, this being machine politics in the Gilded Age—and that it was named in honor of Martin "the Mahatma" Lomasney, the ward boss of Boston's eighth ward, which was set to deliver the race.

The usual contrarian take alleges that Lomasney wasn't in town that night, that his side lost badly in that year's election, that he was a Prohibitionist and wouldn't have been fêted with a new cocktail, and that bartenders wouldn't start using grenadine until the next century.

Both of these accounts are full of myth and nonsense, but kernels of truth keep them in circulation. Lomasney *was* a teetotaler, but not a Prohibitionist. He disliked the associations of the drink and tried for years to persuade people to call it something else. But it is noteworthy that he did not *deny* them. Grenadine, likewise, did not become popular in American cocktails until after 1900, but it was used in an 1895 French cocktail guide called *Bariana*. Considering that Locke-Ober was a French restaurant in a very Europhilic city, they might have been early adopters of the new ingredient—and since the Ward

# Ward Eight

1¾ oz. high-proof rye whiskey

¾ oz. grenadine

½ oz. lemon juice

¼ oz. orange juice

Shake with ice and strain into a chilled cocktail glass. Optionally, garnish with a brandied or maraschino cherry.

Eight was allegedly a new, celebratory creation, it would make sense to reach for the novel syrup when inventing it.

And while Lomasney's party did lose the election in 1898, his faction pulled off some amazing electoral chicanery in the Democratic primary, which he was proud of for years afterward. Stephanie Schorow details the story in *Drinking Boston*, and I find it far more plausible that this was the election that occasioned the Ward Eight's creation.

The unusual variety of Ward Eight recipes further confuses its history. Credit for this high-grenadine, low-orange version belongs to an erstwhile Boston bartender named Chad Arnholt. Brother Cleve, the city's cocktail godfather, has called it his favorite version, and I have to agree. It is best with a whiskey on the order of 100-proof; if using a lower-octane spirit, add an extra quarter ounce.

Orange juice has been maligned for being neither as tart as lemon and lime nor flavorful enough per unit of volume to be used effectively. While it's true that it cannot serve as the sole souring agent in something like a Whiskey Sour or Daiquiri, it can nevertheless be a delightful accent, as it is here. A drink that is otherwise soured and sweetened along familiar lines is transformed by this technique of blending juices. Keep it in mind; it will become very important in later chapters.

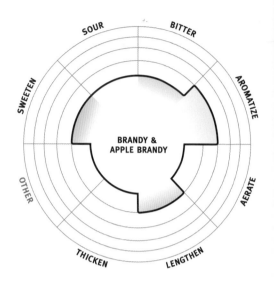

# 1.15

**Where** the Ward Eight blends two juices to change the way it's soured and the flavor of the final result, the Corpse Reviver No. 1 employs a combination of spirits as its core. This technique will also recur—in progressively more intricate ways—but its expression here is particularly simple and elegant. Brandy and apple brandy are distilled from different fruits, yet their flavors are reasonably complementary. They produce a more layered and complex drink when combined with sweet vermouth than either would do on its own.

Notably, this is true even in the absence of bitters or aromatic garnishes, which are not traditional in the Corpse Reviver in contrast to all the other vermouth drinks we've encountered so far. On the one hand, there is more going on here in terms of flavor than there would be in a Manhattan without bitters, for the simple reason that there are more ingredients trying to harmonize. The added complexity of a further aromatizing agent is simply not necessary. It is, however, also the case that we will later encounter split-base recipes with many other aromatic inputs, and one might reasonably ask why the same choice is not always made in similar circumstances.

To that I say, wouldn't it be boring if it were? Think of it this way: the above explains why the Corpse Reviver No. 1 *can* work without bitters

# Corpse Reviver No. 1

1½ oz. brandy

¾ oz. apple brandy

¾ oz. sweet vermouth

Stir with ice. Strain into a
chilled cocktail glass.

or garnishes, but the reason it *does* work is that there are times when one wants something subtle, spiritous, and spare. The variety of fruit and tannic notes in the spirits and vermouth are given space to play off one another, without the intrusion of citrus or spice. We can recognize that less is sometimes more without doubting that more can also be more at times.

As for its history, the Corpse Reviver No. 1 is first attested in *The Savoy Cocktail Book* by Harry Craddock, a classic of the genre, and in that initial appearance it is paired with a Corpse Reviver No. 2, which has more challenging ingredient requirements and therefore won't be discussed until the third seminar. The No. 1 was not actually a mainstay of midcentury cocktail culture, but it is of the same spirit in many respects and I've found it useful to include it in this section as an example of both the split-base cocktail and the unaromatized wine-driven cocktail. In considering recipes, we should always think both about what the ingredients are doing and what, if anything, is not being done which we might have expected: the lack of bitters here, like the absence of sugar in the Rickey, should spur contemplation about why the alternatives are more common and when they might not be required.

SOUR · BITTER · AROMATIZE · AERATE · LENGTHEN · THICKEN · OTHER · SWEETEN

DRY GIN

**One** of four cocktails named after the boroughs of New York City, the Bronx was the Manhattan's rival for recognition for many years. It was ubiquitous on postwar cocktail menus, and it found international success as a representative of the American beverage canon. I was surprised to find it on the menu of a perfectly ordinary Italian bar in 2015, and flabbergasted to subsequently find that the Bronx had an Italian Wikipedia page—but not an English one.*

An undeniably weird drink—which may account for its waning popularity stateside—the Bronx for our purposes is an innovator, a gateway to more advanced techniques. First, it combines sweet and dry vermouth—two aromatic modifiers more often used in isolation. Mixing fortified wines together can be tricky: each is already an intricate web of flavors, and trying to make one mesh with another can give you something that's less than the sum of its parts. This is a case where the combination works well—in part because the drink produces a palate that is orthogonal to its individual ingredients, drawing flavor elements from each that are not obviously complementary.

The Bronx is also our first recipe to combine a fortified wine with citrus juice. Systems that classify all cocktails as variations on a few template

* The Bronx has since received its due on English-language Wikipedia as well.

# Bronx

1½ oz. London dry gin

½ oz. sweet vermouth

½ oz. dry vermouth

¾ oz. orange juice

Shake with ice. Strain into a chilled cocktail glass.

recipes often begin to break down here. Sour-wine drinks don't quite belong in the wine camp with the Gibson and the Manhattan—for one thing, they're usually shaken—but they also don't really behave the same way as more straightforward sours do. The wine and citrus jockey for position as the defining element. One would have to establish a continuum from the wine drinks to the Daiquiri and assess each intermediate creature on the basis of its proximity to the ends.

Or one could do as we're doing here, and take them individually. So what makes the Bronx tick? Orange is less acidic than other citrus juices, skewing this toward the wine drink end of the spectrum. While it contributes a measure of acidity—and sweetness, as do the vermouths—the fresh juice also offers fragrance. It is more important aromatically than acidically. Gin is often made with citrus botanicals, including orange peels. Fresh orange juice has a floral bouquet, which picks up some of the other gin notes and certain of the sweeter spices in the vermouth. Meanwhile, the baking spice elements common to both are complementary to the juice—think about how orange pairs with cinnamon and cloves—while the hint of citrus acidity helps integrate the more savory components of the wine and the gin. The Bronx is to some extent like grapefruit and beer or oysters and chocolate: you can understand why it works but it's still surprising that it does.

# 1.17

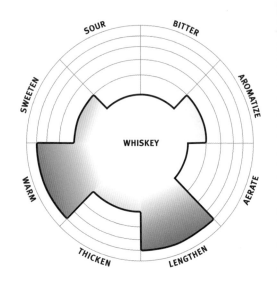

SOUR · BITTER · AROMATIZE · SWEETEN · WHISKEY · AERATE · WARM · THICKEN · LENGTHEN

**A critical** technique in the mixological toolbox is **lengthening**: increasing the volume of a drink while reducing its proof by adding a significant quantity of a less alcoholic or nonalcoholic ingredient. This may be done to minimize the strength or the potency on the palate of the mixed drink, simply to extend the experience of drinking it, or to assist with balancing the other components. In fact, all shaken and stirred drinks are lengthened by the ice that melts into them as they're being made, following Arnold's Fundamental Law of Traditional Cocktails. We have not devoted much time to that so far, because it hasn't been a point of distinction between any of the recipes: the dilution rates are about the same for the Daiquiri as for the Ward Eight, and for the Corpse Reviver as for the Gibson. Nevertheless, while it may not have mattered much in comparing these drinks to one another, the lengthening action of the melting ice has necessarily figured into the internal balance of flavors and textures of each.

In the Hot Toddy, the role of lengthening is made far more obvious by boiling the water that is used to prepare it. Heat accelerates the release of scent chemicals from the surface of the drink, adjusting the perceived flavor profile. It makes thick ingredients like honey runnier and easier to incorporate. It may also speed up the intoxication process. And given that the Hot Toddy is best known as a tonic for warding off illness or else as a drink taken to warm one's bones in the

# Hot Toddy

4 oz. boiling water

1½ oz. whiskey

1 tsp. sugar or honey

cinnamon stick

lemon wheel

Combine all but whiskey in a heat-safe glass or mug and stir until sugar or honey is dissolved. Stir in whiskey.

winter, it makes sense that it would be served hot even if all of this were not true.

Note that heat will also cause alcohol to evaporate, and it will do so at a faster rate than the water does because its boiling point is lower. This is why the whiskey should be added only at the very end of the preparation process. Some amount of vaporization is unavoidable, but we take steps to minimize it nonetheless, as we do with dilution in chilled drinks.

The kinetic action of shaking or stirring is far less necessary when there is a hot medium into which the sugars can dissolve: simply mixing the components and giving them a stir with the cinnamon stick should be sufficient. Note also that this drink, like the Rob Roy and the Mint Julep, has a flavor shaped by the use of an aromatic garnish. In this case, however, multiple such garnishes are used, resulting in a blend of scents, almost as if the cocktail maker had prepared a batch of homemade bitters instead.

I've presented the Hot Toddy as a specific recipe, but the truth is that it's a highly versatile template. It can be made with any spirit, although aged ones are normally preferred, and likewise with any sweetener, although sugar and honey are the most common choices.

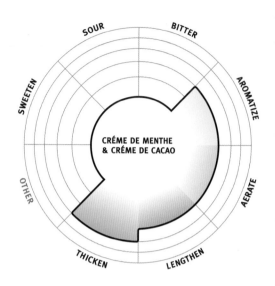

**1.18**

SOUR · BITTER · AROMATIZE · AERATE · LENGTHEN · THICKEN · OTHER · SWEETEN

CRÉME DE MENTHE
& CRÉME DE CACAO

**The Grasshopper** introduces another core technique, which I've termed **thickening**. Many ingredients affect the viscosity of cocktails —sugar increases it, alcohol and water decrease it, and so on—but cream is one of a few that are capable of changing it very noticeably and transforming the resulting drink into something else entirely.

Milk is an emulsion: a combination of liquid ingredients that do not normally like to mix but nevertheless have. It is full of globules of fat and structural proteins that have deigned to be dispersed in water, which account for its richer consistency as compared with the stuff out of the tap. One can think of cream as a kind of distillate of milk, made by partially separating components of different densities to achieve a greater concentration of one of them in the refined product—though in this case, the goal is to concentrate milk fat rather than ethanol. Where whole milk is on the order of 3½ percent fat by weight, cream made from it will have a fat content more like 20 percent. In the United States, half-and-half is between 10½ and 18 percent fat, while light cream is between 18 and 30 percent, meaning that the richest half-and-halfs and the lightest light creams are relatively close to one another.

The use of cream makes the Grasshopper a trio according to the Reganian system: where the duo is a liqueur-driven drink with two

# Grasshopper

1 oz. crème de menthe

1 oz. crème de cacao

1½ oz. light cream or half-and-half

Shake with ice. Strain into a chilled cocktail glass. Optionally, garnish with shaved chocolate.

ingredients, the trio is a liqueur-driven drink with three, of which one is cream or a comparable product like a cream liqueur. Unlike the Stinger, this trio's status as a dessert drink is not seriously disputed— the Grasshopper is more adult milkshake than aperitif.

Both crème de menthe and crème de cacao come in "white" varieties, which are clear, as well as ones colored green or brown, respectively. The Grasshopper traditionally calls for green crème de menthe to match the color of its namesake, but the clear expression tastes the same and a bit of food coloring will give you the right hue. That will save you the trouble of keeping two bottles of different colors in your house or of making peculiarly green-accented Stingers.

The system of parsing drinks I've used thus far presumes that there is such a thing as a base ingredient, which may not even be clear in this case. I've treated the Grasshopper as having the two liqueurs as a mixed base, much like we did with the spirits in the Corpse Reviver No. 1; this makes the cream the sole modifier. Other interpretations would be no less valid, and it is not necessarily even the case that our system of analysis applies to this recipe. I use it as a heuristic, and do not claim that it describes any foundational Truth about Cocktails. Cocktails can be understood in many ways and ultimately are only experienced as finished products when they are already the sum of their parts.

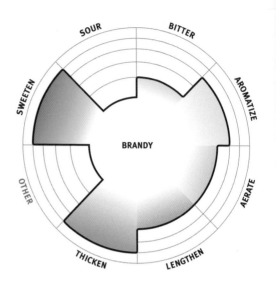

**1.19**

**If the Bronx** is our great example of a drink that doesn't seem like it would work, the Brandy Alexander may be the archetype of the cocktail that looks delicious on paper. Sometimes our preconceived notions are absolutely spot-on.

Interestingly, though, the original Alexander did not look good on paper: it was made with gin rather than brandy. That did not prevent it from being popular well into the heart of the twentieth century. Cream drinks in general were in vogue in the atomic age, and the Alexander appeared on menus nearly as often as the Martini—which is to say, it was on almost all of them. The brandy version could often be found alongside it, and in subsequent years this much more obvious combination of flavors has outstripped its progenitor in popularity.

Another practical consequence of adding cream to drinks is that it suppresses certain flavors. Cream contains the milk protein casein, which can bind to bitter or astringent compounds like tannins so that we perceive them less, while to a certain extent it also simply outmuscles other flavors with its own sweet fattiness, which makes an enticing distraction for your senses. Cream drinks can therefore mellow out bold ingredients, drown out delicate ones, and simplify the experience of ones that hit multiple notes, allowing only the loudest to be perceived clearly.

# Brandy Alexander

1 oz. brandy

1 oz. crème de cacao

1½ oz. light cream or half-and-half

Shake with ice and strain into a chilled cocktail glass. Garnish with a sprinkle of grated nutmeg.

We are broadly folding the mouthfeel component one might describe as *silkiness* or *creaminess* into the "thickening" category in this book. While there is a strong correlation there, creaminess is a distinct sensation, caused by the suspension in the liquid of droplets of fat too small to be individually distinguished by our senses. The movement of these tiny drops makes the liquid feel slippery even as the fats make it more viscous overall.

Where the Grasshopper uses these characteristics to turn the robustness of crème de menthe into the delicacy of an after-dinner chocolate mint, the Brandy Alexander stratifies the flavors of its titular ingredient, letting the rich vanilla and caramel notes the barrel-aging process imparts predominate while the subtler fruit flavors become accents at most. It is more spiritous than the Grasshopper, and while it is not unlike an alcoholic dessert, it is also much more like the other cocktails we've discussed so far than the Grasshopper is. It can be clearly recognized as a brandy drink, the other components serving primarily to enhance, complement, or otherwise affect the flavor of that spirit. It even has an aromatic garnish: the sprinkle of nutmeg, much as one would put on a mug of eggnog, which ties together the dessert notes of the other ingredients and finishes the drink with a hint of spice and complexity.

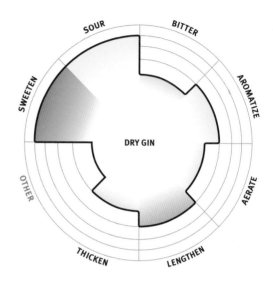

SOUR BITTER AROMATIZE AERATE LENGTHEN THICKEN OTHER SWEETEN

**DRY GIN**

# SOLUTION

No drink that we've covered is quite like the Gimlet, but it resembles the Stinger and the Daiquiri. Like the Stinger, it's a two-ingredient cocktail, a spirit paired with a sweet aromatic component. But unlike crème de menthe, lime cordial is nonalcoholic and sour, properties more in line with the modifiers in a Daiquiri.

That the Gimlet is served with ice suggests that it should be built in the glass, but the word *syrup* and the viscosity of lime cordial are a cue to shake it instead. How to square this circle? Split the difference: give your Gimlet a **short shake** of some 5–6 seconds to fully mix the ingredients, then strain it into a rocks glass and serve with ice, to be sipped slowly like a built cocktail. This isn't a common technique; the point here is less to learn it than to practice working through mixological problems. If you recognized that the Gimlet doesn't seem quite like a built drink or a shaken one, you're doing fine.

2 oz. London dry gin

¾ oz. lime cordial

Shake briefly with ice and strain into a rocks glass with ice. Optionally, garnish with a lime wheel.

# EXERCISE
# Gimlet

London dry gin

lime cordial

*Using the given ingredients, determine the proportions of the Gimlet and its method of preparation.*

**This** will be the final short drink of this seminar. A rock-solid cocktail order for most of the last century, the Gimlet has made appearances in everything from Raymond Chandler's novel *The Long Goodbye* to the HBO series *Six Feet Under*.* Its legendary etymology connects it with Sir Thomas Gimlette, a Royal Navy doctor who purportedly added lime to sailors' gin rations as an antiscorbutic; this story is implausible, given that he was a child when limes became standard issue on British ships. The Gimlet is more likely named after the small manual drill, following the tendency of cocktails to be named after things that are powerful or piercing. Consider what other drinks the Gimlet is like, how it differs from them, and how those divergences should affect its preparation.

To do so, you'll need to know a little about lime cordial. Patented in 1867 as a way of preserving limes for long voyages, it is a concentrated syrup made from lime juice, lime oil, and sugar, sometimes with citric acid or other flavorings. There's a recipe for a homemade version in the appendix, but many excellent commercial brands are also available. Some modern bartenders will use sugar and lime juice instead, but this is a poor substitute. Note also that the best Gimlets are served with ice, but I'll leave it up to you to interpret that hint before you read on.

* Admittedly in its inferior vodka form in the latter case.

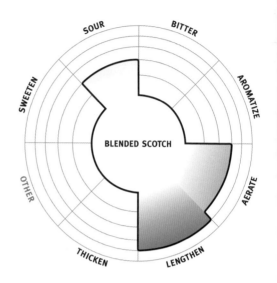

**1.21**

SOUR     BITTER

SWEETEN     AROMATIZE

BLENDED SCOTCH

OTHER     AERATE

THICKEN     LENGTHEN

**Drinks** that have been significantly lengthened to the point that the lengthening agent makes up the majority of the volume are collectively termed *long drinks*. This is a loose categorization, meant merely to distinguish them from *short drinks* in which the base spirit is at least the plurality ingredient by volume or from *cocktails*, which according to some classification systems are definitionally short drinks and long drinks something else entirely.

We have already encountered the Hot Toddy, a rare drink insofar as it is lengthened with plain water. Most of the time, more than that is asked of a lengthening agent: that it add flavor, texture, sweetness, or *something* to the mix beyond volume. Effervescence is a particularly common request, and carbonated lengtheners appear in many cocktails.

Of these, the simplest is seltzer, which is to say water that has been carbonated in some way. And the simplest preparation combines it with a spirit and ice, and nothing else.

There is nowhere to hide in such a drink. The spirit must be of good quality, the balance precisely to taste, and the preparation without fault. Avoid light-bodied spirits: as the minority ingredient in the glass, they can disappear entirely, leaving a glass of what tastes like

# Scotch and Soda

2 oz. blended Scotch

4 oz. seltzer

Combine ingredients in a highball glass with ice and stir.

slightly alcoholic fizzy water. Pick a robustly flavored distillate with a strong middle that can stand up without sugar and punch through a few layers of seltzer to reach the taste buds. A single-malt Scotch is probably not necessary given the number of blends available that meet that standard, but if you choose to experiment with other whiskies, blended American and Canadian ones are best avoided.

I have described the contribution of effervescence as *aeration* in this course of study—the same term I use for other methods that introduce or trap gas bubbles in a cocktail, shaking among them. Carbonated mixers do this on a larger scale and are diagramed appropriately. In a preparation this simple, those bubbles are much of the point, so be careful not to overstir. It is critical that no more carbonation than necessary be lost during preparation. The addition of the seltzer should do much of the mixing work for you if the spirit is already in the glass.

Don't be dilatory about drinking your Scotch and Soda: the longer it sits, the more the dissolved carbon dioxide will reach the surface and evaporate, and the more the melting ice will reduce the relative proportion of the remaining gas in the liquid. In short, do everything you can to maintain the effervescence, and err on the side of having a second drink rather than savoring this one.

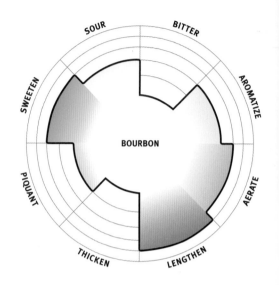

**1.22**

SOUR BITTER AROMATIZE AERATE LENGTHEN THICKEN PIQUANT SWEETEN

BOURBON

**The term** *highball* refers generically to any drink made by combining a spirit with a carbonated lengthener of some type. Thus, the Scotch and Soda described above is a highball, as are the Gin and Tonic and many other common drinks. That said, if someone refers to something they've consumed as a highball without specifying further, chances are they have something like this recipe in mind: the spirit is probably bourbon or another American whiskey, while the lengthener is almost certainly either ginger ale or plain seltzer.

The next step in our study of long drinks is the use of a flavored mixer, so that is what is presented here. Ginger sodas have broad application in mixed drinks going back to the nineteenth century.* They will add sweetness and ginger flavor as well as length and effervescence, consolidating into one component the effects of the Hot Toddy's honey, water, and spices as well as the seltzer in the Scotch and Soda. Ginger is also *piquant*, what we might colloquially call *hot* or *spicy*—it contains a chemical that stimulates the body's temperature sensors, giving a sensation of warmth. This effect is quite mild in ginger ale; spicier, more concentrated ginger sodas are usually called *ginger beer*.

* One can even ferment ginger and sugar to make a naturally carbonated beverage, which is also called ginger beer. It is the ancestor of the nonalcoholic artificially carbonated ginger sodas we know today, and this heritage is the reason we use beer terminology to describe them.

# Bourbon Highball

2 oz. bourbon

4 oz. ginger ale

Combine ingredients in a highball glass with ice and stir.

Ginger ale is, of course, widely available, stocked in every bodega and airplane cart from sea to shining sea and not particularly expensive. I cannot fault you for using a commercial variety, and many of them make very fine drinks. However, there is some benefit to concocting your own from a homemade ginger syrup (see simple instructions in the appendix). First, you can control both the sweetness and the gingeriness of the mixture and adjust them to your personal taste. Second, you can also use the ginger syrup to make the further-concentrated ginger *beer*, saving you the trouble of keeping both in your house, and to mix the cocktails in later seminars that call for ginger syrup specifically. And third, you can enjoy the satisfaction of learning to do something simple that seemed rather difficult and having control over which ingredients you choose to use. If you have read this far, I expect that at least some of those benefits may appeal to you.

The preparation of the Bourbon Highball is identical to that of the Scotch and Soda, and you will find that these proportions and preparations extend further to all drinks in the highball class. You may not prefer my 2:1 ratio, but I am confident that whatever ratio you find you *do* prefer for this drink will also work well for your G&Ts and the like.

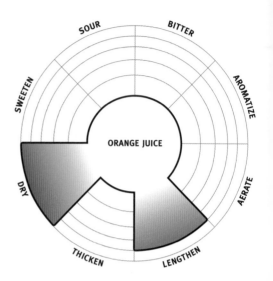

**Surprised** to see the Screwdriver here? I was. It didn't make the cut for Mixology 110b on the grounds that everyone was already sufficiently familiar with it, and I have had few occasions to drink one since then. It is not that it's bad tasting, it is just that there are other more interesting things in the world.

It does, however, provide a template for long drinks driven by juices rather than by sodas. Used this way, fruit juices contribute their usual sweetness and sourness—as well as bitterness, in some cases—but also texture and length, without the effervescence of sodas. At least, that's one way of looking at it.

Another is to consider the juice as the base and the spirit as the modifier, which makes particular sense in the case of vodka. *Pace* the Poles and Russians, but in the United States vodka is rarely made or consumed with much thought to its flavor—it is meant to be as pure a mixture of ethanol and water as possible, with no other tastes to speak of.* Much vodka is made that succeeds in this goal, and vodka drinks therefore operate on that expectation.

---

* Flavored vodkas would seem to be the exception to this, but if anything they reinforce the point: vodka is the most popular base for flavored spirits specifically because no one expects it to have any flavor of its own besides pure ethanol.

# Screwdriver

1½ oz. vodka

4 oz. orange juice

Combine ingredients in a highball glass with ice and stir.

Does that mean vodka serves no role in cocktails other than to make them stronger? Too often that's the case, but it does not have to be. Vodka can be thought of as a modifier that *dries out* the recipes in which it appears, an antidote in some respects to the sweetness and length introduced by other components—or, when vodka is the only spirit ingredient, the sweetness and length of the base. Like sugar or water, it is a pure expression of its category, as close as one can get to a component that affects only one characteristic of the whole. The Screwdriver, viewed thus, is an *orange juice* drink at its core, with vodka added to make it drier.

This is consistent with our instincts about what defines the base ingredient in a drink, as well. In most cases, particularly among short drinks, if a certain ingredient represents the majority or a large plurality of the total volume, that is the one we think of as the base. But the Scotch and Soda belies this description, unless we consider the soda the base and the Scotch the modifier. And so we fall back on a different definition, namely, that the thing which contributes the most essential flavor in the final reckoning is the thing that should be regarded as the base, and the other ingredients as its modifiers. By either standard, the Screwdriver is an orange juice drink in which there happens also to be vodka.

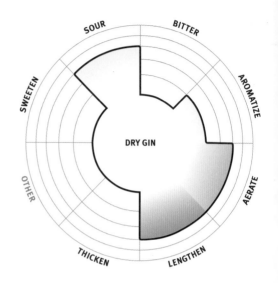

**The commonness** of long drinks means that their elementary expressions have probably been made by many more people than equally rudimentary short drinks have—one certainly sees more Screwdrivers than Daiquiris at undergraduate parties, for example. And for this reason, the last three drinks may have felt like we were stepping back, more reviewing the course prerequisites than introducing new material. I would regard it more like the point in a foreign-language class when one learns a new tense for the first time and suddenly all the practice sentences are just as simple as they were on day one, because familiarity with this new aspect of the language has to be built up from the basics just as the prior material was. It is essential to understand how lengthening and effervescence work in cocktails and what makes a highball or a juice drink tick in order to proceed to more advanced topics. We will now be able to do just that—and rapidly.

The Rickey is another nineteenth-century potation and another one whose history we do actually know. It was invented by a man named Col. Joe Rickey, who sensibly named it after himself. Originally, it was a whiskey drink, which is why gin is specified here. In general, when cocktail names contain elements that might seem redundant,

# Gin Rickey

1½ oz. London dry gin

juice of ½ lime (½ oz.)

3 oz. seltzer

Juice half a lime into a highball glass. Add ice, gin, and seltzer, and stir. Garnish with the spent lime shell.

there are historical explanations to be found—the Mint Julep, the Champagne Cocktail, and the Brandy Alexander are all like this in different ways.

In any case, Col. Joe's invention was rapidly modified into a gin drink, which has attained particular popularity. It is a single step removed from a highball made with plain soda: it has also been soured with lime juice. This is unusual; sweetness is normally added prior to sourness, and so far we have not encountered any drinks that are only soured.

What has changed? In a word, dilution. If we stripped the sugar out of our Daiquiri recipe, it would become overpoweringly sour and horribly unbalanced, because lime juice would be a much higher percentage of the finished cocktail. But the Gin Rickey is a long drink. The lime juice is far more diluted in this case than in that hypothetical diet Daiquiri, and its ability to lower the pH of the solution (i.e., make it more acidic) is consequently reduced. It is still a tart drink, but the lengthening makes it a possible one.

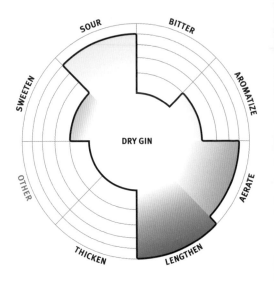

**We have** not directly addressed it, in part because it has been intuitive, but strictly speaking each of the long drinks discussed thus far has been a **built drink**, like the Old Fashioned: prepared in the glass in which it will be served, not chilled in advance but served with ice in the expectation that it will take some time to drink, while the melting ice will both chill it and dilute it. This is second nature when we're mixing whiskey with ginger ale, and so we might not stop to consider that it serves the very same purposes that building does for the Old Fashioned.

This is perhaps more apparent with the Tom Collins, which looks a bit like a shorter drink. If you stopped after the first three ingredients, you would have a Gin Sour—although, as we observed with the Rickey, it would be rather more sour than we have considered palatable in short drinks. Once again, the dilution from the seltzer permits—and indeed necessitates—a relative tilting of the balance among the other ingredients toward the sour.

The Tom Collins's earliest traceable ancestor, the John Collins, dates to the 1830s; the name change seems to have been driven at least in

# Tom Collins

2 oz. London dry gin

juice of ½ lemon (¾ oz.)

1 tsp. sugar

6 oz. seltzer

Combine gin, lemon, and sugar in a Collins glass with ice and stir. Fill with seltzer.

part by the Great Tom Collins Hoax of 1874, when pranksters would tell people about the terrible things a man named Tom Collins was saying about them somewhere nearby until they were provoked to go hunting for their fictional slanderer. It also probably helped that a version of the drink made with Old Tom gin was gaining popularity around then.

In any case, the So-and-So Collins has been around long enough to give its name to the glass, a mixed-drink vessel specifically made large enough to hold it. Consider that the volume of this recipe—some 9 oz.—is far greater than anything else we've discussed so far. It is meant to take some time to sip. In order to keep it cold for all that time, it must be served with plenty of ice. And in order to accommodate all that ice and liquid, a Collins glass holds 14–16 oz. If you are disinclined to go out and buy a dedicated glass just to use for the Tom Collins, recall that 16 oz. is one pint. If you have a pint glass in your house for drinking beer, you have a suitable substitute for a Collins glass.

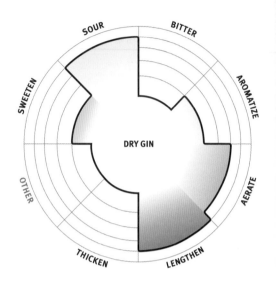

**Cocktail** guides often list the Gin Fizz and the Tom Collins with nearly identical recipes. As you can see, I've done the same: there is slightly more sugar and less seltzer in the Gin Fizz, but other than that the list of ingredients is precisely the same. So what's the difference?

It is entirely about the preparation—and by extension, the purpose for which the drink is intended. Where the Collins is a built drink, meant to be served with ice and drunk over time, the fizz is fundamentally in the spirit of a short drink. It is *shaken*, served without ice, and then topped with seltzer. This means that it cannot stay cold for the *longue durée*, and must be drunk quickly—"while it's still laughing at you," as Harry Craddock would say—in order to maintain the experience of the drink. Temperature affects taste, after all. Sweetness, in particular, is suppressed by the cold, and drinks served cold are balanced with this in mind—one consequence of which is that if they are allowed to warm up, the taste profile can seem imbalanced toward the sugar.

To function as a shorter and faster drink, the fizz uses less seltzer than the Collins does. Because that reduces the dilution of the lemon juice and increases the perceived acidity, the sugar is bumped up to

# Gin Fizz

2 oz. Old Tom gin or London dry gin

juice of ½ lemon (¾ oz.)

¼ oz. sugar

3–4 oz. seltzer

Shake all but seltzer with ice. Strain into a highball glass without ice and top with seltzer.

counterbalance it. The lack of ice and lower volume of seltzer mean it can be served in a much shorter glass. The full extent of the moving parts in these simple-seeming drinks only really becomes clear when the two are examined side by side.

If you have found this analysis of the fizz eye-opening, know that I felt the same way when I first encountered it in *Imbibe!* by David Wondrich, a fabulous book on nineteenth-century drinking practices and my source for the last two recipes. If you remain skeptical about the usefulness of distinguishing the fizz from the Collins, I understand that as well. Consider, though: because fizzes are shaken drinks, you can use the technique to turn many short drinks into long(er) ones. There are even some classic cocktails that have fizz forms as popular as their standard recipes. And because of the fizz's particularly close kinship to other shaken drinks, there are far more recipes for more elaborate fizzes in the world than there are for advanced Collinses. In fact, we will have largely dealt with the Collins by the end of this seminar—it is straightforward and unimpeachable, and little more need now be said—while there is a great deal more discussion of the fizz to come in the later ones.

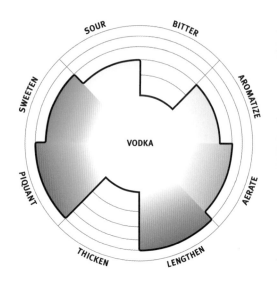

**1.27**

SOUR BITTER AROMATIZE AERATE LENGTHEN THICKEN PIQUANT SWEETEN

VODKA

**Vodka** did not appear in quantity in the U.S. until the 1950s. Paul Clarke outlines its trajectory in *The Cocktail Chronicles*: from 40,000 cases imported in 1950, it jumped to 4,000,000 five years later, outselling gin beginning in 1967 and whiskey within another decade. David Embury wrote in 1958 that it had "streaked across the firmament of mixed drinks like Halley's comet." Its rapid change in fortunes—in the early years of the Cold War, no less—was abetted by its use in several highly charismatic cocktail recipes, the Moscow Mule among them.

The Moscow Mule was invented at the Cock'n Bull in Los Angeles in the 1940s, when relations with the Soviet Union were still relatively good.* Like the Screwdriver, it can be thought of as a drink with a non-alcoholic base, to which vodka is added to dry it out and beef it up. But if we think of it as a vodka drink with lime juice and ginger beer to modify it, we can recognize in it an older template called the *buck*, defined as any combination of a spirit with lime and ginger soda. People had been drinking Whiskey Bucks, Rum Bucks (sometimes called Barbados Bucks), and the like since the nineteenth century, but the popularity and effective branding of the Moscow Mule have put

* It did not hurt that Smirnoff, the highest-profile vodka in the U.S., was distilled in Connecticut.

# Moscow Mule

1½ oz. vodka

4 oz. ginger beer

wedge of lime

Combine vodka and ginger beer in a copper mug and stir. Squeeze lime wedge over the glass and drop it in.

them all to shame—so much so that new recipes of this type tend to be called *mules* in its imitation.

It is an excellent vehicle for vodka: not only is there enough else going on that it does not suffer for its deliberately flavorless base, but the piquancy of the ginger beer appeals to the same palate that relishes the bite or burn of spirits—that is, those people for whom the flavor of plain ethanol is itself desirable, even preferable to other tastes. Put another way, the Moscow Mule makes the vodka more interesting while doubling down on some of the qualities that people find attractive in it in the first place.

Note that when a drink is garnished with a wedge of citrus, some percentage of the people who consume it will choose to squeeze the juice out of the wedge into the drink, drop the wedge itself into the glass, or both. Recipes that call for such garnishes should anticipate this, and the drinks should accommodate these end user adjustments. This is achievable in a long drink, for the same reason that the Rickey works: the added juice will have *an* impact, but not an outsize one relative to the volume of the drink. Long drinks are fairly forgiving. One can even think of the wedge garnish as akin to providing salt and pepper shakers with a meal. It is an intentional way to allow the drinker to make adjustments to their personal taste, within safe parameters.

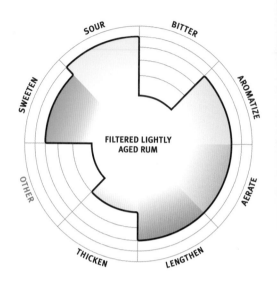

SOUR · BITTER · AROMATIZE · AERATE · LENGTHEN · THICKEN · OTHER · SWEETEN

FILTERED LIGHTLY
AGED RUM

**The Mojito** has been around for ages. David Embury cited it in *The Fine Art of Mixing Drinks*, Ernest Hemingway was a fan, and many sources trace it to a more ancient recipe called El Draque; all agree that the Mojito originated in Cuba. It came to particular prominence in the United States in the 1990s: Paul Harrington plucked it from a Cuban cookbook for the menu at Enrico's in San Francisco, appreciating its then-unusual incorporation of fresh produce. The popularity of both bar and drink grew rapidly after a local article put the spotlight on them, and the Mojito would soon become a nationwide sensation.

The Mojito was, after all, a drink that demanded fresh ingredients, a halfway decent rum, and a certain amount of technique. It was also massively popular, and became the bane of many a bartender. Imagine getting an order for six of them in a packed bar on a Saturday night—that's a lot of muddling, and a lot more time to spend per drink than you'd probably want to. But at the drink's peak popularity, you'd probably be filling that order over and over again until the shift was done.

This version is based on one from Milk & Honey, which in turn was adapted from a Cuban recipe. As we saw in our very first recipe, a mint garnish is the most efficient way to get mint flavor into a drink—it is, however, not the only way, and our Mojito employs two techniques

# Mojito

2 oz. filtered lightly aged rum

1 oz. lime juice

1 oz. simple syrup

3 oz. seltzer

8–10 mint leaves

2–3 mint sprigs

In a rocks glass, gently muddle mint leaves with lime juice and simple syrup. Add rum and swirl to combine. Add ice and fill with seltzer. Garnish with sprigs of mint.

together. We begin by carefully and delicately muddling the mint. It should not be crushed or shredded, only bruised, pressed with the muddler to break open the oil sacs on the surface of the leaf. The mint is a friend, not an enemy. Overly vigorous muddling can break open cells in the rest of the leaf, releasing enzymes that will react with the scent chemicals in the mint oil and break them down—at best reducing the desired mintiness, at worst producing off flavors via unpleasant-smelling metabolites.

Into this are incorporated lime juice and sugar, then rum, then ice and seltzer. Like our other long drinks, the Mojito is built in the same glass in which it will be served—but it is our first muddled drink to be made long, and it looks an awful lot like the short built drinks from the beginning of the seminar before we add the seltzer. The lesson here is that short drinks can sometimes be made into long drinks and vice versa, just as it is possible to convert between duos and trios in some cases. One could make a cocktail using just gin, lemon, and sugar, without lengthening it into a Tom Collins or a Gin Fizz. One could also make a sort of minted sour by leaving out the last step of this recipe, and it would taste quite good. In fact, the Milk & Honey version does just this, getting all its dilution from the crushed ice it's served with. I happen to prefer mine with a bit of effervescence, which is also the way it's usually found in the wild.

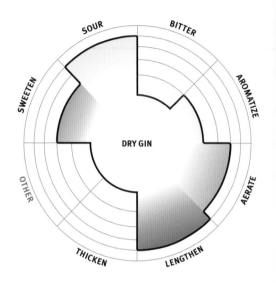

**Named after** a French fieldpiece from World War I, the French 75 packs a punch in a deceptive package. It is crisp, effervescent, citrusy, quaffable—in sum, it cries out to be drunk with brunch—but each one includes a shot of gin and half a glass of sparkling wine. The name is apt.

There is some ongoing debate about whether it should be made with Cognac or gin. The latter is more popular and favored by historical evidence: the gin version appears as far back as 1927, in *Here's How* by Judge Jr; the earliest source for the brandy one is none other than David Embury, writing two decades later.*

We have already encountered sparkling wine as a cocktail base, but here we find it used as a lengthener. It is less alcoholic than gin, so it functions to reduce the proof and increase the volume of the cocktail. It is also carbonated. One could think of it as "a very special kind of fizzy water," which may be a good euphemism to tell small children at weddings.

---

* Embury claims that Cognac was original to the drink, even saying that "we should not call it French" if gin is used. In reality, while there was a drink called the 75 in circulation from 1915 until *Here's How*, it was very unlike the French 75s Embury and Judge Jr describe—and it didn't use Cognac, either!

# French 75

1½ oz. London dry gin
¾ oz. simple syrup
½ oz. lemon juice
2½ oz. sparkling wine

Shake all but the wine with ice. Double-strain into a chilled flute and top with sparkling wine. Garnish with a long, thin twist of lemon.

That mental substitution made, look again at the recipe. What does it resemble that we have previously covered? Yes, that's right, the French 75 is . . . a fizz! Or a close cousin, in any case. It is, like the fizz, shaken rather than served on ice, topped with a squirt of something sparkling, and meant to be drunk at cocktail-speed rather than Collins-speed. The other ingredients are even the same as the ones in the Gin Fizz, although they've been rebalanced once again to account for the sparkling wine. It has its own sweetness, acidity, and bitterness, but above all its own *flavor* to contend with. There is also less of the wine than there is of seltzer in the Gin Fizz, and it is not quite as effective at lowering the proof. In deference to the wine's characteristics, the proportion of citrus juice is pared back and the sweetener increased to avoid overbalancing toward the tart. Likewise, sugar has been swapped out for simple syrup. The Gin Fizz is a nineteenth-century potation and admits a certain amount of rusticity in its preparation, while the French 75 is meant to be beautiful, elegant, and modern; it is a drink that benefits from an unblemished presentation and the preservation of its rather more delicate bubbles. The visual component of appreciation is significant for many cocktails, but it applies as a rule to ones made with sparkling wine. The use of simple syrup ensures that the sugars are well dissolved, keeping the drink silky on the tongue and glittering to the eye.

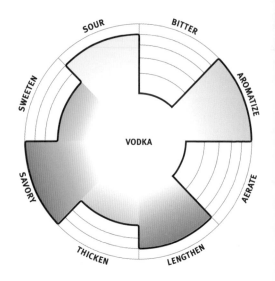

# 1.30

**For our final** examination in this first course in cocktails, we tackle a very different long brunch drink: the Bloody Mary. In his history of the cocktail, *Spirits, Sugar, Water, Bitters*, Derek Brown identifies it as one of three drinks that secured the place of vodka in the American market. The Moscow Mule, which we have seen already, was the second; the Kangaroo, the original name for the Vodka Martini, was the third.*

Brown is correct to observe that cocktails were the "Trojan horse" by which vodka infiltrated the West, but the era was also ideally suited to its widespread adoption. Blended spirits, which at least in the United States were made by combining an ordinary spirit like whiskey or apple brandy with some amount of flavorless neutral grain alcohol (read: *vodka*), were rapidly gaining popularity at the expense of more flavorful offerings. *Bland* became a spirits marketing term, and not one of opprobrium either. That spirit which tasted least was thought best, and vodka tasted least of all.

I should perhaps remind the class that the middle of the twentieth century was not the best time for cocktail drinking in America. It was not chosen as the basis for the seminar because it was exemplary, but

---

* Brown points out that this is a superior name for this drink, which evokes "silly animals that hop around," rather than impinging on the Martini's austere dignity.

# EXAMINATION
# Bloody Mary

vodka

tomato juice

lemon juice

Worcestershire sauce

celery salt

black pepper

simple syrup (optional)

*Using the given ingredients, determine the proportions of the Bloody Mary and its method of preparation.*

because it was not. A strong business may still fail in an economic downturn, but a weak one is unlikely to survive; what widespread failures leave behind, we can reasonably assume had good reasons to make it. Cocktails are very much the same. We have the canon we do because most of the drinks failed during the twentieth century, and that left us with a short list of the most important ones.

Whatever vodka's shortcomings in other contexts, we've seen it work in long drinks where the objective is to add a kick to something that tastes good without changing anything else. We have seen it work as a drying agent, and we have seen it paired effectively with savory, piquant, and moderately sour flavors. The Bloody Mary hits many of these notes for a result that is anything but bland. It also requires some adjustments to our standard long drink preparation—in pondering what those might be, bear in mind that the solid spices are meant to be fully incorporated, but the drink should never become foamy.

As always, consider the nearest analogues among the preceding recipes and how the balance is affected by the changes in this one. The Bloody Mary, like the Margarita, deals with some modifications to the base that do not appear frequently; and like the Gimlet, it will require you to think creatively about your technique. It will also make an excellent basis for future experiments if you wish to undertake them.

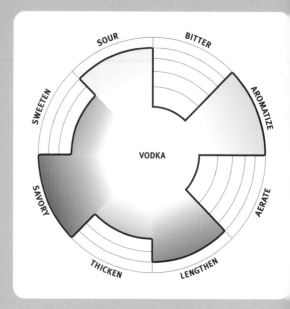

**1.30**

SOUR · BITTER · AROMATIZE · AERATE · LENGTHEN · THICKEN · SAVORY · SWEETEN

VODKA

The first step is to identify the Bloody Mary as a juice drink, like the Screwdriver. We have not dealt with any complicated ones until now, but the presence of a couple of solid ingredients should be a clue that the build-and-stir system we used for the Screwdriver will not be sufficient. But shaking risks making it foamy, an unpleasant texture you've been told to avoid—to say nothing of the fact that drinks this size are not generally shaken.

My recommendation is to **roll** the cocktail, which is to pour it back and forth between two shaker tins with ice half a dozen times or until it reaches the desired consistency. The whole mixture, ice included, is then poured into the glass—you've probably seen bartenders do this. It's not as efficient as shaking, but it aerates the mixture far less, which stops foams from forming when they are not desired.

The flavor balance is informed by the presence of salty and savory ingredients. The Margarita's salt could square off against the tequila, but these need something else because the vodka is no match for them. Tomato juice is savory, but it is also sweet and sour. To set up sufficient contrast, we incorporate a lemon juice accent—somewhat as we incorporated an orange juice accent into the Ward Eight, although in this case we are trying to raise the level of acidity rather than lower it. A quarter ounce of simple syrup can optionally balance the sourness.

# SOLUTION
# Bloody Mary

2 oz. vodka

4 oz. tomato juice

½ oz. lemon juice

3 dashes Worcestershire sauce

1 pinch celery salt

1 pinch black pepper

1 tsp. simple syrup (optional)

Roll between two tins with ice. Pour unstrained into a highball glass with a salted rim.

I recommend 2 oz. of vodka for every 4 oz. of tomato juice—a higher ratio than we used for the Screwdriver, but the Bloody Mary is a taller drink and the vodka functions as a kind of drying lengthener, diluting the strong flavors across the board and ensuring they play well together.

Note that we can't fit all the Bloody Mary's characteristics into its chart: it is savory *and* piquant, and if analyzed as juice-based it's dried as well. Not to belabor the point, but this should remind us that mixing cocktails is not about making this or that modification but the *act* of modification. The Bloody Mary draws more on salty and savory flavors than most recipes, taking its cues from the kitchen as much as the bar.

It also tends to beget house versions. This list of ingredients is far from encompassing everything one might find in a Bloody Mary, although it does cover the core group—rarely will one be made that leaves any of these out. For extra credit, develop your own personal recipe.

This concludes our first course. You should by now have a solid grounding in the essential tools and techniques of the cocktail and be equipped for more advanced study. Subsequent chapters will provide just that, but for now, I advise closing the book and having some drinks. You've earned it.

# The Hidden Patrimony

**The recipes** in our first lesson are not merely respectable drinks, but represent some of the *most* respectable drinks in the canon. Why, then, have I used them to represent an era I call the Cocktail Dark Ages? There are two ways to answer this question: one of quality and one of quantity.

In short, the quality of the canon in this period doesn't reflect the overall quality of midcentury drinking. Lighter-bodied spirits were in vogue, while flavorsome ones were suspect. The picture does not improve when one moves beyond the spirit bases to the other components of a cocktail. In the era of Campbell's *Cooking with Soup*, prepackaged ingredients were preferred: grenadine and sour mix were in, fresh juice and produce were not. The James Bond films began their long assault on the Martini, which gradually persuaded the public that shaken vodka with a few drops of vermouth was the height of sophistication. The changing tastes of the country led to declining sales for once-essential ingredients and eventually to their disappearance; even orange bitters—a ubiquitous item for most of a century—would vanish from store shelves.

Perhaps the greatest issue is that cocktails themselves were not popular in this era. They were stodgy, stuffy—the sort of thing one's father might have drunk. Youth would not reclaim cocktails as their own until the neon-colored drinks of the disco era arrived to handicap their insulin production, and even then the drinks would not be called *cocktails* but instead generically *Martinis*—as entirely wrong as that may have been.

It was after years of such extremes of bad drinking that the Cocktail Renaissance began. Cocktails were no longer what your father drank, but what your *grandparents* drank, and everyone prefers their grandparents' culture to that of their parents. Moreover, there was a sense that something critical to the culture was being lost with the passing of that generation. Cocktails acquired a whiff of nostalgia, as well as a sense of mystery, with information about them being too scattered to be easily discovered.

Place yourself in the position of one of these early Renaissanciers. The world around you is filled with the tantalizing evidence of this lost art. In every liquor store and nearly every bar, there are dust-encrusted bottles with strange, evocative names like Campari and Chartreuse. They're there for a reason, but damn if the bartender can tell you what it is—it's been years since someone came in looking for any of them.

Reviving the mixological arts from near-extinction began with these questions. Most people who came to cocktails before about 2010 began their journeys in much the same way, tugging on a thread without realizing just how far it would take them. An old, dog-eared book, a passing allusion to an unfamiliar drink, a bottle that nobody seemed to use but that was still somehow on every backbar in America—in noticing these kinds of things, one could easily be pulled into the orbit of curiosity that surrounded the cocktail.

This suggests another answer to this seminar's initial question: even if we have no problems with the postwar period's overall mixological quality, even if we contend that there was nothing wrong per se with the way its drinks were compounded, to put it simply *there were not enough of them*. A canon of thirty-odd drinks is hardly adequate to sustain the medium—imagine, if there were only thirty plays or novels in common circulation, what the state of those art forms would be. If absolutely nothing else, the Dark Ages were mixologically *insufficient*.

This course will brush the cobwebs off those untouched bottles and ingredients and allow us to fill out the canon beyond the skeleton of recipes from seminar one. By the end, you will know some of the energizing fire in the soul that drove the revivalist enthusiasm for cocktails at the end of the last millennium. You will also experience some of the yearning—for ingredients that could not be so easily restored to common use and for the unmakeable cocktails of bygone days that require them. In short, you will understand the zeitgeist that helped turn a niche artistic and culinary interest into an explosive cultural phenomenon. Be patient; the cocktailians of the world got what they were longing for, and you will, too.

# Ingredients for This Course

## GROCERY

| | |
|---|---|
| Angostura bitters | 14, 17, 24, 29 |
| coffee* | 10 |
| eggs* | 5–7, 11, 21, 25, 28, 30 |
| ginger syrup/soda | 9 |
| grapefruit* | 3, 8, 15 |
| grenadine | 3, 25, 27 |
| heavy cream/whipping cream* | 10, 30 |
| honey/honey syrup | 8, 12 |
| lemons | 4–6, 11, 14, 16, 18–20, 25, 27, 28, 30 |
| limes | 9, 12, 15, 23, 30 |
| orange flower water* | 30 |
| oranges | 2, 12, 13, 18 |
| Peychaud's Bitters* | 17, 18, 29 |
| raspberry syrup* | 9, 18, 22, 28 |
| rich demerara syrup* | 10 |
| seltzer | 11, 20, 30 |
| sugar/simple syrup | 5, 7, 11, 14, 15, 21, 25, 30 |

## ALCOHOL

| | |
|---|---|
| apple brandy | 24–26 |
| Bénédictine* | 4, 13, 16, 17, 19, 24 |
| bourbon | 2, 29 |
| brandy | 7, 14, 17, 18, 21, 27 |
| Campari* | 2, 20 |
| curaçao/triple sec | 6, 16, 29 |
| dry vermouth | 13, 22, 28 |
| filtered lightly aged rum | 15 |
| Green Chartreuse* | 1, 14, 23 |
| high-proof apple brandy* | 16 |
| high-proof bourbon* | 5, 8 |
| high-proof rye whiskey | 26 |
| Irish whiskey* | 1, 10, 13 |
| kirschwasser* | 19, 22 |
| London dry gin | 2, 6, 9, 11, 19, 23, 25, 28, 30 |
| maraschino* | 15, 23 |
| moderately aged rum* | 12, 18, 27 |
| ruby port* | 21 |
| rye whiskey | 3, 4, 17, 27 |
| sparkling wine/Champagne | 12, 29 |
| sweet vermouth | 1, 2, 17, 20 |
| Yellow Chartreuse* | 24, 26 |

* indicates new ingredients

**The Tipperary**, one of the best cocktails made with Irish whiskey, is an apt place to begin our second lesson. It is not unlike the Manhattan, a whiskey-and-sweet-vermouth drink with a further aromatic component, so there is a familiarity to it. But it also introduces some concepts that we will see repeated throughout this seminar.

Most notably, it derives a complex aroma from a liqueur element. We have seen orange, mint, and chocolate liqueurs already, but in this case we are dealing with what is sometimes called an **herbal liqueur**, a sweetened spirit infused with a large number of herbs and spices which does not attempt to replicate the flavor of some solid ingredient but rather to create a profile all its own. And we are off to a strong start in that department with Green Chartreuse, one of the most potent in the category. Produced by monks of the Carthusian order using a recipe that dates back some 400 years, it employs nearly 130 botanicals and is bottled at a whopping 110 proof—roughly double what we would otherwise think of as "liqueur-strength." There is nothing that tastes quite like Green Chartreuse, with the exception of Yellow Chartreuse, a milder 80-proof expression developed by the same monks in the 1830s. Both versions are common in classic cocktail recipes, and unlike many other traditional ingredients, their production has been fairly consistent since the age of the cocktail began—despite

# Tipperary

2 oz. Irish whiskey

¾ oz. sweet vermouth

¼ oz. Green Chartreuse

Stir with ice. Strain into a chilled cocktail glass.

two expropriations of the Carthusian monastery by the French government since the Revolution. In this recipe, it is sweetener, bitterer, and aromatizer all at once. It is also the highest-proof ingredient. Liqueurs at this level of complexity can be difficult to wrangle, which is why it is used at an accent-level ¼ oz. here—but note that we will see them show up in steadily increasing proportions over the coming pages.

Irish whiskey is a slightly different story. The classic style is known today as "single pot still Irish whiskey," made from a mixture of malted and unmalted barley with a minimum of 30 percent of each. This is unique among barley-whiskey traditions, which elsewhere—and in a few instances in Ireland as well—tend toward single malts, i.e., whiskies made from 100 percent malted barley. Most Irish whiskey available today belongs to a lighter blended style developed in the middle of the last century, in part to cater to the questionable American tastes of the day. Recipes in this book can survive the use of such things, but they will be vastly improved by employing the more traditional single pot still style or an Irish single malt. Those are the only types that would have been available in 1917, when Hugo Ensslin first published an early version of this recipe; we will not be *bound* by historical authenticity in this section, but we will be guided by it!

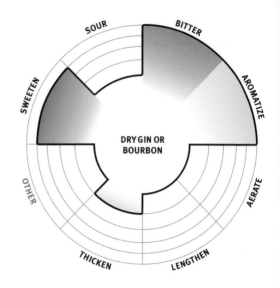

**Campari** is another herbal liqueur, belonging to a particular class known as *amari* (singular *amaro*). These are traditional Italian products that are appreciably bitter in addition to their sweetness and aromaticity. Historically, they have been meant as digestifs: tonics one takes after supper to help everything settle. The herbs involved may have medicinal properties, actual or alleged. And for many years, Campari was the flagship of the category in the United States, achieving such popular recognition as to be used as a rhyme for *sorry* in a Broadway musical.* Its pronounced bitterness makes it polarizing, while its brilliantly red color—originally from cochineal, a dye made from crushed red beetles—makes it impossible to miss.

The Campari-sweet vermouth axis is critical to two classic drinks. To the vermouth, Campari adds bitterness and the aroma of herbs and citrus. To the Campari, the vermouth adds body, texture, and relative sweetness, tempering it so that the pair can play well with others.

To this, we can add bourbon to make a Boulevardier. Invented by Erskine Gwynne and named after the literary magazine he published in Paris during Prohibition, the Boulevardier comes to us via Harry MacElhone—in whose books Gwynne also advertised. As it is most

* *Urinetown*, if you were wondering.

# Negroni

1 oz. London dry gin

1 oz. Campari

1 oz. sweet vermouth

Combine ingredients in a rocks glass with ice and stir. Garnish with an orange peel.

# Boulevardier

1½ oz. bourbon

¾ oz. Campari

¾ oz. sweet vermouth

Stir with ice and strain into a chilled cocktail glass. Optionally, garnish with an orange peel.

often made, the drink takes a step beyond the Tipperary in making the herbal liqueur a substantial part of its final balance, using a 2:1:1 ratio in which the bourbon writes the script but the vermouth and Campari have major roles. If the Campari's bitter orange note is not enough for you, an optional garnish can make up the difference.

Or, we can add gin for a Negroni, which traditionally goes even further with a 1:1 ratio. It has a very big presence on the palate, the herbaceous and citrus botanicals in the gin discoursing loudly with their sweeter partners. It is most commonly built rather than stirred, which allows the drinker to let it dilute to the intensity they desire.

Though the Negroni was not previously a top-tier classic, it took off like a rocket during the Cocktail Renaissance and spent some time as the secret handshake of the mixologically in-the-know. These days, it's mainstream to the point of ubiquity: Campari even sponsors a whole Negroni Week each year, at which bars raise money for charities.

It's worth noting that the original Boulevardier was also an equal-parts recipe, and many still prefer it that way or with proportions of 1½:1:1. Likewise, the Negroni is often found with a more gin-forward tilt. But the probability distribution favors Negronis in equal parts and Boulevardiers that are more generous with the whiskey.

**The Blinker** is not a particularly elaborate creation, and it looks at first glance as though it could have been in our first unit. There are a few reasons it was not—including its use of grapefruit juice, which was available to midcentury imbibers but also appears in enough revived recipes that it was easier to fit in here. Grapefruit occupies a middle position in the citrus family: with an acidity about 40 percent that of lemons and limes, it can be used to sour drinks on its own if there's enough of it or in smaller doses to temper the sourness of its cousins. The juice is still three times more acidic than orange juice, but it is nearly as sweet, so it remains suitable to drink on its own.*

More to the point, the Blinker was emphatically not on drinkers' radars during the Cocktail Dark Ages. It owes its contemporary popularity in large measure to Ted Haigh, nicknamed "Dr. Cocktail," whose book *Vintage Spirits and Forgotten Cocktails* did much to galvanize interest in the recipes in this seminar and the next one. The good

---

* I had trouble getting the hang of this fact when I first began working with cocktails, because I was used to the idea that grapefruit juice is extremely sour. It is, but only by the standards of juices we ordinarily drink plain. Other, sourer juices are usually diluted, sweetened, or otherwise mixed before we consume them—we think of lemonade when we think of lemons, but we think of straight grapefruit juice when we think about grapefruit. It's easy to end up associating the latter with higher acidity as a result.

# Blinker

2 oz. rye whiskey

1 oz. grapefruit juice

½ oz. grenadine

Shake with ice. Strain into a chilled cocktail glass.

doctor also popularized a variation using raspberry syrup in lieu of grenadine, which is sometimes published as the Blinker but is better called the Dr. Cocktail's Blinker, the Dr. Blinker, or some equally clarifying neologism.

Raspberry syrup has been used in cocktails since the nineteenth century, but grenadine gradually replaced it in most of its traditional recipes after becoming widely available in the early 1900s. The two can usually be substituted for one another without doing too much harm, but raspberry syrup is easy to make and phenomenally delicious. Having both in your arsenal is worth it, and in this book I've specified each where I think them best.

Grenadine's good fortune is quite impressive in retrospect. It was nowhere in 1890, crept into recipes over the next twenty years, began displacing other sweeteners, and had become the overwhelming favorite by the time of the last pre-Prohibition cocktail guides. Many recipes that it and raspberry syrup had been fighting over were decided in its favor in *The Savoy Cocktail Book*, the influence of which probably helped to cement it as the go-to red sweetener for many subsequent years. That bottled versions were widely available undoubtedly helped it in the age of convenience foods.

SOUR BITTER AROMATIZE AERATE LENGTHEN THICKEN OTHER SWEETEN

RYE WHISKEY

**With the Frisco Sour**, we resume our discussion of herbal liqueurs and introduce Bénédictine. Several that we cover in this chapter are coextensive with their categories—that is, there is really nothing that can be used as a substitute if one wants to preserve the flavor. There are good curaçaos and bad ones—and expressions that substitute poorly for one another—but many will make drinks that taste similar, and the drinker of curaçao will have many reasonable options to choose from. There is only one Bénédictine.

A French liqueur sweetened with honey, flavored with twenty-seven spices, and aged in oak for a year in total before bottling, Bénédictine has been in production for at least two hundred years. Beyond that point, there is some dispute. The producer has long claimed that the recipe originated centuries earlier and had come from a monastery shuttered by the French Revolution. This has never been publicly substantiated, and it's easy to imagine that it was never more than a marketing ploy—although it has also never been conclusively disproved. In any case, the last two hundred years present plenty for the makers of Bénédictine to be proud of. Their product has achieved wide international success and established itself as indispensable to classic mixology.

# Frisco Sour

2 oz. rye whiskey

½ oz. Bénédictine

½ oz. lemon juice

Shake with ice. Strain into a chilled cocktail glass.

We know it contains saffron and angelica root and that it draws flavor from its barrel-aging process. The honey gives it a robust sweetness, which is put to good use in this cocktail. Where the Sidecar and the Margarita may need a bit of additional sugar to reinforce their orange liqueurs as sweeteners, the Frisco Sour has no such requirement. Even at a nontrivial 80-proof, the Bénédictine holds up against the lemon juice. It contributes aroma as well; where our previous herbal cocktails have been wine-driven, focused on incorporating the complex liqueur into a harmonious environment, the Frisco Sour holds it in counterpoint with the bright, sour assertiveness of the lemon. This environment shows off the Bénédictine well, but as we go on, we will see it matched with increasingly bold ingredients that demonstrate how even something this intricate can still play well with others.

The Frisco Sour is also a shining example of cocktail revivalism at work. Having tasted it once at an event, but not knowing the name, *New York Times* columnist Frank Bruni set about trying to identify and recreate it—the fruits of which the paper eventually published. While it has a classic pedigree, it had failed to catch fire like other old recipes, and confusion reigned about the difference between the Frisco (a duo of whiskey with Bénédictine and a lemon peel garnish) and the Frisco Sour. Having consulted contemporary cocktail luminaries like Audrey Saunders and Jim Meehan, Bruni settled on the recipe above.

## 2.5

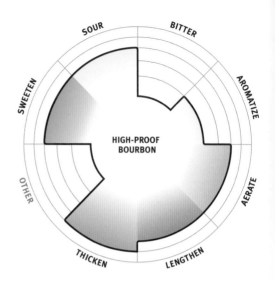

**If one wished** to capture the *geist* of this seminar in a single technique or ingredient, the egg drink would do it best, and the Boston Sour is the flagship of that fleet.

Eggs have been popular in mixed drinks for the last two centuries. In sour cocktails like this one, the egg white is generally used sans yolk, to texturize the drink and make it foamy without adding much flavor itself. It can also bind to a variety of bitter compounds, stripping them out of the mixture and softening the final taste. In short, egg cocktails are relatively forgiving and quite attractive tactilely. They are also more delicate than other cocktails, their foamy heads becoming rather less appealing if they sit too long and dissipate.

For the best foam, we use a modern technique called the **dry shake**: combine all your ingredients in the shaker *without* ice, shake, then add ice and shake again. In the egg white, proteins are twisted into balls. You want them to unravel, stick to each other, and form a lattice, trapping bubbles of air. This is easier at room temperature than when they're cold, and the dry shake gives them the room to do it.*

* As it happens, the dry shake was developed by a bartender named Chad Solomon to make the punishing task of being a high-volume craft bartender a bit easier on his body. The benefits to the drinks' texture were serendipitous.

# Boston Sour

2 oz. high-proof bourbon

1 oz. simple syrup

¾ oz. lemon juice

egg white

Shake without ice, then again with ice. Strain into a chilled cocktail glass.

An average-sized egg white will also add about an ounce of water to your cocktail. Between this and the tempering effects of the proteins, egg drinks can accommodate more intense ingredients, like the higher-proof bourbon I recommend for this recipe. In the United States, the gold standard is **bonded spirits**, certified by their makers—to us and to the government—as having been made by a single distillery in a single half-year period, aged no less than four years in oak barrels, and bottled at precisely 100 proof. Bonded spirits are statements of confidence by the distiller and usually quite flavorful. If none is available, substitute a nonbonded 100-proof whiskey; to use an 80-proof one, add an extra quarter ounce.

As for the Boston Sour, in my own extensive research I have found no consensus on how or why it came to have that name. As a Massachusite myself, I would love to claim it as a native concoction, but I find that exceedingly unlikely. Egg whites have been a common addition to sours for nearly as long as there have been sours; even if it had been "invented" by some Bostonian or other, it would have assuredly also been invented by scores of other barkeeps in as many other cities at various points. I am fond of the name and it is reasonably widely known, but it is worth noting that simply ordering a "Whiskey Sour" will in many places get you a drink that looks like this one.

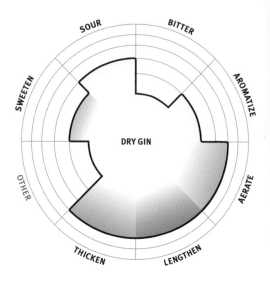

**2.6**

SOUR · BITTER · AROMATIZE · AERATE · LENGTHEN · THICKEN · OTHER · SWEETEN

DRY GIN

**Just as** the building blocks that give us the plain Whiskey Sour have parallels in those that yield the Sidecar, the Boston Sour finds a liqueur-driven analogue in the White Lady.

Americans who fled the sober tyranny of the Volstead Act and washed ashore in Europe had their choice of two recognized masters named Harry to serve them cocktails: Harry MacElhone of Harry's New York Bar in Paris and Harry Craddock of the Savoy Hotel's American Bar in London. Each produced at least one cocktail book for the benefit of posterity and good press. Each also produced a cocktail called the White Lady. MacElhone's version was the first to market, a teetering combination of crème de menthe with brandy and orange liqueur that did not survive the competition with his namesake neighbor to the north. Craddock's White Lady looked more like the one printed here, but he had not quite won the day: his recipe was eggless, yet in subsequent years the White Lady was solidly established as an egg white drink.

If not common per se, such a change is at least precedented. Once given the capacity to add egg whites to cocktails, it seems that people have at least some tendency to do so whenever a drink appears to

# White Lady

2 oz. London dry gin

½ oz. curaçao or triple sec

½ oz. lemon juice

egg white

Shake without ice, then again with ice. Strain into a chilled cocktail glass.

work somewhat like other egg drinks do. With the notable exception of the Daiquiri, the basic sours of most spirit classes are often made with an egg white, and this predilection has gone far enough that now and then a recipe with a living progenitor is rewritten to make it "more of a sour" by the addition of egg.

This became the standard for the White Lady with good reason. The completed cocktail gives one something of the sense of drinking a meringue that has been lightly perfumed with orange—which, in a chemical sense, is not too far off from what's happening. The action of the shaker, particularly during the dry shake, serves to beat the egg in the presence of sugars and flavors that will be combined into it. Egg drinks are the place where mixology and baking come closest to one another.

Always be especially careful when dry shaking a drink. Without ice, the tins will not form as tight a seal as they otherwise do. There is some risk that the drink will splash out if the pieces are not firmly together—and if you neglect to keep a hand on each tin while shaking, there is an even better chance than usual that the top half will fly off at the apogee of the shake and be followed across the room by a stream of wasted cocktail.

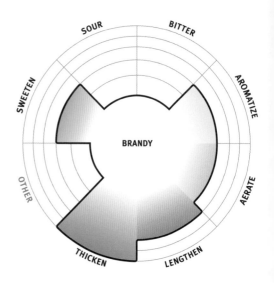

SOUR BITTER AROMATIZE SWEETEN BRANDY AERATE OTHER THICKEN LENGTHEN

**Even** before there were egg white sours, there were flips. Strictly speaking, there were also flips before there were flips: the first drinks by this name were concoctions of beer and rum, cooked in their mugs by inserting red-hot pokers fresh from the fireplace, which caused the mixtures to bubble and, yes, to flip. This was the sort of thing one might have sampled at a tavern during the Revolutionary War.

By the same alchemical process that turned a word for rose water into the Mint Julep, flips evolved considerably in a short period: eggs came in, eventually beer dropped out, the whole thing acquired ice when Frederic Tudor brought it to the world, and by the middle of the nineteenth century the flip had stabilized as a cold drink made by shaking spirits with a whole egg.

Where egg whites are added to drinks for texture—and to some extent for the flavors they can strip *out*—while being treated as largely flavorless themselves, the egg yolks in flips unavoidably contribute flavor. They do not, however, taste eggy. The yolk of an egg is dense with rich fats and proteins, in which respect it is not unlike cream. As a result, the finished flip has significantly more of the character of a boozy milkshake than the noninitiate would expect. Despite being on the heavy side and having very little volume that is neither hard liquor nor raw egg, flips are downright quaffable.

# Brandy Flip

1½ oz. brandy

½ oz. sugar

whole egg

Shake without ice, then again with ice. Strain into a chilled cocktail glass and garnish with a sprinkle of grated nutmeg.

True, eggs do lack milk's sugars, but flips make up for it. They're commonly prepared with a **rich simple syrup**, made with sugar and water in a 2:1 ratio. **Demerara sugar**, which is less refined than white sugar and retains some molasses characteristics, is often used for this purpose. Rich demerara syrup will appear often throughout the book, so this is not a bad time to prepare some. However, the Brandy Flip can be made just as well and will have the same sugar content with another rich simple syrup, maple syrup, or plain sugar. I have recommended the last here for simplicity's sake.

A word about egg foaming: while flips will generate a head, it does not work in quite the same way as it does for an egg white sour. Egg whites love to form foams—in *On Food and Cooking*, Harold McGee estimates that you can increase the volume of egg whites by eight times through whipping alone—but egg yolks are more reluctant. The proteins are less inclined to bond with one another than those in the albumen, because they are fairly stable as they are. Whole-egg foams tend to be less dramatic and shorter-lived than ones that use the egg white alone.* In short, drink your flips quickly and don't expect them to be as visually striking as your sours.

* To address this, separate the egg, beat the white until fluffy, beat the yolk separately, and then combine them while working in the other ingredients.

## 2.8

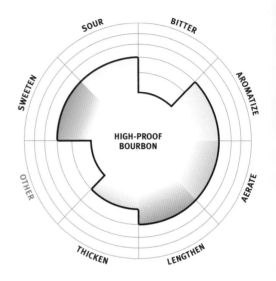

**Eggs** are not the only ingredients conducive to foam. All you need is something in the mixture that can hold an architecture of bubbles together. Even lemon and lime juice have enough plant matter in them to help with foam formation, although they work best in conjunction with other, frothier ingredients.

Honey foams up well, and is an ideal candidate for dry shaking. Its protein density is impressive for a sweetener, and it's full of foam-stabilizing sugars. A honey drink will never build up the kind of head one sees on an egg cocktail, but it can certainly get closer than the average sour.

Dry shaking also makes undiluted honey easier to work with, because you're mixing it at room-temperature viscosity rather than trying to chill and incorporate it at the same time. Its effects on the flavor are even more impressive: wonderfully fragrant, floral scents come wafting off ordinary grocery store honey when it's shaken unchilled, and the foam ends up full of them.

I realized this while working on my previous book, but I can't imagine no one else has thought of it—it seems obvious in retrospect, and I've yet to find a recipe it doesn't improve. For extra credit, see how much dry shaking a Bee's Knees or a Gold Rush changes it.

# De Rigueur, alias Brown Derby No. 2

2 oz. high-proof bourbon

1 oz. grapefruit juice

⅓ oz. honey

Shake without ice, then again with ice. Strain into a chilled cocktail glass.

The Brown Derby first appears in *Hollywood Cocktails*, a 1933 book by George Buzza Jr. He claimed to be revealing the house drinks of Hollywood hot spots, but lifted many entries word for word from *The Savoy Cocktail Book*, with the De Rigueur renamed after the Brown Derby, a famous hat-shaped restaurant. Culinary historian Robert F. Moss has found press coverage of the big hat's actual specialty, a brandy drink completely unlike this one. No other sources have been found that suggest a "Brown Derby" was even being served in L.A.

Not so in New York, where a briefly trendy combination of rum, maple, and lime bore the name. Only Buzza would use it for the honey-grapefruit recipe until Dale Degroff picked it up for his book in 2002.

Both Brown Derbies are worth knowing, but we need a clearer way to distinguish them. One option is to resume calling this one the De Rigueur. Another would be to assign them numbers, as Harry Craddock did for the Corpse Revivers: let this recipe be the Brown Derby No. 2, and the New York version be the Brown Derby No. 1.

### FURTHER READING

For the Brown Derby No. 1: shake 2 oz. moderately aged rum, ¾ oz. lime juice, and ⅓ oz. maple syrup with ice and double strain into a chilled cocktail glass.

2.9

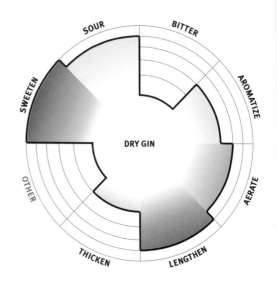

**Returning** for a moment to the topic of long drinks, we find as we did in the last seminar that the techniques and ingredients we have covered lend themselves as well to this format as they do to shorter preparations. The Florodora is the simplest case of this, one that you can probably classify on sight as belonging to the extended clan of the buck.

As extremely specific stories about the origins of cocktails go, the Florodora's is relatively plausible. In 1900, a show called *Florodora* was must-see material in New York City. Or, more specifically, six of the actresses were: the "Florodora Sextette" were comely brunettes of equal height dressed in matching costumes, whose involvement in the storyline was entirely beside the point.

Naturally, the women who played these roles were the toast of the town. The Florodora is reputed to have taken place at a post-performance gathering in a successful effort to get one of the six to switch from lemonade to something stronger. Mission accomplished: David Wondrich writes in *Imbibe!* that this drink is "a fragrant, slightly silly one that hits like a roll of quarters in a clutch purse."

Made with ginger soda, a spirit, and lime juice, the Florodora is manifestly a cousin to the buck we discussed in the first seminar. What makes it more interesting is the use of raspberry syrup. Bucks do not

# Florodora

1½ oz. London dry gin

½ oz. lime juice

⅓ oz. raspberry syrup

4 oz. ginger ale

Combine gin, lime, and raspberry syrup in a highball glass with ice and stir. Fill with ginger ale.

generally add any sweetener beyond what the soda provides and pare even that back through citrus juice. Why, then, does the Florodora impose this extra sugar on the template?

If its origin story is to be believed, the more than adequate reason is that the drink was meant to appeal to someone whose first choice had been lemonade. Of course the replacement drink would be sweeter than the average buck, if that is the standard to which it was being designed. This, however, does not explain why it works well enough that we continue to drink it, including those of us who would not sooner have had lemonade.

Raspberry syrup is sweet, yes, but it is also tart. If in the course of preparing this drink, one finds that it is causing more of a pucker in the mouth than seems desirable, the usual response of adding more of the sweetener will not help matters—and will instead likely exacerbate the problem. A consequence of this is that we must be judicious with both the raspberry syrup and the lime juice, allowing both to settle in as accents to a drink with a central axis determined by the gin and ginger ale, bowed only slightly by the sourness of the other two ingredients. In this sense, the Florodora is as much a spiritual cousin to the Rickey as it is a structural relation of the buck: a refreshing soda drink, tilted a bit more than one might expect toward the sour.

# 2.10

# SOLUTION

The Irish Coffee is most similar to the Hot Toddy: a long drink, served hot and built in the glass. What distinguishes it is the use of a flavorful lengthener, as in a juice drink—but unlike juice, coffee is bitter and not especially sweet, so we offset it with sugar and cream.

Cream is filled with globules of fat, which the whisk breaks apart. The molecules try to regroup, forming a connective network that traps the air bubbles whipping introduces—and also traps liquid, meaning that whipped cream is more solid and less prone to flow than unwhipped cream is. The higher the cream's fat content, the better all this works.

The dollop of freshly whipped cream fattens, thickens, and sweetens all at once. It's kept separate so each sip of piping hot cocktail comes topped with cool, rich cream. The drinker chooses how much of each experience to have in a given sip, as with a sugared rim.

1¼ oz. Irish whiskey

3½ oz. hot coffee

½ oz. rich demerara syrup

1 oz. heavy cream

Whisk cream gently in a bowl until bubbles dissipate. Stir coffee, whiskey, and demerara syrup together in a heat-safe glass or mug. Float cream on top.

# EXERCISE
# Irish Coffee

Irish whiskey

hot coffee

rich demerara syrup

heavy cream

*Using the given ingredients, determine the proportions of the Irish Coffee and its method of preparation.*

**I've based** our Irish Coffee recipe on one developed by Jillian Vose at the Dead Rabbit, an acclaimed modern cocktail bar that's also an Irish pub. Vose took their widely praised version back to the drawing board in 2016—she describes the bar's mentality as "if it isn't broken, fix it anyway"—and brought in Dale Degroff for a day of workshopping.

Following Vose, we'll use the rich demerara syrup touched on with the Brandy Flip. She calls for a lighter-bodied blended Irish whiskey, but the single pot still we've been using will do just fine. The cream is the trickiest piece technique-wise: you'll want to whip it in a separate bowl and float it on top of the cocktail, preserving the temperature gradient of hot coffee and cold cream for the drinker. Use a cream of at least 30 percent fat—look for heavy cream or *whipping cream*—and stop whisking when there are no visible bubbles left.

Vose advises that most Irish Coffee makers go wrong by using too large a glass. Six ounces is plenty. Now, consider what makes the drink work, what each of its pieces does, and what we've seen before that it resembles—our course is cumulative, so keep your wits about you! When you have your answers, proceed and see how well you did.

**I promised** that we had not seen the last of the fizz. I keep my word in matters of cocktails and pedagogy: the Silver Fizz is merely one of several more which are scattered throughout this text.

Historically, fizzes have incorporated eggs nearly as often as plain sours have. The textural dynamics at play in the foam of an egg sour are kicked into high gear when carbonated water is introduced. If shaking alone is enough to aerate an egg white into a foam, imagine how much further the introduction of bubbly water can take that.

The Silver Fizz unites the dry shaking technique to unfold egg proteins with the fizz technique of effervescing a shaken cocktail, making a medium-length drink that's meant to be swiftly dispatched in the manner of a shorter one. It is a lighter and more refreshing take on the egg sour, with an even more intriguing mouthfeel.

Other long egg drinks exist. One can make a Golden Fizz using the yolk of the egg instead of the white or a Diamond Fizz by using both. The latter may particularly appeal to fans of flips, the former to those who have been wondering this whole chapter what they are meant to do with the leftover yolks from their egg white cocktails. In practice, they are often just discarded, because there are too few egg yolk drinks

# Silver Fizz

2 oz. London dry gin

juice of ½ lemon (¾ oz.)

¼ oz. sugar

egg white

3 oz. seltzer

Shake all but seltzer without ice, then again with ice. Strain into a highball glass without ice and top with seltzer.

to keep up. But an advantage of domestic mixology is that one need not include the yolks in cocktails in order to find a use for them. Add them to spaghetti carbonara or scrambled eggs; use them to make homemade mayonnaise, hollandaise sauce, custard, pudding, or any number of other things that I will freely admit to not having tried myself. Those inclined toward pastries may already have answers to this question already and appreciate the chance to work through their surfeit of albumen.

This may also be a good point to discuss the health concerns some people have about consuming raw eggs in cocktails. *Salmonella* is the usual worry, but it's relatively hard to get *Salmonella* from eggs these days: the bacteria live on the outside of the shell, not the inside, and eggs have to undergo a sterilizing wash before they reach U.S. grocery stores. More to the point, if you've had poached, soft-boiled, over easy, or sunny-side up eggs you've already eaten eggs that were "undercooked" according to CDC guidelines, and chances are you didn't get sick. Now, if your doctor tells you not to have raw eggs, do listen to them. They can cause problems if you're allergic, and if you have a compromised immune system it may simply not be worth accepting *any* risk of *Salmonella* infection. But if you're otherwise healthy, raw eggs are nothing to fear.

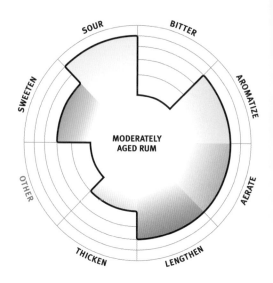

**If you** are skimming through this book without making the recipes, drop what you're doing and make an Air Mail right now. I had never made one prior to the research process for my last book, and while I remembered generally enjoying the cocktail when I had it at this or that bar, I did not recall it as remarkable. It was by far the greatest pleasant surprise of that round of research, and made as described here, it now ranks among my very favorite drinks.

Just as the French 75 may be regarded as using the fizz technique with sparkling wine in lieu of seltzer, the Air Mail borrows the dry shake fizz technique for a bit of honey and a bit of bubbly. In this respect, we are borrowing from both the De Rigueur and the Silver Fizz as well.

What is it that makes the Air Mail so special? It is—and I cannot stress this enough—the dry shake. Honey does not foam up quite as well as egg whites do, but the addition of a carbonated ingredient gooses it nicely, giving the honey even more of a textural role than it has in its other appearances. But unlike egg whites, honey is an *aromatic* foaming agent. Its wonderful floral characteristics are accentuated in a foam, with a series of little Champagne bubbles periodically popping and bursting its aromatic chemicals right up into your nose. That is to say nothing of how well the lovely aromas of honey complement the fruity notes of sparkling wines, nor of how surprisingly well the

# Air Mail

1½ oz. moderately aged rum
¾ oz. lime juice
½ oz. honey
1½ oz. sparkling wine

Shake all but the wine without ice, then again with ice. Strain into a chilled cocktail glass. Top with the sparkling wine and garnish with an orange peel.

richness of honey bridges the gap between the lighter wine flavors and the deep notes of the aged rum. It's a drink with a two-octave range.

Had I not chanced upon the technique of dry shaking honey drinks, I very much doubt I would have realized how delicious the Air Mail can be. Make no mistake, it is a perfectly delightful cocktail otherwise, but releasing the full aromatic power of the honey unlocks the drink to a degree I would never have imagined.

By **moderately aged rum**, I mean any rum that has been aged on the order of 5–12 years. Relative to the filtered rums from seminar one, they will have more wood flavor because of their time in oak, but also more rum flavor. Extended aging in tropical climates provides many opportunities for olfactorily interesting chemical reactions to occur, and these aromas are neither stripped out by filtration nor disincentivized by the market's taste in clear spirits.

The categorization of rums is surprisingly fraught. The common terms—white, amber, gold, silver, dark—are meaningless as indicators for age or flavor. Aged rums can be filtered to remove color, while some of the darkest "dark" rums are hardly aged at all but have instead been heavily colored and sweetened to suggest richness. Stick to age statements for now; we'll discuss rum at greater length in seminar four.

**Having** established most of the core techniques and ingredients of this unit, we can now begin to assemble them in more complex ways as we did in seminar one. The Brainstorm's kinship with the Tipperary should be evident. Let us consider its points of subtle distinction.

First, it uses dry rather than sweet vermouth. We have so far tended not to find dry vermouth paired with whiskey or other aged spirits, but this tells us more about tendency than essence. In addition to having a lower sugar content than its red Italian cousin, dry vermouth is also more comfortable in an accent role, accepting a more diminished presence in the Gibson than sweet vermouth does in the Manhattan. The flavor is not necessarily lighter, but the body is, and the presence of dry vermouth ordinarily betokens a more delicate cocktail than sweet vermouth does.

If we proceed under this assumption, we see how this recipe takes shape. Chartreuse finds a reasonable match in the sweet vermouth

# Brainstorm

2 oz. Irish whiskey

½ oz. dry vermouth

½ oz. Bénédictine

Stir with ice. Strain into a chilled cocktail glass. Express an orange peel over the top and discard.

of the Tipperary (albeit with a 3:1 handicap), but it would shred any subtlety we hoped to achieve by using dry vermouth in this case. Out it goes, with the lower-proof and more agreeable herbal liqueur Bénédictine arriving in its place. The Brainstorm's vermouth is too dry to sweeten the cocktail on its own, so its proportion with the liqueur is evened out to compensate. The orange peel garnish draws out the fruit notes in the wine while complementing the spice of the liqueur and the wood and malt of the whiskey, tying it all together and finishing the drink.

We end up with an alternative execution of some themes we saw in the Tipperary, a liqueur-wine cocktail done differently and further aromatized by means of a garnish. The variations are subtle—but as with the Rob Roy in the last seminar, small-seeming changes can work out to substantial differences in the profile of the resulting cocktail.

## 2.14

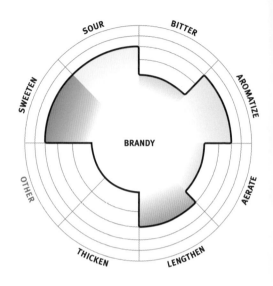

**Another** European creation of the Prohibition era, the Champs-Élysées both takes its name from that tony Parisian neighborhood and highlights two of France's national products. Amusingly, it appears to have originated across the Channel, first appearing in a British cocktail guide called *Drinks Long and Short* in 1925.

Where the Brainstorm was a liqueur-and-vermouth cocktail further aromatized, the Champs-Élysées adds aroma to an herbal sour along the lines of the Frisco Sour. We can get a sense of how it ought to work by reversing our steps from last time to get back to Chartreuse from the Frisco Sour's Bénédictine.

A cardinal rule of the mixological arts is that bold flavors should be matched with bold flavors and mild with mild to maintain balance in a recipe. Green Chartreuse is about as bold as they come. Rather than attempt to find proportions that will fit it into the Frisco Sour's template, we recognize instead that it may take a battalion to keep it contained. The lemon juice—no slouch of a flavor in its own right—will do the bulk of this work, providing a counterpoint to the heavy herbaceousness of the liqueur. That dose of sourness and the high proportion of alcohol per unit of sweetness that the Chartreuse delivers means that the cocktail needs some sugar to reinforce it. In goes simple syrup, in

# Champs-Élysées

1½ oz. brandy

½ oz. Green Chartreuse

½ oz. simple syrup

¾ oz. lemon juice

1 dash Angostura bitters

Shake with ice. Strain into a chilled cocktail glass.

a proportion to keep the lemon-liqueur contest evenly matched. The brandy serves almost as the field of battle.

Here again, we need to finish the drink—to offer a tweak toward bitterness to balance the sugar that balances the lemon that balances the Chartreuse. Our reliable old friend Angostura can do this for us, although this is an unusual preparation: we have yet to encounter a shaken drink that incorporates bitters. In fact, it may seem counterintuitive to do so, given the importance of smelling the tiny dose of bitters—surely it would be better if it were dashed right onto the surface? Will we even still be able to detect the bitters after shaking? Not exactly, but then, that is the point. One can almost conceive of the Angostura in the Champs-Élysées as slightly doctoring one of the other ingredients, making it more bitter and adding Trinidad's finest blend of spices to its flavor—in much the way that we have used simple syrup to amend our orange liqueurs when a cocktail needed it. The bitters, in other words, will still be there, affecting how the drink smells and tastes, but probably not in a way that is individually discernible. Like the Brainstorm's orange peel—or the Rob Roy's—it is a finishing agent, helping to tie the rest together into the subtly accented, spiced, and herbaceous lemonade that is the result of the titanic battle being waged within the Champs-Élysées.

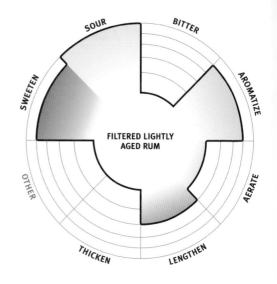

**FILTERED LIGHTLY AGED RUM**

SOUR · BITTER · AROMATIZE · AERATE · LENGTHEN · THICKEN · OTHER · SWEETEN

**Like** the Ward Eight, the Hemingway Daiquiri uses a blend of citrus juices. Unlike the Ward Eight, it draws its sweetness primarily from a liqueur—and one we have not previously seen at that. Maraschino is made from marasca cherries, a traditional product of the Dalmatian coast, by a process that combines infusion with distillation. Maraschino is at once a liqueur and a cherry spirit, its flavor coming heavily from its heady, potent fragrance. It is not fruity in the slightest, and its flavor is difficult to describe in the abstract. Some would call it floral. If you've had kirschwasser, that's the closest-tasting thing I've seen, because a cherry distillate is present in both.

Maraschino makes a disproportionate contribution to any cocktail in which it appears. This recipe uses extra citrus to keep it in check, lest it overpower and unbalance the whole. Maraschino is nevertheless a welcome accent flavor in many contexts, having an ethereal character that makes the overall flavor harder to place and more evocative.

Considerable confusion surrounds the name of this drink. It hails from Havana's famous Bar La Florida, nicknamed El Floridita by its patrons. Ernest Hemingway was one of them—and so much a fixture of the place that a statue of him now occupies one of the barstools. The proprietor was Constantino Ribalaigua Vert, known as "El Rey de los Coteleros" for his mastery behind the stick. Ribalaigua's Daiquiris

# Hemingway Daiquiri

1¾ oz. filtered lightly aged rum

¾ oz. maraschino liqueur

1 oz. lime juice

¾ oz. grapefruit juice

¼ oz. simple syrup

Shake with ice and strain into a chilled cocktail glass. Garnish with a lime wheel, a brandied cherry, or both.

were particularly lauded, and his menu included five signature house variations. What's known today as the Hemingway Daiquiri is essentially the Floridita Daiquiri No. 3.

Ribalaigua does seem to have named a drink after his famous regular, but its recipe and spelling differed from what we have today, the "E. Henmiway Special" was sugar-free. This is variously attributed to a personal preference or a medical necessity on Hemingway's part; if the latter, the maraschino's sugar content likely undid any benefit. This drink is also sometimes called the "Hemingway Special" or "Hemingway Daiquiri."

Further muddying the waters is the so-called "Papa Doble." "Papa" was Hemingway's nickname in Cuba, which makes this the "Hemingway Double." To prepare one, double the rum in the E. Henmiway Special.

The recipe most often called the Hemingway Daiquiri is none of these, but it's quite close to the E. Henmiway Special, albeit better balanced for most tastes and easier to spell. It also came from the same hand, and it seems very probable that Hemingway drank a few of them before he settled on his adjusted version. But if it irks you to use Hemingway's name for a drink that wasn't created specifically for him, keep the sugar and just call it the Floridita Daiquiri No. 3.

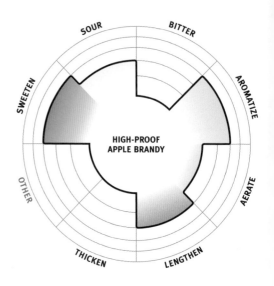

**2.16**

SOUR  BITTER

SWEETEN  AROMATIZE

HIGH-PROOF
APPLE BRANDY

OTHER  AERATE

THICKEN  LENGTHEN

**Where** the Ward Eight and the Hemingway Daiquiri subdivide their sour element and the Corpse Reviver uses a split spirit base, the Honeymoon incorporates multiple liqueurs as sweeteners. Until now, we have not had enough liqueurs in circulation to use two of them in a single recipe (except in the sui generis case of the Grasshopper), but make note of this technique, because it will become increasingly common as we discuss more advanced drinks.

As is always the case with liqueur-driven recipes, the curaçao and the Bénédictine in the Honeymoon contribute spirituousness as well as sweetness and flavor. This has historically been a problem for us in cocktails that relied on orange liqueur for sweetness, and we have often found it necessary to supplement the liqueur with simple syrup. Not so here: as it did in the Frisco Sour, the sweetness of the Bénédictine is enough to balance out the sourness of the lemon juice, relieving its partner of that burden. While the curaçao contributes some sugar, it does not strain credulity too far to think of it as primarily an aromatizer in this context, its orange scent helping to frame the other ingredients. Its effect in combination with the Bénédictine is akin to a clove-studded orange peel. Add in the woody apple flavor of the brandy, the Bénédictine's honey notes, and a bit of fresh juice, and overall, the Honeymoon is a fabulously autumnal cocktail.

# Honeymoon

1¾ oz. high-proof apple brandy

½ oz. Bénédictine

½ oz. curaçao or triple sec

½ oz. lemon juice

Shake with ice. Strain into a chilled cocktail glass.

It is also a good use of apple brandy specifically. One of the traps that that spirit can fall into is failing to sufficiently distinguish itself from grape brandy in cocktails. Many recipe guides lump all the drinks made with either of them together in a single section and give the general impression—or sometimes explicitly state—that the two are interchangeable. When this occurs, it is clear which one is the also-ran.

Such mistaken thinking undercuts apple brandy's position in the hierarchy of spirits—in a just world, more homes would stock it than vodka—as does its substitution into grape brandy drinks that fail to fully utilize its strengths. The Honeymoon is an excellent example of a cocktail that relies on the warm, subtle, wood-accented apple blossom flavor which this and only this spirit can provide to tie its pieces together. In a way, it is at once the base and the finishing element of the cocktail.

Somewhat amusingly, given our previous discussion of the De Rigueur, Ted Haigh reports that the Honeymoon was a specialty of the Brown Derby restaurant chain in Los Angeles, although they did not invent it and never claimed to. It first appeared in print in *Recipes for Mixed Drinks*, published in 1917 by Hugo Ensslin; it would be another nine years before the Brown Derby opened its hatband to Angelenos.

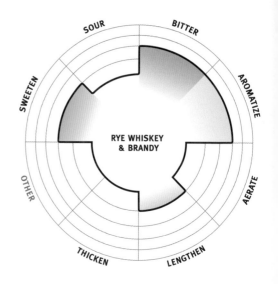

**We have** already dealt with recipes which do something interesting by doubling up on some type of ingredient. The Vieux Carré is a double-double: it uses two base spirits, as well as two kinds of bitters. This is our first encounter with a drink that blends multiple bitters. Peychaud's is the traditional aromatic style of New Orleans, aniseed-forward with undertones of fruit and other spices. It is our new bitters for the chapter, and one of the three varieties essential for any serious home cocktail bar.

Which prompts the question: why use two kinds of bitters, especially in a drink also embracing an herbal liqueur and a vermouth? As always, it is a matter of taste, but one reason these components can function together is that they approach a similar palate from different angles. *Baking spice* is a term one might use for Angostura, Peychaud's, *or* Bénédictine, meaning the subset of sweet spices that we associate with fall, winter, and assorted baked goods. If using any of these ingredients is like reaching into the spice cupboard, mixing them all into one drink is akin to using a bit of everything on the shelf.

The Vieux Carré, moreover, represents those flavors associated strongly with New Orleans. Peychaud's Bitters, absinthe, and Bénédictine all appear disproportionately in the native drinks of the Big Easy, and frequently at least two of them will co-occur. Vieux Carré is the French

# Vieux Carré

1 oz. rye whiskey

1 oz. brandy

1 oz. sweet vermouth

1 tsp. Bénédictine

2 dashes Angostura bitters

2 dashes Peychaud's Bitters

Stir with ice. Strain into a chilled rocks glass. Optionally, garnish with a lemon peel.

name for what the rest of us call the French Quarter. Not so long ago, the drink was forgotten even in its namesake neighborhood—indeed, even at the Hotel Monteleone, where it was first compounded in 1938. Thankfully, it has been restored to its rightful prominence and is now recognized both within the city and without as belonging to a pantheon of exceptional creations by New Orleanian bartenders.

It is also, in my view, a great counterweight against the reduction of cocktails to templates. Most schools of thought that attempt this assign the Vieux Carré to the type of the Manhattan. What, we must ask, does such a claim serve to illuminate? That it uses vermouth and bitters with a spirit base? Does it teach us anything about the cocktail's flavor, the reason it works, the spirit that motivated its creation, or the things partaking of one evokes? Of course not. It may at most provide a basis for estimating the relative proportions of whiskey, brandy, and vermouth, but if you understand how those ingredients work in cocktails, you will not need the Manhattan comparison to know how to use them here. In the Vieux Carré are six pieces working together, producing something greater than the sum of their parts. To understand what it does and why it works, *drink* it. The totalities of the Vieux Carré and the Manhattan, viewed side by side, give the lie to any deconstruction that names one a mere variation on the other.

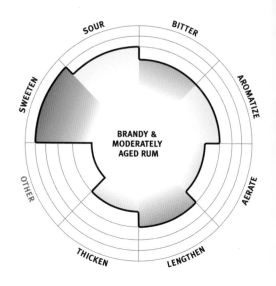

**The Cocktail** Renaissance has made mining old bartenders' guides for recipes a cornerstone of entire careers. Sometimes truly stunning recipes are found discarded on the ash heap of history and returned more or less directly to stalwart service at the bar. Other times, the archaeo-mixologist must spot the vein of precious metal in the ore, adapting an old recipe to suit modern tastes and ingredients. This second possibility is the reason that the canon of classic cocktail books is not entirely picked over even after nearly thirty years of work. The Fighting Quaker is the fruit of my own endeavor in this area.

A drink called the Quaker's Cocktail appeared in one of Harry Mac-Elhone's books, but I first encountered it under Harry Craddock's by-line in *The Savoy Cocktail Book*. Both provide for a ratio of 1 part each of brandy and rum, to ½ part each lemon juice and raspberry syrup. Although I had never heard of the drink before, I felt sure it would be a good one.

As written in the classic texts, it was a bit disappointing—pleasant, but not especially compelling or novel. I tried refracting it through the lens of Chad Arnholt's Ward Eight recipe, dialing up the fragrant syrup while splitting the lemon with an orange juice accent to mellow out the tartness. It was nearly there, but it needed one additional dimension to complement all that fruit while setting off the sugar and the acidity. I reached for Peychaud's.

# Fighting Quaker

1 oz. brandy

1 oz. moderately aged rum

¾ oz. raspberry syrup

½ oz. lemon juice

¼ oz. orange juice

2 dashes Peychaud's Bitters

Shake with ice and double-strain into a chilled cocktail glass.

The essence of this cocktail—a brandy and rum base with a raspberry-forward fruit sour layered on top—has not changed that much with these modifications. One could argue that this version tastes more the way the Quaker's Cocktail ought to taste than the Quaker's Cocktail actually does. But it is different enough that I feel an amended name is appropriate; I have chosen the nickname of General Nathanael Greene of Rhode Island, whose successes in the Revolutionary War also earned him the title of "Savior of the South."

The Fighting Quaker opens interesting philosophical questions about when a cocktail ceases to be itself and becomes something else. The only serious treatment of the Quaker's Cocktail's history I have found is remarkably extensive, but also in German. Armin Zimmermann has documented every available reference to it, with recipes, from its creation to the present. Orange juice is attested elsewhere in this canon, favored by no less a mixological mind than Trader Vic, but oddly neither the Trader nor anyone else has used it in conjunction with lemon juice, only as its replacement. Bitters, however, appear nowhere else, and that I consider a substantial enough change to the structure of the recipe to warrant renaming. That is, after all, a whole different building block that does not appear in the original.

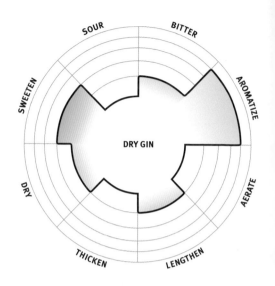

**2.19**

SOUR · BITTER · AROMATIZE · AERATE · LENGTHEN · THICKEN · DRY · SWEETEN

**DRY GIN**

**To consider** mixing spirits from a slightly different angle, we turn to the Acacia, a drink that is as criminally overlooked as it is alphabetically prominent.

This is another drink that uses a single herbal liqueur for much of its heavy lifting, akin to the Reganian duos we discussed in seminar one, where the liqueur is responsible for all of the modifications: here, Bénédictine sweetens, bitters, and aromatizes. The lemon peel to finish it—essential to the balance, let there be no doubt—is likewise a familiar addition.

The wild card is the kirschwasser, an unaged cherry brandy historically associated with the German-speaking areas of the Alps and surrounding regions and sometimes called *kirsch* by its friends. Because it is a spirit, like brandy and gin and rum, our study of split-base drinks thus far suggests that it should appear in a 1:1 or perhaps a 2:1 ratio with the gin in this cocktail, but we find instead we have eight times as much gin as kirschwasser. Why is it relegated to such a small role?

# Acacia

2 oz. London dry gin

¾ oz. Bénédictine

¼ oz. kirschwasser

Stir with ice and strain into a chilled cocktail glass. Express a lemon peel over the top and drop it in.

Think back to our earlier discussion of maraschino liqueur, another cherry-derived product. It turns out that the flavor of cherry distillates is *potent*. One can use kirschwasser as the sole spirit in a cocktail, but if mixed with another class of hard liquor in equal proportions, it can easily overwhelm its partner. To even ensure that both are tasted, the kirsch must be reined in. In other words, it must be made an accent.

We will see more of this in future recipes, but in general one should consider such a strategy when dealing with any sort of irascible ingredient. A particularly loud spirit mixed into a much larger amount of a more conventionally voiced one is a bit like a house blend—one could choose to think of the Acacia as being made with a base of 2¼ oz. of kirsch-infused gin, if one wished to take this premise to the extreme. However you care to parse it, kirsch is the kind of spirit that can be either the star of the show or a scene-stealing character actor, but chafes in an intermediate supporting role. The Acacia strikes a masterful balance, using its big presence in small doses to elevate what otherwise looks like a fairly straightforward duo.

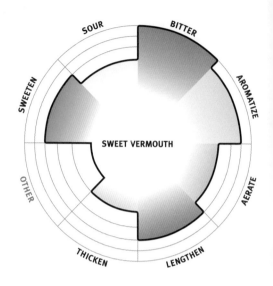

**In a sense**, we are approaching the Campari drinks backward. The Negroni was reputedly invented when a count by that name popped into a Florentine bar he frequented and asked the bartender to make him a stronger twist on the Americano. But the Americano is the more complicated of the two to address in our curriculum, so it comes later.

After all, what kind of thing is this? A longish drink with no base spirit, rooted in wine and amaro. How on earth should we approach it?

As with the Negroni and the Boulevardier, the core of this cocktail is the Campari–sweet vermouth axis. If we wished to assign a base spirit, we could think of this as a split-base drink with those two being the constituent parties—much as we can consider the Corpse Reviver as having a mixture of apple brandy and grape brandy as its core.

And like its red relations, this one is designed to make its still-potent principal pairing a bit more palatable for most people. Where the Boulevardier and the Negroni achieve this balance by setting the Campari off against other strong flavors, the Americano uses seltzer to dilute it. The length and effervescence lighten the overall experience, even making it refreshing. The Americano, like the Champagne Cocktail, is a low-ABV drink, and its flavors dance delicately on the tongue with the burst of each tiny bubble. Together, these qualities

# Americano

1 oz. Campari

1 oz. sweet vermouth

2 oz. seltzer

Combine ingredients in a rocks glass with ice and stir. Garnish with a lemon peel.

suit it to a long afternoon of casual imbibing. Drinkers who got their start on stronger stuff may consider reversing Count Negroni's course and using the Americano as a road map for easier-drinking options.

Note also that the Americano and Negroni are garnished with different citrus peels. This helps a busy bartender quickly tell which drink is which, but the scents of these garnishes also match the cocktails they go with. Lemon is bright and assertive, something that pops through in a long drink and complements the snap of effervescence. Orange is warm and welcoming, harmonizing readily with other ingredients and helping to meld their flavors together. The Americano is light and refreshing, the Negroni contemplative and normally a longer drinking experience. These garnishes stuck for a reason.

### FURTHER READING

A modern but pre-Renaissance drink called the Negroni Sbagliato (zbal–YAH–toh) was allegedly created when an absentminded bartender accidentally put sparkling wine into a Negroni ("sbagliato" means "mistaken" or "screwed up" in Italian). The story is implausible, but the drink is good, though it's structurally much closer to the Americano than the Negroni. The directions are even the same—just swap out the Americano's seltzer for sparkling wine.

# 2.21

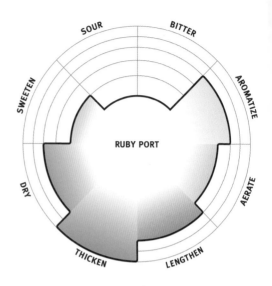

## SOLUTION

Unsurprisingly, the Coffee Cocktail resembles the Brandy Flip. It's made the same way: shaken first without ice to abet protein unfolding, then again to chill and dilute; it even shares the wintry nutmeg garnish we've used to aromatize creamy cocktails since the Brandy Alexander.

The presence of both a spirit *and* a fortified wine affects our calculations a bit. We know that the wine is sweeter than the spirit, and so we can hit our target sugar level with less added sugar than we use in the Brandy Flip.

It is not immediately apparent why there should be more wine than spirit in this recipe. For the answer, consider the drink's mouthfeel. Flips are meant to be rich, creamy, silky—characteristics enhanced by using relatively more of the sweet, viscous wine. There is nothing wrong with reversing the ratio, but I find that this version feels somehow *flippier*.

2 oz. ruby port

1 oz. brandy

1 tsp. sugar

whole egg

Shake without ice, then again with ice. Strain into a chilled cocktail glass and garnish with a sprinkle of grated nutmeg.

# EXERCISE
# Coffee Cocktail

ruby port

brandy

sugar

whole egg

*Using the given ingredients, determine the proportions of the Coffee Cocktail and its method of preparation.*

**The Coffee Cocktail** is somewhat notorious among mixographers, all of whom seem to feel obliged to include some commentary about its name and why it hasn't got any coffee in it. Simply put, many drinks are named by their appearances, and the Coffee Cocktail looks quite a bit like coffee. There need be no confusion about this.

Historically, the greater controversy was the use of the word *cocktail*. In the 1880s, when this recipe was first kicking around, the traditional view was still that a cocktail had to have bitters to be worthy of the name. The Coffee Cocktail was an early challenge to this policy. Its name offended further by being impossible to truncate: one could say either "Manhattan Cocktail" or "Manhattan" with equal clarity, but this drink could never be ordered without calling it the Coffee *Cocktail*, "coffee" having a rather different meaning on its own.

All of the ingredients will be familiar except for one: port is a forti-fied dessert wine from Portugal, made by adding distilled spirits to the wine before fermentation is complete. This means that the natural sugars in the fermenting juice are not completely broken down, and the wine is both sweeter and stronger as a result. Tawny port is the slightly drier expression, usually aged longer, while ruby is younger and sweeter. Think about these qualities, the drinks that resemble this one, and how it differs. What can you infer about its preparation?

# 2.22

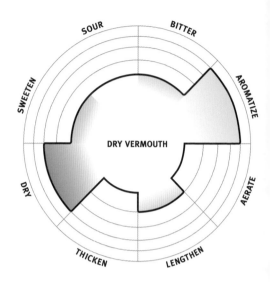

**Even** unluckier than raspberry syrup is groseille syrup, a preparation of sugar and red currants that saw particular use in France during the American diaspora following the passage of the Volstead Act. A handful of recipes from that period appear on the odd list of mixological worthies, but most of us will never try them as they were originally intended and many will never even encounter their approximations.

Alone among them, we have the Rose, a sleeper-hit cocktail plucked from obscurity by David Wondrich. In its original form, it came out of the American Bar at Paris's Hotel Chatham, across the way from Harry's New York Bar. The recipe was as listed here with groseille syrup in lieu of the raspberry, the latter being Wondrich's modern substitution for a rather hard-to-scrounge-up ingredient. As usual, his recommendation is spot-on. The sweet-tartness of the raspberry brightens a mixture full of savory and herbaceous notes, downplaying these while elevating the fruitiness and acidity already present in the other ingredients but somewhat muffled by their stronger flavors.

Like the Coffee Cocktail, the Rose can be thought of as an "upside-down drink," because it flips our expectations about the proportions of spirits and fortified wines in cocktails. Where a Manhattan, for example, uses a 2:1 ratio of whiskey to vermouth, the Rose reverses that, making the vermouth the base and the spirit the modifier.

# Rose

2 oz. dry vermouth

1 oz. kirschwasser

1 tsp. raspberry syrup

Stir with ice and strain into a chilled cocktail glass. Optionally, garnish with a brandied or maraschino cherry.

There are two ways to look at this. One is to focus on the spirit itself: kirschwasser comes with a very strong flavor, rather like maraschino without the sugar. It would be hard to wrangle as the base of a cocktail—it's unusual enough that there's a full ounce of it in this recipe, rather than the smaller portion we used in the Acacia. One could parse the Rose like a long drink, with the kirsch as the base and the vermouth standing in for the milder, nonalcoholic mixer.

Another approach would be to consider the intent behind the drink. If one's goal is to mix a relatively low-proof beverage that still captures the sense of a cocktail, one might very well begin with a fortified wine as the base, and use modifiers with a high flavor-to-alcohol ratio.

That type of structure will not be common in this course, but it will appear again. Recipes compounded along these lines make particularly good aperitifs, being light and pleasant and tickling the senses without supplying too much liquor. In theory, many cocktails *can* whet one's appetite for a meal, but in practice they often appear in other contexts, priming palates less for dinner and more for the next round of drinks. I cannot find fault with this practice, but if one wishes to experiment with a more old-fashioned form of cocktail drinking in which a mixed beverage or two precedes a substantial meal and its associated wines, the Rose and cocktails like it do a splendid job.

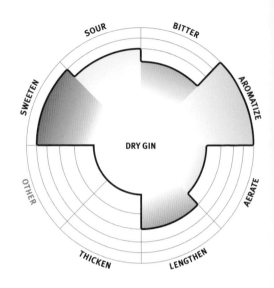

SOUR · BITTER · AROMATIZE · SWEETEN · DRY GIN · OTHER · AERATE · THICKEN · LENGTHEN

**One of the** best-named drinks in the canon—if not quite as evocative as the Widow's Kiss is—the Last Word transcended its own midcentury obscurity to become a much-riffed-on modern favorite. Whether that is ironic or apt for a drink so named is hard to say.

It had never been a wildly popular recipe in its heyday—and stood no chance of surviving the ill midcentury wind that scattered the canon to the corners of the earth. Sheer happenstance saved it, when Murray Stenson plucked it out of *Bottoms Up* by Ted Saucier and put it on the menu at the Zig Zag Cafe in Seattle. His place was influential enough that the recipe rapidly circumnavigated the globe. That Seattle was also home to other influential Renaissance figures like Paul Clarke of *The Cocktail Chronicles* and Robert Hess of *DrinkBoy* did not hurt. The Last Word may have been invented at the Detroit Athletic Club, but these days it's an icon of the Emerald City's cocktail revival.

How does the Last Word work, proportioned as it is unlike anything we have seen thus far? It takes cues from multiple-liqueur drinks, to be sure, as well as from the Negroni, which traditionally blends three ingredients in equal proportions. There is a certain bartenders'

# Last Word

¾ oz. London dry gin

¾ oz. lime juice

¾ oz. maraschino liqueur

¾ oz. Green Chartreuse

Shake with ice. Strain into a chilled cocktail glass.

fascination with equal-parts drinks, to some extent because they are easy to make and their recipes easy to remember, but also because getting three or four disparate items to harmonize while singing at the same volume is proof of the creator's mixological prowess. This is particularly apparent in the Last Word, where in the words of Joaquín Simó, "Every ingredient is a haymaker." We have already seen recipes that had to work to counterbalance maraschino or Green Chartreuse. Lemon juice has gotten the same treatment, and lime juice is no less acidic. If anything, it is the *gin* we would expect to be the least-pushy ingredient—but remember, it can hold its own in a 1:1:1 Negroni; even the Boulevardier is ordinarily more spirit-forward than that.

All this is to say that the Last Word succeeds for the same reason any equal-parts drink will: it uses four ingredients that are equally assertive. In other contexts, they must be accounted for, accommodated, adjusted. In the Last Word, they are given free rein, held back not by the subtle leashes of delicate balances but by the blunt force of the other three. The result is a bold, bracing cocktail, ideal for the end of an evening when one's palate is dulled from tasting too many others. In this respect, the name is entirely appropriate.

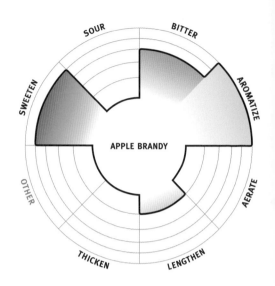

**We have** now seen several recipes that double up on something. The Last Word even doubles up on liqueurs, although one of them is herbaceous while the other is more floral. The Widow's Kiss is our first encounter with a two-liqueur drink in which *both* of them are herbal.

It is also our first opportunity to discuss Yellow Chartreuse. While it is similar in overall bouquet to its green forerunner, it is neither as strong, nor as sweet, nor as bold in its pronouncements. If Green Chartreuse is a haymaker, Yellow Chartreuse is impeccable footwork.

That is one of the reasons the Widow's Kiss is possible. It also helps that Bénédictine is extremely amicable as ingredients go and both liqueurs benefit from a subtle infusion of apple.

Note that our previous multi-liqueur cocktails have been sours, relying on citrus to balance out the liqueurs' flavor and sugar, while the Widow's Kiss does nothing of the kind. It is, if anything, more like the

# Widow's Kiss

1½ oz. apple brandy
¾ oz. Bénédictine
¾ oz. Yellow Chartreuse
2 dashes Angostura bitters

Stir with ice. Strain into a chilled cocktail glass.

duo type we discussed when we covered the Stinger in the previous seminar: a spirit, sweetened and aromatized by the presence of a liqueur. In this case, it happens that there are two of them.

What makes this work? As in the Honeymoon, Bénédictine can do most of the sweetening work on its own and is partially counterbalanced by the more spirit-forwardness of the Chartreuse. We know from the Champs-Élysées that a bit of Angostura can strategically offset the sugar-Chartreuse axis and bring balance to the whole. Here we use an extra dash, because without lemon juice to assist it, it has a bit more work to do. Of course, the relative mildness of Yellow Chartreuse—strong emphasis on *relative*—is necessary for the drink's success: the bolder, sweeter Green could not so easily be brought in without its overtaking everything else. This is a corollary to the lesson of the Last Word: when mixing herbal liqueurs, match their levels of assertiveness, whether or not the cocktail you are making is an equal-parts recipe.

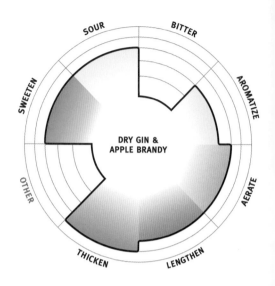

**Now that** we have explored a couple of multi-liqueur combinations, let us return for a moment to split-base cocktails. On that front, the Pink Lady is interesting in two ways.

First, it is a split-base egg sour, which is something we have not yet considered. And second, the two bases it employs are not an intuitive match, in no small part because one is an aged spirit while the other is not.

Until now, all our mixed-base cocktails have involved two spirits which were aged for some time in oak—in fact, each of them has featured brandy so far—and one can surmise that the typical flavors of oak aging enable a certain agreeableness between them. If vanilla, wood, and a hint of coconut can be found in both bases, of course they can mix decently well, right? So how does gin come into it?

This is as good a time as any to note that apple brandy often has savory undertones. There is a bit of residual plant matter on the palate—subtle, noticeable chiefly when one is looking for it, but there all the same.

# Pink Lady

1½ oz. London dry gin
½ oz. apple brandy
¾ oz. lemon juice
½ oz. simple syrup
½ oz. grenadine
egg white

Shake without ice, then again with ice. Strain into a chilled cocktail glass.

This gives it a particular penchant for playing nicely with ingredients that might surprise us, including gin—and for that matter, Chartreuse.

It is also the case that gin complements fruit better than we might assume. It is loaded up with citrus notes from a variety of its botanicals, while the earthy-spicy ones are at least compatible—cinnamon and nutmeg are not so strange to imagine in a pie, for example. The evergreen flavors are more easily admitted into this club than one might expect: they dovetail nicely with citrus notes—which often co-occur in actual evergreen trees—while sweet alpine flavors can be complementary to fruits in more savory contexts. Rosemary may not belong in a pie, but in an apple or pomegranate dressing for a roast? Absolutely.

There is, in sum, a lot going on in the Pink Lady's kitchen. The egg white does as it always does and mellows everything out; any stray off notes that might not jibe will tend to be silenced when the volume gets turned down. The egg also gives us more texture to play with, which cannot hurt our ability to parse this drink more in the way we would food.

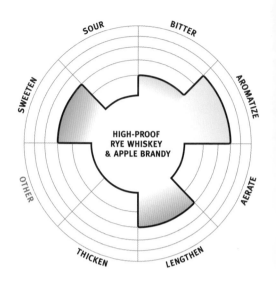

**2.26**

SOUR · BITTER · AROMATIZE · AERATE · LENGTHEN · THICKEN · OTHER · SWEETEN

HIGH-PROOF
RYE WHISKEY
& APPLE BRANDY

**The modern** Diamondback is notorious. Often made with bonded spirits and Green Chartreuse—and nothing under 100 proof—it has become a poster child for the triumph of the flavorful and high-proof over the anemic bland beverages of the Cocktail Dark Ages.

Ironically, the Diamondback is itself a mid-twentieth-century cocktail, first appearing in *Bottoms Up* by Ted Saucier in the 1950s. His version was lower proof, specifying Yellow Chartreuse and opening the door to standard-proof whiskey and apple brandy.

The trend toward higher-proof spirits in cocktails was in theory restorationist, but in this case it "restored" a recipe into something entirely new—and, it can reasonably be argued, unnecessary. Saucier's original may not be as combustible as its modern cousin, but it is still a potent drink. It has merely had its rough edges sanded down.

We can tell from the ingredients what kind of thing this is: it uses two different distilled spirits, so we may want to parse the apple brandy as either accenting the whiskey or as part of a split base with it; for more aroma, it uses a liqueur, the selection being spiritous enough that it can only go so far in counterbalancing the liquor with sweetness; there are no other modifiers. If you have something in mind that's like a duo, but with more herbal complexity, you have the right idea.

# Diamondback

1½ oz. high-proof rye whiskey

¾ oz. apple brandy

¾ oz. Yellow Chartreuse

Shake with ice. Strain into a chilled cocktail glass. Optionally, garnish with a brandied or maraschino cherry.

With that in mind, one would picture a built or stirred drink, but this one is shaken. Why? There are no particularly viscous ingredients, nothing solid, and nothing that foams—none of the indicators we normally turn to in order to determine whether shaking is necessary.

The answer lies in the chief reason we normally do *not* shake: it dilutes the drink more. Remember that stirring and shaking are normally done for about the same length of time, but shaking is more efficient. In practice, it will achieve more chilling and dilution in the same period than stirring would. We often regard that by default as a disadvantage, something to accept when necessary and otherwise avoid. Here, though, it is the goal: even this milder, 1950s-style Diamondback is fairly high-octane. Shaking waters it down just enough to give its flavors the space to breathe. It's not so much that it would be out of balance otherwise, as that the volume on everything would be turned up too high to fully appreciate the experience.

This is a rare technique, but it's used time to time when a cocktail is at risk of coming out too spirit-forward. In this case, I must credit Saucier himself for the recommendation. I've tried the Diamondback many ways and at various alcoholic strengths, but learning that it had originally been shaken was the key that made it work.

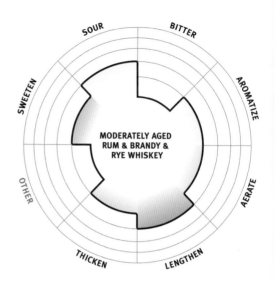

**We have** seen a number of two-spirit cocktails, but this is our first containing three. Tripling up on base liquors is unusual in most of our curriculum, though the technique will come roaring back when we discuss tiki drinks in the fourth seminar.

In one sense, understanding this recipe is merely a problem of addition. Coincidentally, that's also how the Twelve-Mile Limit came to be.

When the United States began its questionable experiment in mandatory national sobriety, it claimed the right to enforce it up to three miles off the coast, as was standard international law at the time. Those with access to boats quickly discovered that four miles offshore was an ideal place for a party. This upset the Prohibition authorities, who promptly extended that claim to twelve miles.

American expatriates enjoyed naming new drinks at the Drys' expense, and a Three-Mile Limit* cocktail circulated when that jurisdictional boundary was obtained. Once the authorities extended their reach another nine miles into the ocean, those scamps across the pond matched them with a Twelve-Mile Limit. To demonstrate their

---

* This drink underwent its own odd metamorphosis thanks to *The Savoy Cocktail Book*, in which a typo rechristened it the "Three *Miller*."

# Twelve-Mile Limit

1 oz. moderately aged rum

½ oz. brandy

½ oz. rye whiskey

½ oz. grenadine

½ oz. lemon juice

Shake with ice and strain into a chilled cocktail glass. Garnish with a brandied or maraschino cherry.

commitment to this game of brinksmanship, the new drink added whiskey to the brandy and rum of its predecessor. Fortunately, the U.S. government blinked, and extended their territorial claims no further.

In *Barflies and Cocktails*, Harry MacElhone attributes the Three-Mile Limit to Chips Brighton, who tended his eponymous New York Bar in Paris, while the Twelve-Mile Limit had come all the way from Tommy Millard in Shanghai. Interestingly, where the Three-Mile was a brandy drink accented by rum, the Twelve-Mile turns that upside down, making the rum the major player and the rye and brandy accents.

There is a good lesson in higher-order spirits blending here: ingredients should be used in inverse proportion to the strength of their flavors. The type of rum we employ in this recipe is flavorful but not overpowering. It has a broad range of possible proportions in which it will register but not drown out anything else. It's consequently a good choice for the largest single component in a mixture of three base spirits. The whiskey and brandy will still make themselves known, but won't silence their counterparts. It can be a tricky balance to strike, and this is a good recipe to practice matching brands of spirits. Find a reliable rum-brandy-rye combination that suits your tastes; the exercise will help you identify spirits brands that work well together going forward.

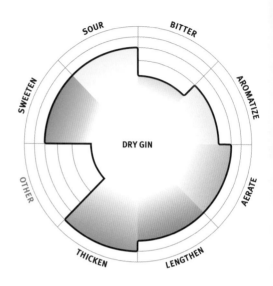

**For much** of the second half of the last century, the Clover Club was defined in the negative, as a Pink Lady without applejack. Grenadine had been swapped in for raspberry syrup years prior, and they were regarded as substantially similar pink egg sours as a result.

This recipe is a triumph of mixological archaeology and one of the great success stories of the revival era. It begins with Julie Reiner, a major modern talent whose establishments had a significant influence upon the developing Cocktail Renaissance in Manhattan. In 2008, with New York's cultural center of gravity shifting across the East River, Reiner opened a neighborhood cocktail lounge called the Clover Club in Brooklyn. She has sensibly observed that if you're going to name a bar after a cocktail, it should be one that most people will enjoy.

Restoring the raspberry syrup was essential to reinvigorating the Clover Club. The second piece of the puzzle was supplied by Reiner's friend and neighbor David Wondrich, the preeminent cocktail historian whom I have already quoted liberally in this book. He unearthed the earliest known printed recipe for the drink and found it contained a dollop of dry vermouth, unattested since that time.

We've seen almost no drinks that use both citrus and vermouth, and certainly no egg sours that do. A case could be made that the Pink

# Clover Club

1½ oz. London dry gin
½ oz. dry vermouth
½ oz. lemon juice
½ oz. raspberry syrup
egg white

Shake without ice, then again with ice. Strain into a chilled cocktail glass. Optionally, garnish with 2–3 raspberries speared on a toothpick.

Lady is its closest analogue, but the Bronx and the Coffee Cocktail seem nearly as relevant. What do you do with a cocktail that seems to pull in so many directions at once? Go back to basics.

Vermouth adds acidity, sweetness, aroma, and body. It's in a way a concentration of the effects of multiple other cocktail ingredients. Notice that our Pink Lady recipe used both more citrus and more syrup than our Clover Club does. The vermouth partially accounts for this, as does the tartness of the raspberry and the slight reduction in the volume of base spirit. The flavor of the fortified wine sinks into our perception of the other ingredients, its silky texture enhancing the egg foam. Like salt in food, the vermouth will not be noticed when it is doing its job. This is a reason to prefer the dry stuff here rather than the more assertive sweet—that, and a flavor that pairs well with both gin and raspberry, as we have seen. Dry vermouth also makes the Clover Club a great example of a cocktail that appears less complex than it is. The casual consumer may read it as simply a grown-up pink lemonade. If one takes the time to sit with it, the details of its other flavors can come into focus, but even then, the mechanism is concealed behind the harmony of the whole.

This recipe is one Reiner and Wondrich developed for the Clover Club's namesake bar, where it's a fittingly popular house specialty.

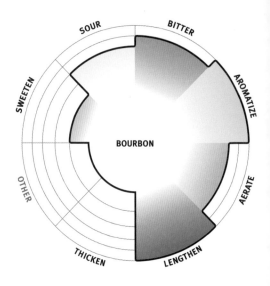

## 2.29

SOUR · BITTER · AROMATIZE · AERATE · LENGTHEN · THICKEN · OTHER · SWEETEN

BOURBON

**The house** cocktail of its namesake hotel in Kentucky, the Seelbach is a baroque pre-Prohibition potation that calls for a whopping fourteen dashes of bitters, split evenly between Peychaud's and Angostura. It dates to 1917, first made by accident when a busy bartender spilled some Champagne into a Manhattan and decided to go with it. Sadly, it did not survive Prohibition, but the Seelbach Hotel did, and its resident barman-historian Adam Seger unearthed the recipe in 1995 and restored it to its rightful place on the menu.

A dramatic tale, and not a word of it is true: Seger invented the drink himself and spun a yarn to get some press for his hotel. While happy accidents do happen in the mixological world, they are rare, and rarer still are the ones that someone bothers to record after the fact.

Unfortunately for him, Gary Regan and Mardee Haidin Regan caught wind of the Seelbach and persuaded him to let them print it in *New Classic Cocktails* in 1997. Its reputation took off, the novelty of its fourteen dashes and its hard-luck "history" perfectly riding the wave of the Cocktail Renaissance to prominence. When the thing did not go away on its own, Seger maintained the lie for *twenty-one years* before coming clean in 2016. A drink that had sounded the clarion call for cocktail revivalism and archival research was in fact the highest-profile fraud in the canon. In the end, the truth is a better story than the myth.

# Seelbach

1 oz. bourbon

½ oz. curaçao or triple sec

7 dashes Angostura bitters

7 dashes Peychaud's Bitters

3–4 oz. sparkling wine

Combine bourbon, liqueur, and bitters in a chilled flute. Fill with chilled sparkling wine. Garnish with an orange twist.

As a recipe, the Seelbach is interesting in two ways: first, unlike the Air Mail and the French 75, it does not follow our fizz structure, making it our first Champagne cocktail other than the Champagne Cocktail to belong to some other school. Lacking citrus juice or really any texturizing element besides the sparkling wine, it shares with the Champagne Cocktail a certain sense of being an Old Fashioned made large and effervescent. It is sweetened, but not much—the curaçao's dry side is an asset this time—it is bittered and heavily aromatized for its size. Remember that even the Champagne Cocktail went in for four dashes of bitters, and there, all they had to stand up to was the delicate flavor of the world's most famous sparkling wine. The Seelbach can be made with something a bit beefier, and in any case the bourbon and liqueur give the bitters something else to bounce off of.

Make no mistake, fourteen dashes is still a lot, an extravagant choice that will be revisited and even expanded on in later chapters. But much as the Rickey caters to those who like things sour, the Seelbach is there for the lover of the bitter and anyone who questions whether a drink can be challenging and refreshing at once.

## 2.30

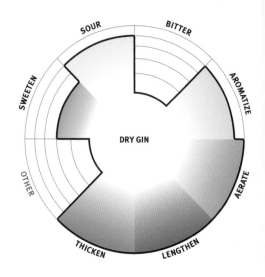

**The Ramos Gin Fizz** is a legendary New Orleans cocktail, famous for a preparation technique that is tricky to the point of grueling. Various sources require it be shaken for ten or fifteen minutes, until all the ice has melted, or until "ropey," whatever that means. In its heyday, teams of "shaker boys" were employed to keep the legendarily labor-intensive cocktail in constant production and (barely) meet demand.

In *On Food and Cooking*, Harold McGee calls beating egg whites "cooking with the wrist," and that description is an apt one here as well. We are making structure out of fluids by mechanical action—even more so than in a normal egg drink, because of the added cream.

I have mentioned previously that the fats in egg yolks keep them from foaming up as well as the albumen does—but we have already *made* a milkfat foam: the Irish Coffee's whipped cream. Milk products and eggs simply have opposite foaming tendencies.

Egg foams depend on the proteins in the whites having lots of contact with one another to build an air-trapping lattice, cream foams on their dispersed globules of fat breaking apart and reforming around bubbles of gas. The Ramos Gin Fizz takes the most froth-inducing elements of each, the proteinaceous white and the lipid-dense heavy cream, and attempts to harness them both at once.

# EXAMINATION
# Ramos Gin Fizz

London dry gin

simple syrup

heavy cream

lemon juice

lime juice

orange flower water

egg white

seltzer

*Using the given ingredients, determine the proportions of the Ramos Gin Fizz and its method of preparation.*

Egg whites are slightly to moderately alkaline, depending on their age. The more alkaline they are, the more the protein molecules repel one another, inhibiting foam formation. An acidic juice can counteract this. (Don't worry, the cream is fatty enough that it won't curdle.)

Sugar helps stabilize foams by providing structure, although it slows down their formation. Simple syrup saves us the trouble of dissolving the solid sugar, but it also adds water. Each addition increases the agitative effort required to realize its full foaming potential.

Henry Charles "Carl" Ramos's fizz won national fame in the 1890s. It was the signature drink at the Imperial Cabinet on Carondelet, which he ran, and tourism to New Orleans was booming. By 1899, he was slinging enough of them to go through five thousand egg whites every week, putting the unused yolks into flips, omelets, and trucks that shipped them to bakeries all over the U.S.; he kept a hennery north of the city, which was said to be the nation's largest. The fizz's fortunes would not change until the passage of the Eighteenth Amendment.

While the combinations and technique may be novel, the only unfamiliar ingredient here is orange flower water, a hydrosol of aromatic chemicals from the orange blossom suspended in ordinary water. Everything else you will have seen before—but never quite like this.

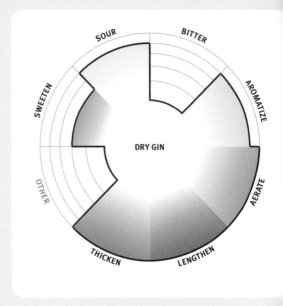

## 2.30

In 1925, presumably having concluded that Prohibition wasn't getting repealed anytime soon, Ramos gave his recipe to the *New Orleans Item-Tribune*. Even so, the cocktail as it is known today is less a recipe than a tradition. Certain aspects are inviolable, while others are tweaked, usually in response to the effort required to make the drink.

That the Ramos is a fizz is no secret—it's right there in the name. The paucity of orange flower water should call to mind the other floral ingredient we've encountered thus far: maraschino. Both can predominate if injudiciously used. This gives us our first application of the **drop**, the dash's more precise and limited cousin. I'd stick to three here.

Thinking back to the first seminar, we can recall that the citrus split reflects the different extents to which lemon and lime juice linger on the tongue. So far, we are discussing something a bit like the White Lady in its orange-perfumed meringue-ness, but fizzed and fancied up.

Then we introduce the cream, the eggs, and the construction of the drink's famous foam. Ramos's original advice was to "shake and shake and shake until there is not a bubble left"; he also added the seltzer to the shaker, so there were more bubbles to dissipate. Remember, too, that the dry shake is a modern technique: Ramos's shaker boys had to mechanically emulsify the ingredients while *cold*.

# SOLUTION
# Ramos Gin Fizz

2 oz. London dry gin

¾ oz. simple syrup

¾ oz. heavy cream

½ oz. lemon juice

½ oz. lime juice

3 drops orange flower water

egg white

1½ oz. seltzer

Pour seltzer into a chilled Collins glass. Shake remaining ingredients without ice for a full minute, then shake again with large ice cubes. Strain into the Collins glass.

Jim Meehan of PDT advises shaking with two 1¼ inch ice cubes "until they disintegrate," and then pouring unstrained over the seltzer. I find that a minute of shaking is a good benchmark irrespective of the size of your ice or how much remains, but I have taken that second piece of advice, which Meehan attributes to Don Lee: adding the cocktail to the seltzer rather than the other way around gives you more control over the fizzing-up process.

Make no mistake, the Ramos Gin Fizz builds volume explosively when introduced to the carbonated mixer—all that work does pay off—and it can be useful to slow it down, and even pause a moment so some of the liquid can settle back out of the foam before building it up more. Modern Ramoses are often served in tall, slender highball glasses, with the foam carefully built to stand, meringue-like, a full-inch higher than the top of the glass.

The laboriousness of the Ramos is one of its charms. It is much more satisfying to drink something that you had to put so much effort into. It also means the drink tends to get saved for special occasions—for a long time I would make it exactly once per year—and that scarcity heightens the pleasure of the experience. In other words, take your time making it, take your time drinking it, and then take a little break to savor what you've learned before you begin the third seminar.

# Renaissance Revivals

**Our journey** has come to a turning point. For two chapters, we have considered only those cocktails that could easily have been made when the Renaissance began. Now we begin to consider the ingredients, recipes, and techniques that reflect the triumph of that movement, the recovery of what had been lost from the days of our foremixers and its restoration to the cultural mainstream today. Cocktails foreshadowed in previous chapters will appear at last—unlike the cocktailians of the last millennium, you will not need to wait years or decades to try them.

By now, you should understand the rudiments of how cocktails fit together. This seminar will therefore proceed at a quicker pace. Rather than describing each cocktail's structure and balance from the ground up, I will refer to previously covered recipes and identify iterations that get us from those to these, noting the consequences of each choice and any additional compensations they may require.

For so much of the period we are considering, everything old was new—and moreover it was *exciting*, whether it was a forgotten recipe, a defunct liqueur, or simply an old-fashioned set of standards to which the drinking experience could be held. Mixologists revived some of the greatest hits of the pre-war backbar, with absinthe, Old Tom gin, crème de violette, Kina Lillet (or something close to it), and orange bitters among them. Bars elevated their standards of service and some even posted rules for their patrons' behavior. These efforts not only made cocktails cool again but also revived the respectability of hospitality as a profession.

Consider: Bartenders were being quoted in newspapers of record. Serious journalists were bothering to write about their experiences with the mixological revival. Watershed books—Gary Regan's *The Joy of Mixology*, Dale Degroff's *The Craft of the Cocktail*—appeared in stores alongside glossy coffee-table recipe guides produced by actual bars. Authors who had long been out of print, from Harry Craddock to David Embury to Jerry Thomas, found new audiences through printed facsimile editions, and cocktail books and pamphlets of every level of obscurity were scanned and shared. The popular image of the bartender was no longer *Cheers*'s womanizing Sam Malone or Tom Cruise's doggerel poetry-spouting flairtender in *Cocktail* but a real-life figure like Sasha Petraske, warm and welcoming to his guests but holding exacting standards for himself and his craft—and looking like he'd just gotten back from a 1940s tailor shop.

The clientele matured as the bars did, with the trendy speakeasy style—quiet, dimly lit, intimate, and private—inspiring better behavior than the fern bars of the previous era. The religious magazine *First Things* even published "The Virtues of the Speakeasy," in which the author approvingly called such bars "an island for adult behavior in a world of perpetual adolescence." At the same time, bartending was gaining respect in the eyes of the public, as bartenders became owners and impresarios and people like Don Lee left jobs in lucrative industries to pursue soul-gladdening work in hospitality. (Did I mention David Wondrich has a PhD?) Other eras may equal the Renaissance in their widespread celebration of the cocktail as an art form, but none have surpassed it.

Necessarily, the Cocktail Renaissance was limited, as all such movements are, by the amount of revivable material it had to work with and by how well it prepared its adherents to create the movements that would replace it. Simultaneous with their study of the past, contemporary cocktail enthusiasts were inventing new recipes of their own, and when in time they felt they could surpass their predecessors behind the stick, the impulse to excavate mixological history began to dry up. A heavy focus on the classics came to seem hidebound and stuffy, and bartenders sought less serious alternatives.

In these ways the Renaissance sowed the seeds of its own succession by the Cocktail Baroque Period, a history we will unspool in the next two seminars. For now, though, we are in the High Renaissance and can experience it in its full flower, fleeting though that bloom may be.

# Ingredients for This Course

## GROCERY

| | |
|---|---|
| Angostura bitters | 1, 6, 7, 11, 16, 21, 25 |
| Boker's Bitters* | 16, 25 |
| eggs | 29 |
| grenadine | 8, 20 |
| lemons | 1, 7, 8, 10, 13, 16–18, 21–23, 26, 27, 29, 30 |
| limes | 6, 29 |
| mint | 18 |
| orange bitters* | 2, 3, 5, 6, 8, 9, 12, 18, 21 |
| oranges | 14, 20, 21, 24, 28 |
| orgeat* | 7, 16, 26 |
| Peychaud's Bitters | 1, 4 |
| rich demerara syrup | 21 |
| seltzer | 18, 29 |
| sugar/simple syrup | 1, 10, 14, 18, 29 |

## ALCOHOL

| | |
|---|---|
| absinthe* | 1, 4, 13, 15, 19, 23, 28, 29 |
| Amer Picon*† | 30 |
| Bénédictine | 4, 28, 30 |
| blanc vermouth* | 20 |
| blended Scotch | 24, 26, 29 |
| brandy | 16, 23 |
| Cherry Heering* | 15, 24 |
| crème de cacao | 27 |
| crème de violette* | 11, 22 |
| curaçao/triple sec | 6, 13, 20 |
| dry red wine* | 10 |
| dry vermouth | 3, 8, 9, 11, 21, 28, 30 |
| filtered lightly aged rum | 20 |
| Green Chartreuse | 12 |
| high-proof rye whiskey | 10 |
| Irish whiskey | 26 |
| Kina apéritif wine* | 13, 17, 27 |
| London dry gin | 3, 6, 7, 11–13, 17, 18, 22, 27 |
| maraschino | 22, 25, 30 |
| moderately aged rum | 2 |
| Old Tom gin | 5, 25 |
| rye whiskey | 1, 4, 8, 15, 30 |
| sherry* | 14, 21 |
| sparkling wine/Champagne | 19 |
| sweet vermouth | 2, 4, 9, 12, 15, 21, 24, 25, 30 |
| vodka | 17 |
| Yellow Chartreuse | 5 |

* indicates new ingredients
† bottled or homemade for final project

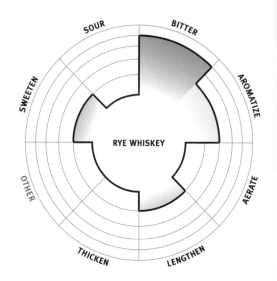

**To begin**, we return to the simplest and earliest cocktail templates: a bittered sling in the style of the Old Fashioned. Our standard-bearer for this seminar is the Sazerac, that most classic potation of New Orleans. The Sazerac and its absinthe-laced cousins are so much the lifeblood of the Crescent City that when the Green Fairy was unavailable in the United States, a domestic imitation called Herbsaint was put into market specifically for the sake of New Orleans.

Absinthe proper is a very high-proof spirit—usually at least 70% ABV—flavored with a variety of herbs and spices but particularly aniseed, wormwood, and fennel. Wormwood is the source of absinthe's alleged hallucinogenic properties, because it contains thujone. It's true that consuming enough thujone will cause hallucinations, but so will eating enough nutmeg. Given that hallucination is *also* a side effect of severe alcohol withdrawal, the widespread casual consumption of a 140-proof spirit may have been the issue irrespective of what was infused into it. While absinthe has certainly been consumed straight, it is not meant to be—it's traditionally diluted and sweetened due to its strength and concentration of flavor.

For similar reasons, the Sazerac uses a **rinse** of absinthe: one pours a bit of it into a glass, swirls it around to coat as much of the interior as possible, pours out any excess, and then adds the drink. This is by far

# Sazerac

2 oz. rye whiskey

1 tsp. simple syrup

4 dashes Peychaud's Bitters

1 dash Angostura bitters

1 tsp. absinthe (rinse)

Combine all but the absinthe in a rocks glass and stir with ice. Strain into a second, chilled rocks glass rinsed with absinthe. Express a lemon peel over the glass and discard.

the most common use of absinthe in cocktails, and sometimes other highly fragrant ingredients will be employed in the same manner. This is not unlike finishing a cocktail with an expressed citrus peel—although looked at in this way, the Sazerac would be "finished" twice, which puts a substantial strain upon the English language.

If built in the glass like an Old Fashioned, any agitation to combine the ingredients will tend to wash off this aromatic layer, so the Sazerac is stirred and then strained into a rinsed glass instead. Despite this, rocks glasses are traditionally used both to make and serve it. The experience of drinking a Sazerac is enough like having an Old Fashioned that this glassware selection seems appropriate.

Although sometimes claimed to be far more ancient, this drink is only a sprightly 120 or so years old. Wondrich writes that it was first compounded in the late nineteenth century, a (slight) modification from the Improved Whiskey Cocktail recipe published by Jerry Thomas, likely developed by either Billy Wilkinson or Vincent Miret, and then skillfully marketed by their employer, Handy and Co. of New Orleans. It also appears that weaving a little Angostura in with the Peychaud's has always been the practice. It's still under debate today—and one may certainly prepare a Peychaud's-only version to great effect—but I find that my tastes and others' incline more toward the both-and version.

# 3.2

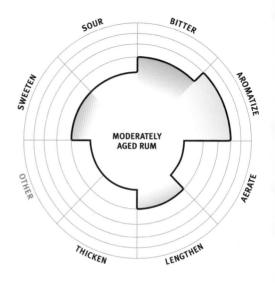

SOUR · BITTER · AROMATIZE · SWEETEN · AERATE · OTHER · MODERATELY AGED RUM · THICKEN · LENGTHEN

**Ingredient** revivalists clamored for orange bitters in large part due to its ubiquity in old cocktail guides, which stems in turn from its incredible versatility. There is no class of spirit which it cannot befriend, and rare is the ingredient it doesn't agree with. Consider how often we have used orange peels as garnishes already, to say nothing of our frequent use of orange liqueurs. Their flavors are not the same as that of orange bitters, but there is enough similarity for the comparison to be instructive: the scent of orange can complement, enhance, or otherwise tie together any number of spice, fruit, and spirit flavors. It seeps natively into herbaceous palates, brightens up crisp and refreshing ones, snuggles warmly into rich, deep ones. It alights gently atop fizz foams and bulks out the middle of sparkling wine cocktails. Any attempt to determine which flavors are most important in classic drinks must place orange near the top. It sees serious recipe use in four formats, appearing as juice, bitters, aromatic garnish, and liqueur. No other fruit can match that feat.*

* I gave the question some thought, and determined that the next-closest analogue might be the *peach*, which appears pureed in one classic (the Bellini), has historically wide currency as a bitters and a distillate, and also appears reasonably often as a liqueur. We consume far more grapes than peaches or oranges in cocktails, of course, but most of us would describe vermouths and brandies as having winelike rather than grapelike flavors, while everything we make from oranges still very much tastes like oranges.

# Palmetto

1½ oz. moderately aged rum

1 oz. sweet vermouth

2 dashes orange bitters

Stir with ice. Strain into a chilled cocktail glass.

The Palmetto, which is structurally akin to the Manhattan, combining as it does a spirit with sweet vermouth and bitters, is nevertheless an entirely different drinking experience. While there is a certain amount of push and pull between rye whiskey and vermouth, aged rum embraces its vinous partner entirely, in much the same way that it formed the most agreeable base in the Twelve-Mile Limit. I find that Palmettos tend to taste better with a higher proportion of vermouth, in part because it helps fill in a middle that in the Manhattan is occupied by the adversarial tension between whiskey and wine. The orange bitters does some of the work of the Angostura and the orange peel from the Rob Roy. They bitter and aromatize the drink—both helpful at keeping the vermouth from overpromoting itself—while also triggering a certain palate sense of the citrus-oil sweetness and mild sourness we expect from oranges. Scent memory is powerful and highly associative; part of the magic of aromatizing agents in cocktails, including orange bitters, is their capacity to imply flavors that we incorporate into our perceptions of the whole. The result is not unlike a barbershop harmony, which can produce a five-note chord using only four voices.

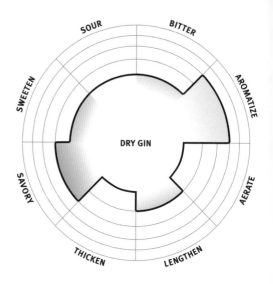

**Every cocktail** writer must eventually write about the Martini—Robert Simonson has even dedicated a whole book to the task. Doing it justice is no easy feat. The Martini has a nigh-untouchable reputation; it is also the only drink the patron will presume to tell the bartender how to make every time it is ordered. No other cocktail provokes such strong opinions, and none may be quite as iconic, the Old Fashioned being its only possible rival for either title.

It is a bit ironic, then, how much the Martini has changed in its history. No fewer than three stages of its evolution appear in this book, their recipes plucked from choice moments in its 150 years of evolution: the Gibson, the Martinez, and the Martini here presented, which is based on the Dry Martini recipes from the turn of the twentieth century.

It should be noted that none of these dates to after World War II. The midcentury formulation used vermouth as if it were bitters, resulting in a glass of chilled gin—or, worse, vodka—masquerading under the name, while later years brought cloying, luminescent concoctions served in cocktail glasses with -*tini* tacked onto the ends of their names. These are equal heresies of Martiniology. Eschew them both.

Despite its complicated journey to the present, the Martini did retain a few consistent features for long enough to give clear shape to what it is

# Dry Martini

3 oz. London dry gin

1 oz. dry vermouth

1 dash orange bitters (optional)

Stir with ice. Strain into a chilled cocktail glass and garnish with an olive or a lemon twist.

and is not. Its earliest versions combined Old Tom gin and Italian vermouth with bitters—a sweeter gin and vermouth than would later come into favor, but gin and vermouth nevertheless. The circa 1900 development of the Dry Martini, aptly named for its substitution of London dry gin and Marseilles dry vermouth, was initially recognized as the genesis of something new, rather than a tweak to an existing recipe, despite having more in common with its progenitor than either has with the fruit and chocolate concoctions found on "Martini menus" in our fallen age.

Let there be no confusion on this point: A Martini is a cocktail made with gin—or another base spirit *if and only if so specified*—and vermouth or a reasonably similar fortified wine. Nothing, however well-intentioned or pleasant tasting, should be considered a Martini if it fails this rudimentary test. You will find no such abuses of nomenclature in this book.

What we have instead is the Dry Martini in its circa 1900 glory. The subtleties of gin and vermouth play off one another, enhanced by bittersweet citrus—a clean, crisp cocktail, neither so dry as not to be refreshing nor so sweet as to fail to be bracing, and finished, according to the drinker's preference, with the brightness of a lemon peel or the salt-savoriness of an olive, each aromatic garnish pulling the drink in a different direction, each bringing it to its own satisfying conclusion.

**3.4**

SOUR  BITTER  AROMATIZE  AERATE  LENGTHEN  THICKEN  OTHER  SWEETEN

RYE WHISKEY

**In the last** seminar, I observed that Peychaud's, Bénédictine, and absinthe crop up frequently in New Orleans cocktails, sketching the outlines of a local signature flavor palette. The Vieux Carré employs two of these, as does the Sazerac. In the De La Louisiane, we have all three pulling together.

Also known as La Louisiane, À la Louisiane, Cocktail à la Louisiane—and various permutations of these—this recipe is a genuine specialty of the La Louisiane restaurant, which served the French Quarter for over a century beginning in 1881. It is also an opportunity to consider some structural novelties, in particular the application of the absinthe rinse technique to a liqueur-wine cocktail of the type discussed in the previous seminar.

Consider how this cocktail is compounded. To a base of rye whiskey we add vermouth for sweetness, bitterness, acidity, and aroma. While their relative proportions are the same as in a Manhattan, we reduce the volume of each and fill the gap with Bénédictine; it adds a certain amount of spirit and a third dimension of flavor, but it also tilts the balance toward sweetness overall. To compensate, we incorporate bitter elements that are aromatically complementary: first Peychaud's, which gets three dashes rather than Angostura's usual one or two, because its flavor is not quite as strong, and then absinthe, which

# De La Louisiane

1½ oz. rye whiskey

¾ oz. sweet vermouth

¾ oz. Bénédictine

3 dashes Peychaud's Bitters

1 tsp. absinthe (rinse)

Stir first four ingredients with ice. Strain into a chilled cocktail glass rinsed with absinthe.

reinforces the aniseed note from the bitters while laying the whole mixture down in a herbaceous garden bed, its wormwood note serving to further counterbalance the sweetness of the Bénédictine. All the classic seasonings of Louisiana cocktails accenting and enhancing one another, in much the same way that gumbo comes together.

Here as in the Sazerac, the absinthe rinse is crucial, but it is likewise essential not to overdo it. In intensity, absinthe ranks behind bitters but ahead of kirschwasser: it will take over the drink if too much is used. As a result, it almost always appears in rinses or teaspoonfuls rather than larger proportions. Some excellent craft absinthes are available in half-bottle sizes, but even so, a bottle of absinthe will normally last a very long time if it is only used in cocktails.

### FURTHER READING

One classic New Orleans method for going through absinthe faster is the Absinthe Frappé. Recipes for it differ, but based on Stanley Clisby Arthur's in *Famous New Orleans Drinks and How to Mix 'Em* and a survey of others, I would recommend combining 1 oz. absinthe, 1 oz. seltzer, and 1 tsp. simple syrup in a highball glass with crushed ice and stirring gently to combine. Mint garnishes appear to be a more recent addition, but are likely to improve the drink.

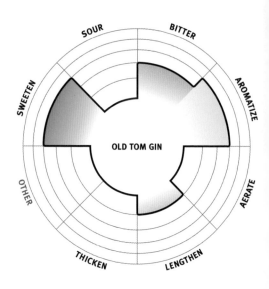

**Our third** revived ingredient for this section is Old Tom gin. Sadly not as popular today as absinthe or orange bitters, it was monstrously successful in the nineteenth century, and a number of cocktails, including the Martini, were originally made with it.

So what is it? That's a harder question than it sounds. The first modern Old Toms, Hayman's in 2007 and Ransom in 2008, differed in their interpretations of the style, with one sweetened and the other aged. Each has had some influence on subsequent products.

Either approach will result in a higher proportion of sugars in the finished product than in an unaged, unsweetened gin, because the barrels used for aging spirits are generally toasted or charred, which breaks down some of the wood cellulose into sugars. Both spirits will therefore register as at least a hair sweeter and more viscous than the average dry gin. This, incidentally, is why we use the term *dry gin*—to contrast with the sweeter Old Tom style.

The botanicals one might use in an Old Tom bottling are also likely to be different, or at least differently balanced, from the ones employed in drier styles of gin, because sugar enhances our perception of certain flavors while tamping down bitterness. This may argue for both aging and sweetening, the added sugar offsetting the tannins of the

# Alaska

2 oz. Old Tom gin

1 oz. Yellow Chartreuse

2 dashes orange bitters

Stir with ice. Strain into a chilled cocktail glass.

wood and letting more of the vanilla, clove, and coconut flavors from the toasted oak come through to mingle with the gin's botanicals.

Old Tom gin can work in a liqueur-driven cocktail when paired with Yellow Chartreuse, which is high enough in alcohol relative to its sugariness that each ingredient can fill in some of the other's gaps: the gin's sweetness compensates for the Chartreuse's lack of it, while the liqueur's spirituousness does some of the gin's job of drying out the mixture. The Alaska is often made with London dry gin, but I agree with Simonson that Old Tom makes a better drink. The orange bitters, meanwhile, does a bit of what it was doing in the Martini as well as in the Palmetto, the Alaska's profile having elements of both.

In 1910 Alaska was exciting news, having been the site of a series of gold rushes since the 1890s. Simonson speculates that the name could have been connected to the drink's shimmery yellow color. He notes it wasn't popular in its heyday, winning modest acclaim only during the Cocktail Renaissance. It was, however, included in *The Savoy Cocktail Book*, which conveyed it to posterity.

We've already encountered a few Old Tom gin recipes in disguise: the Gin Fizz, Silver Fizz, and Gin Rickey all predate the widespread use of dry gin in cocktails. Try them with your new bottle of Old Tom!

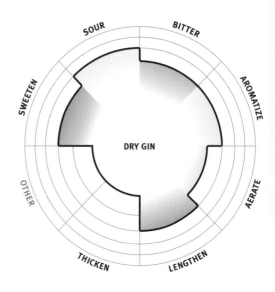

**You will notice** that even our early recipes get more complex as we proceed through the five seminars. This unit's very first sour is liqueur-sweetened and bittered—and it doubles up on its bitters to boot. This reflects the cumulative structure of our course of study: you should by now be comfortable enough with liqueur-sweetening and bittering that we can use both techniques incidentally while investigating a new ingredient. (Granted, this is already our fourth orange bitters cocktail, but there is still much exploring to be done.)

The Pegu Club takes its name from a British officers' club in Rangoon (now Yangon), Burma (now Myanmar), back before the sun set on the British Empire. It also gave its name to a legendary Manhattan bar opened by Audrey Saunders with Julie Reiner and Susan Fedroff, which was the Cocktail Renaissance's global ambassador from its much-heralded opening in 2005 until COVID-19 pulled the rug out from under New York's hospitality industry.

The namesake cocktail was chosen by Saunders in part because it was an underrated classic and in part because it was an accessible gin cocktail, and Saunders had made it a personal mission to rehabilitate gin in the eyes of the general public. Obviously, quite a lot has changed since then, in no small part because talented people like Saunders and Co. have continued to push the envelope.

# Pegu Club

1½ oz. London dry gin
¾ oz. curaçao or triple sec
¾ oz. lime juice
1 dash Angostura bitters
1 dash orange bitters

Shake with ice and strain into a chilled cocktail glass. Optionally, garnish with a lime peel.

But to return to the cocktail, one interesting feature of the Pegu Club is that it is our first recipe sweetened with an orange liqueur that does not call for or suggest reinforcing it with more sugar. Remember, the Honeymoon gets plenty of sweetness from the Bénédictine, and even the Seelbach can take advantage of the sugars in the wine. What distinguishes the Pegu Club from all the rest? The bitters.

Understand, we've never wanted to minimize sourness per se in our recipes, only to keep it from predominating. The most common and probably easiest method is to counter it with sugar—a task orange liqueur is often not up to on its own. The Rickey has shown us that this isn't the only way to keep sourness in check. The Pegu Club presents another alternative: to the dimensions of sweet and sour, add a third of bitter. So long as the sweet and bitter elements are in balance with one another, each can serve as a partial counterpoint to the sourness, thereby balancing the whole. The usual harmonies of spice and citrus are likewise in play, both among the modifiers and within the gin, while the orange bitters carries elements in common with all the other ingredients sufficient to tie them together. The optional lime peel garnish is a matter of taste, like the lemon peel in a Martini. Add it if you prefer the drink limier; if orangier, leave it out.

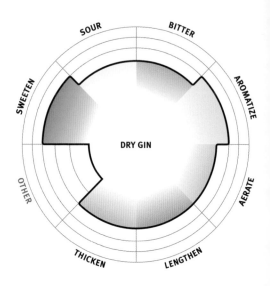

**Like** the Pegu Club, the Army & Navy is a shaken drink with bitters. It is also our first syrup-sweetened cocktail in a little while, and it introduces us to orgeat (pronounced "or–ZHAH"), a traditional French almond syrup that has been incorporated into cocktails since the mid-1800s. It is generally seasoned with orange flower water, giving it a blossomy bouquet in addition to its nuttiness. This enhances its versatility in cocktails, helping it to dovetail with the flavors of flower and citrus present in other cocktail components.

This is perhaps a good moment to think about gin more generally. We will take a variety of gastronomic cross sections of gin throughout this chapter as we consider it in different contexts; part of the reason it is so popular in classic recipes is that this can be done in the first place. The shape of its flavor is irregular, undulant, even changeable from brand to brand. It contributes juniper, but even juniper has some variety to it, containing as it does not only the pinene and myrcene that are typical of evergreen scents, but also the woodier sabinene and cadinene. Likewise, every gin further backs up its juniper with other spices, commonly including lemon and orange peel, cinnamon or its close cousin cassia, nutmeg (which evokes all of the foregoing as

# Army & Navy

1¾ oz. London dry gin

¾ oz. orgeat

½ oz. lemon juice

2 dashes Angostura bitters

Shake with ice. Strain into a chilled cocktail glass.

well as camphor), earthy angelica root, piney-floral cardamom, and any number of other herbs, spices, and flowers the distiller cares to blend together. Gin, in a sense, is like Chartreuse on a lighter plan. Its botanical richness enables it to go toe-to-toe with heavyweights like Campari, where other ingredients need a 2:1 ratio to keep the match fair. But the neutral base, lack of sugar, more streamlined blend of spices, and, frankly, lower proof, also permit gin to play gently with more delicate partners.

Orgeat offers an interesting mixture of elements, the heavier flavor of the almond accompanied by the more fragile orange flower fragrance—and each in turn is a good partner for the gin, picking up respectively on its winter spices and its citrus or floral botanicals. In understanding what makes a gin cocktail work, we should always consider not only the overall flavor balance of the recipe, but how it employs the balance that exists within the gin itself. Ingredients enhance and suppress the botanicals such that a given gin is never quite the same in two different cocktails. Having a good handle on this will also help in deciding which gin brands will work best in particular recipes.

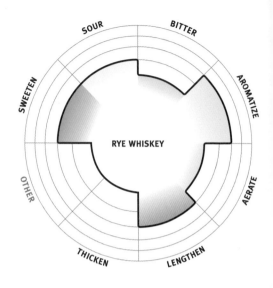

**3.8**

SOUR · BITTER · AROMATIZE · AERATE · LENGTHEN · THICKEN · OTHER · SWEETEN

RYE WHISKEY

**Iterating** one step beyond the last two recipes, we have in the Scofflaw another shaken drink with bitters—as well as one of our elusive sour-wine cocktails. Notice that the proportion of wine is a bit higher relative to the spirit than in the Clover Club. This is a sign that we want to be more aware of it than we were last time, in part because we have to be: sans egg white, it would be harder for the vermouth in the Scofflaw to fade into twilight subtlety the way it can in the Clover Club. Rather than have a small but recognizable component continually pop up when we taste the cocktail, we instead use enough of it to leave no doubt about its presence and adjust the rest accordingly. The larger slug of vermouth also provides body to the cocktail in the egg white's absence. It contributes a hair more sweetness, and grenadine is normally not as tart as raspberry syrup, so the proportion of lemon juice is slightly higher than is required in the Clover Club. The lack of egg also means that all the ingredients can be heard at full volume, which is tempered by the additional dimension of flavor the orange bitters provides.

Like the Twelve-Mile Limit, the things that make the Scofflaw most interesting are outside the syrup-citrus axis—note, for example, that this is our first recipe to pair dry vermouth with an *aged* spirit—and consequently, we stick to the basics of lemon and grenadine in that

# Scofflaw

1½ oz. rye whiskey

1 oz. dry vermouth

¾ oz. lemon juice

½ oz. grenadine

1 dash orange bitters

Shake with ice and strain into a chilled cocktail glass. Optionally, garnish with an orange peel.

department, rather than using a blend of juices or one of our more complex sweeteners.

Also like the Twelve-Mile Limit, this is an international cocktail that owes its name to Volstead-era developments in the States. Not long after Prohibition became the law of the land, a Massachusetts man by the name of Delcevare King decided that a new word should be coined to describe the people who were ignoring it and held a competition to devise one.* King, who was involved with the Anti-Saloon League, offered a prize of $200 in gold to the person with the best response.† He stipulated that the word must also begin with *s*, on the grounds that it had a particular sting. In the end, out of some 25,000 submissions, two people came up with *scofflaw* and split the prize money. A cocktail by that name was swiftly devised at Harry's New York Bar.

Sadly, the scofflaws' counter-coinage for the promoters of enforced teetotalism, "spigot-bigot," never quite caught on. Perhaps because no cocktail was ever invented with that name.

* It should be noted for posterity that the sponsor of this killjoy contest was a Harvard man.

† In 2021 money, that's over $2,500. King was *very* serious about this.

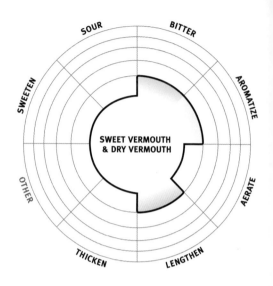

## 3.9

**The Vermouth Cocktail**, as venerable as it is and as easy to compound, may look a bit odd arriving this late to *The Cocktail Seminars*. We have, after all, seen plenty of vermouth by now. We have even seen lots of orange bitters, despite only meeting it nine drinks ago. In truth, there are lots of recipes for the Vermouth Cocktail, many made with Angostura rather than orange bitters and frequently just a single type of vermouth. However, this is the most agreeable version I know, and it also serves to introduce another new approach to making cocktails.

Presented as it is here, the Vermouth Cocktail employs a split base of fortified wines. We have occasionally dealt with multiwine drinks, going back as far as the Bronx; we have likewise seen cocktails with wine bases. But we have yet to see a pair of wines sharing the main spotlight in a recipe.

As was the case with herbal liqueurs, fortified wines can be challenging to blend with one another, simply because they each have so many things going on. The keys to effectively combining them are selecting

# Vermouth Cocktail

1 oz. sweet vermouth

1 oz. dry vermouth

1 dash orange bitters

Stir with ice. Strain into a chilled cocktail glass. Optionally, garnish with a brandied or maraschino cherry.

wines with complementary or overlapping flavors and employing them in a structure in which each enhances the other, as we did with the Alaska.

One reason I favor this recipe for the Vermouth Cocktail rather than the abounding single-vermouth variations is that the sweet and dry vermouths do complement one another. The lighter acidity and savoriness of the dry, when combined with the deeper spice and more robust sugar of the sweet, forms a more complete picture than either does alone. The orange bitters, as we have seen, appeals to both sides and helps them to join effectively.

To be clear, there is nothing wrong with other preparations. The earliest Vermouth cocktails, compounded not long after the sweet Italian variety reached U.S. shores and made with no admixture of any other wines, were enough to give Americans a taste for vermouth in the first place. This book is evidence enough of their success.

# 3.10

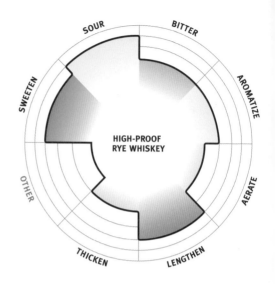

SOUR · BITTER · AROMATIZE · AERATE · LENGTHEN · THICKEN · OTHER · SWEETEN

**HIGH-PROOF
RYE WHISKEY**

## SOLUTION

The Irish Coffee showed us how a float provides the drinker a gradient of experiences. Like a sugared rim or a citrus wedge garnish, it affords a measure of sip-by-sip control over how the drink tastes.

In this recipe, each sip exists on a spectrum from Whiskey Sour to dry red wine, the relative admixture determined by him or her who sips. Because the wine's position and aromatic strength make it impossible to avoid getting a whiff, the float also functions a bit like a rinse here.

To keep the wine from predominating, I recommend serving the New York Sour on ice. We haven't seen a shaken-rocks drink since the Gimlet, but think about it: this recipe is nearly the same as our Whiskey Sour, but with added wine and a stronger whiskey. Adding dilution counterbalances the extra ethanol and the wine's flavors without having to muck around with the proportions. Shaken-rocks drinks are sometimes called *fixes*, but strictly speaking the fix was a specific drink historically; we can use this shorthand if we are careful to distinguish fix-as-technique from fix-as-recipe.

2 oz. high-proof rye whiskey

1 oz. simple syrup

¾ oz. lemon juice

½ oz. dry red wine (float)

Shake all but the wine with ice.
Strain into a rocks glass with ice and float wine on top.

# EXERCISE
# New York Sour

high-proof rye whiskey

simple syrup

lemon juice

dry red wine

*Using the given ingredients, determine the proportions of the New York Sour and its method of preparation.*

This exercise's special ingredient is plain red wine. Unlike vermouth, which is traditionally bittered with wormwood and laden with other spices, it adds astringency to the mix and lets us explore a more oenological blend of scents. Its fragrant qualities are key to this drink. Our third iteration of the Whiskey Sour, the New York Sour provides an opportunity to experiment with **floating** one ingredient on top of another.* This is best accomplished by pouring it over the back of a barspoon or very gently down the side of the glass, so that it forms a layer on top of the finished drink. Consider: Where have we seen a technique like this in use before? To what end was it employed then, and what does that tell us about how it should be used here? What are the salient differences between the two applications? And what kind of role do the red wine's properties suggest that it should play?

* The New York Sour's first three attestations, which span a period of decades, all come from Boston-area publications. As Wondrich points out in *Imbibe!*, this may indicate that the drink was accepted without dispute as a specialty of the Empire State, or that it was derisively named by Bostonians who found neither the drink nor its namesake to their liking. In either case, the consequence has been that the New York Sour has a stronger documented association with Massachusetts than the Boston Sour does, or than either has with New York!

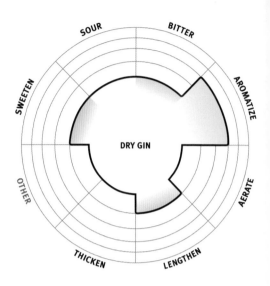

**I have** long held the opinion that, under any other name, the Yale would have become a widespread favorite during the Cocktail Renaissance. Its Ivy League association instead rendered it a curiosity, grouped with other drinks with collegiate names in listicles but appearing in few other places. Its novelty did, however, bring it to its namesake university, where in 2012 I was teaching Mixology 110b. Including it was an easy choice. Since then, I believe I have become the world expert on its history, largely for lack of competition.

The first cocktail to be called the Yale dates to 1895, in *Modern American Drinks* by George Kappeler. A glass of gin with a few dashes of bitters and a lemon twist, it may have reflected the spirit of the sons of Eli—indeed, every Yale Cocktail I've seen is strongly gin-forward—but it was neither particularly tasty, imaginative, nor blue.

Crème de violette changed the landscape. When mixed into a cocktail (and diluted), its purple hue becomes a steely blue-gray, sometimes even a lovely light blue if the right balance is struck. When it and the similarly colored but more elaborate-tasting Creme Yvette reached American shores in the early twentieth century, there was a scramble to find drinks that could be given blue-themed names. Recipes floated around that we might today recognize as the Yale, Aviation, and Blue Moon before landing on those names somewhat arbitrarily.

# Yale Cocktail

2 oz. London dry gin

⅓ oz. dry vermouth

⅓ oz. crème de violette

1 dash Angostura bitters

Stir with ice. Strain into a chilled cocktail glass.

Kappeler's version from '95 and similar variations remained in circulation, not seriously displaced until New Haven barman Jere Sullivan wrote his cocktail guide—during Prohibition at that!—and offered a very indigo recipe of equal parts gin, vermouth, and violette. It was entirely too sweet for modern tastes. The recipe above comes from Haus Alpenz, the company that imported crème de violette to the U.S. in 2007 after a half-century hiatus. I had been using their drier and Angostura-ed version for years before I managed to trace its history back to a contemporary of Sullivan's: as far as I can tell it was Leo Cotton, the first and longtime editor of *Mr. Boston Bartender's Guide*, who adapted Sullivan's recipe into more palatable proportions.

Its closest cousin is a Gibson before the onion goes in, while it's just gin and dry vermouth. The Yale takes a different path to get further aroma and requires no garnishes. Crème de violette, flavored and colored with violet petals, provides a floral accent that's easier to place than maraschino's. It draws out the subtle common notes in the floral palates of vermouth and gin. It's sweet, so the wine is dialed back and bitters added to keep the whole in balance. In a surprising collaboration, the Angostura keeps the spice notes in the gin from too great a subordination to the crème de violette, and violets make an excellent addition to that bouquet.

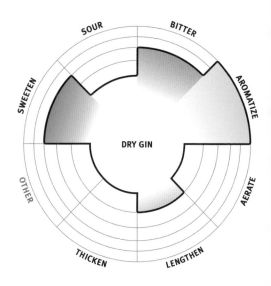

# 3.12

SOUR

BITTER

SWEETEN

AROMATIZE

DRY GIN

OTHER

AERATE

THICKEN

LENGTHEN

**By repute**, the Bijou—which is French for "jewel"—gets its name in homage to its ingredients: the gin represents diamond, the vermouth ruby, and the Chartreuse emerald. (The orange bitters represents orange bitters.) It dates back to the late nineteenth century and first appears in the bartender's manuals of Harry Johnson. A consummate professional as a bartender and a bar manager, whose books were successful enough for new editions to be issued every few years and whose precepts are no less valuable today than they were then, Johnson is also remembered for making exaggerated, unlikely, and in some cases impossible claims about his authorship of certain drinks. Strangely enough, he never claimed to have invented the Bijou; take from that what you will.

We have seen orange bitters at play in a liqueur-and-vermouth cocktail and pitted against an herbal liqueur in the Alaska. Here we find it in something more on the Negroni plan, a drink made with gin and

# Bijou

1 oz. London dry gin

1 oz. sweet vermouth

¾ oz. Green Chartreuse

1 dash orange bitters

Stir with ice. Strain into a chilled cocktail glass. Optionally, garnish with a brandied or maraschino cherry.

vermouth and a potent herbal, closely matched in both strength and volume. Many recipes for the Bijou call for equal parts of the three, but I find the Chartreuse a bit too much in that case.

Let us consider what to do to apply the Negroni's lessons to the Bijou. The boldness and sweetness of Green Chartreuse are helpfully checked by using ¾ oz. instead of a full ounce. It is less bitter than Campari and lacks the latter's citrus note, so if we are trying to strike a balance as close to that of the Negroni in terms of flavor, we will need to adjust the structure, incorporating a further aromatizing agent. Orange bitters would seem to be the natural solution to both problems, as well as a third: Green Chartreuse is quite strong. Its spiritousness needs to be checked somehow. Normally, we use sugar or dilution for this, but as we saw in the Pegu Club, bitters can offset more than just sweetness; our dash of orange at once serves to hold the Chartreuse to an acceptable level of assertion and to finish the Bijou.

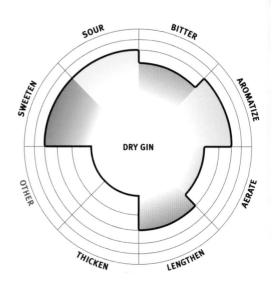

SOUR · BITTER · AROMATIZE · AERATE · LENGTHEN · THICKEN · OTHER · SWEETEN

DRY GIN

**We have** experimented with absinthe rinses in a built Old Fashioned–style cocktail and in a liqueur-wine cocktail already. The Corpse Reviver No. 2 adds it to an otherwise equal-parts recipe in the style of the Last Word. It is also our first introduction to what I am calling "Kina apéritif wine," a clumsy circumlocution that I promise I would not use if it could be avoided. The original recipe called for Kina Lillet, a defunct product that appears often in the old bar guides—especially *The Savoy Cocktail Book*.

Historically, Kina Lillet was a brand of quinquina, which in turn is a class of aromatized wine that has been flavored and bittered using cinchona bark or quinine. It was discontinued in the 1960s, leaving us with Lillet Blanc, a perfectly pleasant-tasting wine made by the same house that nevertheless lacks entirely the bitter punch its predecessor's recipes require. There are other quinquinas on the market, including Byrrh and Dubonnet, but these do not tend to make good substitutes for one another or for Kina Lillet, and all were generally called for by name rather than by category in the old recipe books.

The modern cocktail revival has brought us viable alternatives, beginning with Cocchi Americano. Confusingly, Cocchi's product is both a quinquina and an americano, a type of aromatized wine flavored and bittered with gentian, among other things. Some sources classify

# Corpse Reviver No. 2

¾ oz. London dry gin

¾ oz. curaçao or triple sec

¾ oz. Kina apéritif wine

¾ oz. lemon juice

1 tsp. absinthe (rinse)

Shake first four ingredients with ice. Strain into a chilled cocktail glass rinsed with absinthe.

quinquina and americano as wholly separate; others consider americano to be a subtype of quinquina—the truth is that they can overlap but often do not. In any case, Cocchi had the best substitute for a number of years, but the market has gradually filled up with new or newly imported aperitifs gunning for their spot atop the pyramid.

Interestingly, Kina Lillet makes a higher percentage of its appearances in soured cocktails than vermouth does. The flavor is bright and crisp, and it turns out that cinchona pairs well with lemon. The comparison with the Last Word is apt: there is nearly as much going on here as there, but the result is light enough overall to be conceivably taken at brunch. The same cannot really be said for the No. 1 from the first seminar.

We owe the numbering scheme for the Corpse Reviver cocktails to Craddock's magnum opus, *The Savoy Cocktail Book*. The name being a natural enough one for a cocktail, especially a morning cocktail, it had been applied to a handful of pre-Craddock recipes, none of which much mattered after his landmark text established this and the Corpse Reviver No. 1 as the canonical pair. Similar things have happened with other sets of numbered cocktails, but rarely do both recipes under a given name merit inclusion in the canon's greatest hits. The Corpse Revivers are the exception.

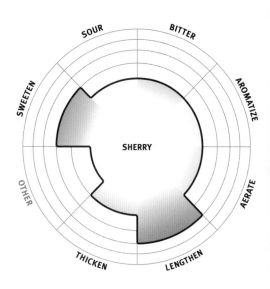

**3.14**

SOUR · BITTER · AROMATIZE · AERATE · LENGTHEN · THICKEN · OTHER · SWEETEN

SHERRY

**A scrumptious** expression of sherry and a stupendously popular cocktail of the nineteenth century, the Sherry Cobbler was so in vogue from the 1840s well into the 1880s that it forever gave its name to a patented cocktail shaker developed in 1884.*

It's an appropriate introduction to sherry, a style of fortified wine traditional to Spain and famously produced using a solera method, in which casks are partially emptied and then topped up with new wine, making each bottle a blend of many different ages. Its major styles, from dry to sweet, are fino/manzanilla, amontillado, palo cortado, and oloroso; the drier ones spend more barrel time under the *flor*, a natural protective layer of sherry-loving yeasts that minimizes oxidation during the aging process. For cocktails, amontillado is a safe middle-of-the-road bet, and the recipes in this book are tailored to work with it. If you want something richer—say, for a Sherry Flip— oloroso is the way to go.

The Sherry Cobbler also gives us a chance to discuss another new preparation technique. It was "invented" in 2010 by Theo Lieberman

---

* This is merely an interesting bit of history—there is no requirement to use a cobbler shaker to make the Sherry Cobbler. I find them too troublesome for the task, what with their little caps' tendency to vanish like socks in a dryer.

# Sherry Cobbler

4 oz. sherry

½ oz. sugar

3 orange slices

Shake with ice. Pour unstrained into a highball glass, or strain into a highball glass filled with crushed ice. Garnish with seasonal berries, a sprig of mint, and/or more slices of orange or lemon, as desired, and drink through a straw.

and christened by him and Meaghan Dorman as the **regal shake**, a sufficiently appealing name that we shouldn't trouble ourselves that the technique is at least as old as Jerry Thomas.

Simply put, it is using the action of shaking to extract something from a solid ingredient. This is easiest to imagine with a citrus peel: in moving from one end of the shaker to the other and being struck by the ice cubes along the way, the aromatic sacs on the surface of the peel burst and release fragrant oils into the mixture. The peel is then strained out and the drinker none the wiser. This delivers more oil into the cocktail than expressing a peel over the top and enables the peel to contribute taste as well as aroma. In contrast to dropping a peel into the glass before serving, it will not cause the drink to evolve in the drinker's hand. It is a subtle, in-between step.

The Sherry Cobbler extracts juices and oils from its orange slices as it's being shaken, its resulting flavor profile having certain commonalities with the Old Fashioned: a complex base, chilled, sweetened, and bittered, with tantalizing aromatics—in this case from the sherry itself—and a whiff of citrus oil to finish it. That said, the Sherry Cobbler is refreshing, being lower in proof and served with crushed ice and a straw. In fact, it came of age around the same time as commercial ice and straws and did a great deal to popularize them both.

**Where** the Yale takes the model of a vermouth-driven cocktail and uses a liqueur to make it floral and the De La Louisiane achieves a similar effect with its tripling up on herbaceousnesses, the Remember the Maine aims squarely at spiced fruit.

Its signature ingredient is an aged spiced cherry liqueur made in Denmark since 1818, officially known as Heering Cherry Liqueur but most commonly referred to as Cherry Heering. Like Chartreuse and Bénédictine, it remained available throughout the last century, but I have waited until now to introduce it because the ingredients it often accompanies are a prominent part of this seminar. Sumptuous and exceedingly agreeable, it is the sort of thing one could drizzle on a sundae in lieu of hot fudge—or, for that matter, in addition to it.

Heering's flavors are pleasant and familiar, many of them appearing in other ingredients. Still, it does not advertise itself in cocktails, and isn't easily identified. This makes it a capable utility player, adding understated complexities to drinks that appear straightforward at first blush—much like dry vermouth does in the Clover Club.

The model here echoes the De La Louisiane, with a liqueur adding sweetness and a third dimension of flavor to the axis of whiskey and vermouth. However, there is another subtlety of technique at play in

# Remember the Maine

2 oz. rye whiskey

¾ oz. sweet vermouth

½ oz. Cherry Heering

½ tsp. absinthe

Stir with ice and strain into a chilled cocktail glass. Optionally, express a lemon peel over the glass and discard.

the absinthe. So far, we have seen it used exclusively as a rinse, an aromatic finishing agent more like a citrus peel than a bitters. Here it is combined into the drink—fully half a teaspoon of it. As we have done in the past, we can think of it as modifying the liqueur as though we were making a house blend. Our absinthe-infused Heering is a bit drier, more bitter, and certainly more herbaceous than the Heering is alone. It can do all the things the triad of New Orleans ingredients did in the De La Louisiane with no further modifications.

Interestingly, there is another optional aromatic element. If you want your drink drier and crisper, express a lemon peel to finish it. If the sweetness of the Heering and the prominence of the absinthe require no sanding down for your palate, you can skip the citrus.

Remember the Maine comes to us from Charles H. Baker, a globe-trotting American adventurer who published cocktail-laden travel-ogues in the 1930s and '40s. Its name refers to the USS *Maine*, which mysteriously exploded and sank off the coast of Cuba. The Spanish were blamed, and "Remember the Maine, to hell with Spain!" became a rallying cry for war. In his *Gentleman's Companion*, Baker calls the drink "a hazy memory of a night in Havana" during the Sergeants' Revolt of 1933 and says he swigged them down to the sound of artillery fire on the city's promenade.

# 3.16

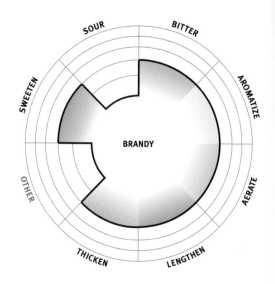

**The Japanese** was likely an original creation of "Professor" Jerry Thomas, who wrote the first known bartender's guide in 1862. Its rare and illustrious pedigree is complemented by its novel approach to the syrup-driven cocktail.

Structurally, the Japanese looks like an Old Fashioned: a healthy pour of spirits, a nonalcoholic sweetener, two dashes of bitters, and even a citrus peel. Why, then, it is shaken rather than built in the glass? The answer lies in the heaviness of orgeat—both gastronomically and in the fluid-mechanical sense. It is heavy on the palate, thick and syrupy; it cries out to be diluted for us to enjoy it, in much the same way that we prefer grating peppercorns onto our food rather than eating them whole. It is also physically heavy: viscous, full of suspended solids, and unwilling to mix easily into other liquids when it could settle on the bottom of the glass instead. Both these factors encourage shaking, making its closest cousin not so much the Old Fashioned as the Gimlet, another stripped-down drink that leaves a syrup to do most of the modifying. Unlike the Gimlet, however, the Japanese relies on an ingredient that does not have a significant sour dimension alongside its sugars, so it requires the external assistance of bitters to not become overly sweet.

# Japanese

2 oz. brandy

½ oz. orgeat

2 dashes Boker's Bitters or Angostura bitters

Shake with ice and double-strain into a chilled cocktail glass. Express a lemon peel over the glass and discard.

Thomas's original recipe calls for Boker's Bitters, a wildly popular brand in his era—overwhelmingly favored in *The Bon-Vivant's Companion*\*—which ceased production in the 1920s. Of the historic bitters brands, it has generated the most interest in modern times, in part because of its connection to the Professor; several versions exist today, of which at least two purport to be based on surviving bottles of the original. Boker's was an aromatic bitters style, meaning it works like Angostura in cocktails—and you can substitute Angostura or your favorite aromatic bitters if necessary. Most reconstructions have a pronounced flavor of cardamom and deep coffeelike notes, which respectively pick up on the floral orange and almond aspects of the orgeat. Depending on the assertiveness of the Boker's expression you have, you may even want to try using ½ tsp. of it instead, as we did with the absinthe in the Remember the Maine—that was how the Professor mixed his originally, but it will only work if the bitters you have is a good deal softer than, say, Angostura.

\* Strictly speaking, he called for "Bogart's Bitters," but it is widely accepted that this was simply a typo for "Boker's." Nevertheless, one of the modern reconstructions uses the "Bogart's" name, in part as an homage to Thomas and probably also because another producer branded its product as "Boker's" first.

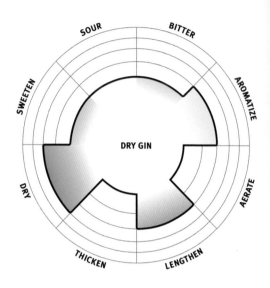

**The Vesper** was the world's introduction to the James Bond catch-phrase, "Shaken, not stirred." Invented by Ian Fleming and inserted into *Casino Royale* as 007's own creation, the recipe is untitled at the beginning of the book but eventually named after Bond's love interest Vesper Lynd. Fleming's original recipe called for Gordon's gin, vodka, and Kina Lillet in a ratio of 3:1:½, shaken, with a lemon twist. Gin and vodka we have still, but a true Vesper could not be had until Kina Lillet found viable modern analogues.

As everyone from Jed Bartlet to yours truly has observed, "shaken not stirred" is a terrible formulation for a Martini. Why, then, does it work for the Vesper? Direct your attention back to the Diamondback from the last seminar, so far our only example of an on-paper stirred drink that we have chosen to shake. We did so to introduce some dilution, to turn the volume down a bit on the ingredients. The Vesper benefits from the same: it's a heavy pour of gin, further dried with vodka, and its "mixers" are a half ounce of wine and a lemon peel. It needs all the dilution it can get! This was even more true in the 1950s when Gordon's was 94 proof and the most available vodkas were 100 proof. At its best, the Vesper is bracing, but still delivered in an elegant package with details worth the effort to examine. It is in this respect not unlike the gun with the mother-of-pearl handle that Fleming also allowed his hero as a personal touch.

# Vesper

3 oz. London dry gin

1 oz. vodka

½ oz. Kina apéritif wine

Shake with ice. Strain into a chilled cocktail glass and garnish with a long, thin twist of lemon.

A final note on the Vesper: Some sources attribute the recipe to Fleming, others to this or that acquaintance of his, but in any case he never tried it himself before *Casino Royale* went to print. When he finally got around to it, he didn't care for it—an ironic twist for the most famous cocktail in literature!

**FURTHER READING**

John Steinbeck also got into the literary cocktail game in his novella *Sweet Thursday*, a sequel to *Cannery Row*. Steinbeck's characters at one point order a drink called the Webster F-Street Layaway Plan, which is described as a Martini with Chartreuse instead of vermouth. As far as I can tell, the first published recipe for it that goes into any greater detail was in a 1998 book called *Atomic Cocktails*, which calls for two ounces of gin to be shaken and poured into a glass rinsed with Green Chartreuse, followed by an expressed lemon peel. The book may have originated the ludicrous claim that the unknown drink—named after a friend of Steinbeck's and included as an inside joke—had been a favorite of F. Scott Fitzgerald's, but the recipe is genuinely good. Whether this is the kind of "Martini" Steinbeck intended or he had something more like the Alaska in mind is harder to say.

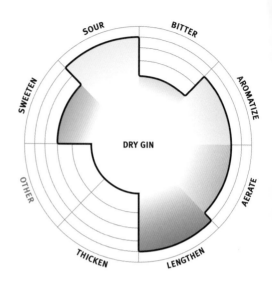

**Like the** Vermouth Cocktail, a version of the Southside could easily have appeared in the first seminar. I have elected to save it until now because this adaptation of a recipe by Joaquin Simó incorporates a number of things we have learned since then and is by a wide margin the best expression of this drink I know.

First, the history: The Southside, so far as we can tell, is not a Chicago drink, although the name has given it some cachet there. It seems likely that this is another one in New York's column, for those keeping score, coming either from one club in New York City or another on Long Island, depending upon whom one asks.

Mechanically, we are dealing with a sour with a gin base and two additional aromatics. Bittered sours have been rare so far, but not unheard of. The mint is what makes this really interesting. As we did with the orange slices in the Sherry Cobbler, we add it directly to the shaker and let the ice do the work of extracting the oils from the leaves.

Most people overmuddle their mint. The goal is to gently bruise it to burst open the aromatic glands on the surface of each leaf, not to make pesto with it. Grinding up the leaves releases enzymes that can break down those lovely aromatic chemicals, reducing their potency at best

# Southside (Fizz)

2 oz. London dry gin

¾ oz. lemon juice

¾ oz. simple syrup

~8 mint leaves

1 dash orange bitters

Shake with ice and strain into a chilled rocks glass. Garnish with a sprig of mint.

and transforming them into unpleasant off-flavors at worst. The regal shake is not quite as gentle as a muddler-wielding human *can* be, but it tends to be far gentler than the average human *is*. It is also easier and less messy. In other words, while this technique is not required for a good Southside, it is a big help.

It is also worth noting that both a Southside and a Southside Fizz are in circulation. As often happens when two close variants of a cocktail exist, they are often confused for one another, and murky half-measures can masquerade as either. Simply put, the Southside is as above, or as above without the orange bitters. The Southside Fizz is the same drink with 2–3 oz. of seltzer added to make it a fizz. No other change is necessary! This incidentally makes the Southside the first fizz-optional cocktail we have seen. In principle, one could make any shaken sour into an equivalent fizz just by adding seltzer, although some will be easier than others.

### FURTHER READING

Just like the dry shake changed our impression of the Bee's Knees, the Southside Fizz gives us another angle of attack on the Mojito. It may not be traditional, but it can absolutely be made as a regal-shaken fizz. Give it a try!

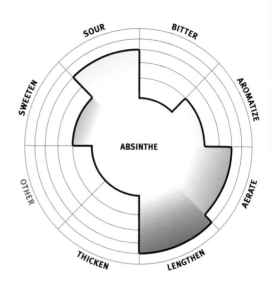

SOUR · BITTER · AROMATIZE · AERATE · LENGTHEN · THICKEN · OTHER · SWEETEN

ABSINTHE

**The Death in the Afternoon** is one of two promised recipes that will help you to work through a bottle of absinthe a bit more rapidly. It is also one of a handful of cocktails personally invented by Ernest Hemingway, in this case for a 1935 compendium of mostly forgettable cocktails by famous writers entitled *So Red the Nose; or, Breath in the Afternoon.* Hemingway's entry was named after his book on bullfighting.

If you have experimented with absinthe service, dripping water through a sugar cube atop an ornate spoon into a waiting glass full of the Green Fairy, you have seen the famous louche effect: absinthe, along with ouzo and other anise-flavored spirits, becomes cloudy when diluted. This is due to trans-anethole, the substance in anise and related spices that gives that licorice-y taste to things. It is about thirteen times sweeter than table sugar, which may account for its popularity in desserts, candies, and liqueurs. It is also very hydrophobic. When water is introduced into a solution that contains it, the anethole molecules collect into tiny clumps as they try to get away from it. When sufficient water is added, the clumps become large enough to scatter light, and numerous enough that the whole mixture grows opalescent.

# Death in the Afternoon

1½ oz. absinthe

4 oz. sparkling wine

Pour absinthe into a chilled flute, followed by sparkling wine. Stir gently to combine.

Absinthe producers are careful to balance the water, ethanol, and anethole contents of their products so that they are translucent green in the bottle rather than opaque white. This is one advantage to absinthe's notoriously high proof: anethole has no problem staying dissolved in alcohol. But another consequence is that virtually any other ingredient mixed with absinthe will raise the proportion of water and, in sufficient quantity, induce at least some amount of louching. This is ultimately unavoidable, because the thing that does the louching is what gives the spirit its flavor; it is regarded instead as one of absinthe's charms.

While the Champagne Cocktail and the Seelbach are instructive in our approach to the Death in the Afternoon, this drink in turn may give us some notion of how to tackle other recipes that combine a sparkling wine with one other thing. The stronger the flavor of the second ingredient, the less of it one needs—but even absinthe wants a full ounce and a half to overcome dilution by the wine. Keep this benchmark in mind for your next Bellini or Kir Royale. Whatever you do, though, do not take literally Hemingway's instruction for the Death in the Afternoon: "Drink 3 to 5 of these, slowly." That is an easy way to make the drink's name a reality.

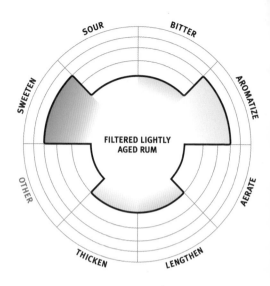

SOUR · BITTER · AROMATIZE · AERATE · LENGTHEN · THICKEN · OTHER · SWEETEN

FILTERED LIGHTLY
AGED RUM

# SOLUTION

The El Presidente most resembles the Palmetto of anything we have seen, but skewed deliberately sweeter. We need not worry that their structures differ. Let's start the El Presidente at square one.

It is vermouth-driven, seasoned with a syrup and a liqueur but no bitters. This technique was in vogue early in the twentieth century, but because contemporary tastes skew more bitter, most liqueur-wine drinks that have entered the Renaissance-era canon have either bitters or citrus in them as well. The El Presidente feels no such compunctions. The vermouth's sweetness joins that of the syrup and the liqueur (conveniently, the triple sec is fairly dry and adds some spirituousness as well), and the cocktail certainly leans in that direction—but not unpleasantly so, nor as much as one might think. The orange peel is just enough to cover any excess.

1½ oz. filtered lightly aged rum

1½ oz. blanc vermouth

1 tsp. curaçao or triple sec

1 tsp. grenadine

Stir with ice and strain into a chilled cocktail glass. Express an orange peel over the glass and discard.

# EXERCISE
# El Presidente

filtered lightly aged rum

blanc vermouth

curaçao or triple sec

grenadine

*Using the given ingredients, determine the proportions of El Presidente and its method of preparation.*

**Believe it** or not, there is a third major type of vermouth. Known as *bianco* (in Italy) or *blanc* (in France), it is sweet but colorless, its botanicals a middle ground between the other styles. It is fragrant but delicate, low on bitter spices and heavy on sweet-floral notes like elderflower. Blanc vermouth isn't seen much in the U.S., where vermouth is mostly used in cocktails tailored to sweet or dry.*

El Presidente recipes do list dry vermouth sometimes, because the earliest printed versions specify "French" vermouth; but Wondrich has established that the blanc style was meant. A Ribalaigua cocktail from circa 1919, it shot to fame on both sides of the Straits of Florida. Its namesake president was likely Mario García Menocal, but it stayed popular into the Machado administration, and was even offered to Calvin Coolidge at a state dinner (he declined).

In this chapter, we've often understood a cocktail's balance by iteration from a previous one. Before we get too far with that, I want to make sure it's clear that balances can be struck in various ways and to various tastes. Expect the El Presidente to be on the sweet side. Everything else should be familiar. Consider, reflect, and read on!

---

* It makes up for it elsewhere: Martini & Rossi reports that its bianco expression is its most popular product worldwide.

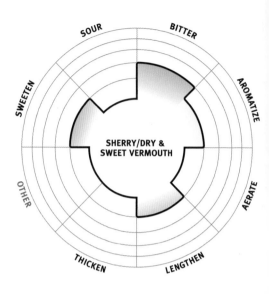

**3.21**

SOUR

BITTER

SWEETEN

AROMATIZE

SHERRY/DRY &
SWEET VERMOUTH

OTHER

AERATE

THICKEN

LENGTHEN

**As we did** with the Negroni and the Boulevardier, we will consider the Adonis and the Bamboo together in light of their similarities. Like the Vermouth Cocktail, the central problem of each is pairing two fortified wines. They address that in two slightly different ways.

The Adonis, named after a Broadway show from 1884, is what *Punch* has called the "classical beefcake" of the two, matching sherry with the viscous goodness of sweet vermouth. That's a lot of body, and to keep it from getting excessive, a couple of dashes of orange bitters are added as a counterbalance; the orange flavor is further enhanced with an expressed peel, no additional bittering needed. It is a straightforward recipe—warm, inviting, and tasty, but also somewhat obvious.

The Bamboo is the subtler of the two. It uses a larger number of ingredients, each of which pulls a smaller number of levers, giving the maker more precise control over the final balance. The vermouth is dry, so sugar can be added to taste. Our choice for that is the demerara syrup introduced for the Irish Coffee last seminar, a far more useful ingredient than it might have appeared at first—its concentration of sugar and depth of comforting molasses-y flavor make it a great replacement for simple syrup in many recipes, and it is going to appear a lot in our unit on tropical drinks. I take my inspiration for it here

# Bamboo

1½ oz. sherry

1½ oz. dry vermouth

1 tsp. rich demerara syrup

1 dash Angostura bitters

1 dash orange bitters

Stir with ice and strain into a chilled cocktail glass. Express a lemon peel over the glass and discard.

# Adonis

1½ oz. sherry

1½ oz. sweet vermouth

2 dashes orange bitters

Stir with ice and strain into a chilled cocktail glass. Garnish with an orange peel.

from Joaquín Simó, whose Bamboo recipe I have also adapted. A dash of Angostura picks up on the syrup's flavor and joins with the orange bitters to keep the sugars of the wines and the syrup in check. The Bamboo is drier and more layered than the Adonis, brought into crisp focus with a spritz of lemon oil across the top. To a trained eye, the Bamboo can be an exceptionally good gauge of its preparer's technical expertise. Unsurprisingly, it has gained some popularity in recent years as a drink for cocktail bartenders to serve one another when they want to show off their skills and their personal styles. In a sense, this is taking it back to its roots at Yokohama's Grand Hotel, where Louis Eppinger built his reputation by specializing it.

**FURTHER READING**

Demerara syrup also unlocks the best version of the Sidecar I know—also by Simó. Where in the first seminar I advised a quarter ounce of simple syrup or a sugared rim, I can now recommend a teaspoon of rich demerara syrup with the same quantities of everything else I gave before. The total amount of sugar is the same in 1 tsp. of 2:1 syrup and ¼ oz. of regular simple syrup (and, for that matter, in 1 tsp. of dry sugar or maple syrup), but the demerara's rich flavors compensate for some of what is lost using a younger Cognac. Simó is one of the Sidecar's greatest modern champions, and this recipe justifies his commitment.

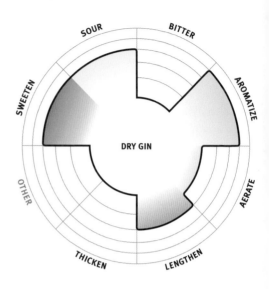

**3.22**

SOUR · BITTER · AROMATIZE · AERATE · LENGTHEN · THICKEN · OTHER · SWEETEN

DRY GIN

**More than** most other recipes in this book, the Aviation captured the imagination of a generation of mixophiles as a drink they yearned to taste but could not. *An* Aviation was known from *The Savoy Cocktail Book*, but it omitted the crème de violette. This version had some currency while the question of "which old drinks are worth reviving" remained open, but after Wondrich found Hugo Ensslin's original 1916 recipe in 2004, the world went gaga over it.

It hit every note of the revival era. The recipe had to be rediscovered *twice*, and only the dedicated efforts of modern sleuths could uncover the gnosis Ensslin bequeathed us. It did not hurt that the crème de violette explained the name, in honor of the then-new field of aviation and the drink's pale indigo color like a wide-open sky. It also did not hurt that crème de violette could not be had in the United States, and was unavailable for decades until Haus Alpenz brought it back in 2007 (it was, at the time, the top item on bartenders' request lists).

With its key ingredient restored, the Aviation enjoyed a moment of unparalleled trendiness. It was an in-the-know drink for the cocktail-literate even as it was popping up on mainstream menus everywhere. Its triumphant return permanently ensconced it in the canon, granted it greater name recognition than 80 percent of the drinks in this book, and made crème de violette a requirement for a serious bar program.

# Aviation

2 oz. London dry gin
3/4 oz. lemon juice
1/2 oz. maraschino liqueur
1/4 oz. crème de violette

Shake with ice and double-strain into a chilled cocktail glass. Optionally, garnish with a brandied or maraschino cherry.

It flew too close to the sun. By 2012, the backlash had begun. Renaissance godfather Dale DeGroff was labeling it "Do Not Resuscitate," and many of its adopters repudiated it as a product of misguided zeal in restoring old drinks.

The Renaissance's blue darling may have been a convenient scapegoat for changing attitudes toward what cocktails should be, but its fall from grace was abetted by its unusual blending of two floral liqueurs. Overdo one or both and the drink escapes the realm of cocktails and enters that of soap or perfume. It does not do this if made well, but its sudden ubiquity meant that it was very often *not* made well, looking borderline purple and tasting like potpourri punch.

As we have seen elsewhere, the secret to using ingredients that can easily become excessive is to apply them sparingly. This is why we make the Yale with just two teaspoons of crème de violette, and the Aviation with even less in light of its maraschino. Made as here, the drink deserves legitimacy as a classic, warranting neither the universal relish of its brief heyday nor the opprobrium it has received since. It should also have a more appropriate color; although crème de violette drinks often come out more blue-gray, sometimes you get it just right and the drink will have the exhilarating pale blue of the sky.

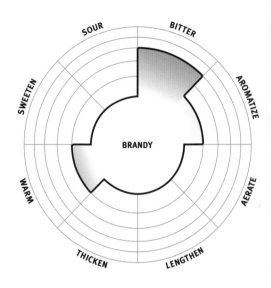

SOUR · BITTER · AROMATIZE · SWEETEN · BRANDY · AERATE · WARM · THICKEN · LENGTHEN

**Mightily** deserving its name, the Earthquake is a creation of the artist and patron of the Parisian demimonde Henri de Toulouse-Lautrec. In his native tongue, it was the rather more evocative *Tremblement de Terre*, and its original form was a combination of brandy and absinthe in equal parts that most moderns would have difficulty choking down.

The Earthquake is an example of a **scaffa**, a rare type of mixed alcoholic drink that is prepared and served at room temperature. Why might one do this? Consider that in our most extensive previous discussion of preparation styles, concerning the Collins and fizz, much was made about the difference between a drink one will sit with for a long time and one that is meant to be drunk more quickly. If we begin with the assumptions that all drinks should be cold and that no more dilution should be accepted than is necessary, we arrive fairly naturally at the methods for those two: one is chilled during preparation and served without ice, to be rapidly consumed; the other is built in the glass, chilled and diluted over the duration of its consumption.

Very well, but what if we eliminate the first assumption? What if we contend that a drink need not be cold, only that it be undiluted? And what if we introduce a third requirement, that the drink not *change* in the time it takes to drink it? The Collins and fizz both do, the former being diluted by its melting ice, the latter gradually warming to

# Earthquake

2½ oz. brandy

¼ oz. absinthe

Combine ingredients in a rocks glass and stir without ice. Express a lemon peel over the glass and discard.

the temperature of your hand, changing the balance of flavors we perceive. Minimizing the change in the cocktail over time is very difficult to do in vivo if we care that it be a particular temperature—unless, of course, that temperature is the same as its surroundings.

The thermodynamics now dispensed with, why would we want such a thing? Perhaps because we're mixing a drink that will take even longer to get through than a Collins, so that if any change is allowed it will be wildly different by the last sip. That makes the most sense when a cocktail demands a few minutes' reflection and recovery after each sip—say, when the drink is half brandy and half unwatered absinthe.

That justifies the original recipe, but why retain it for the modern one? There is a certain amount of romance in historical accuracy in this case*—Lautrec is, after all, the only painter with a recipe included herein, although he joins Hemingway and Fleming in the broader ranks of artists with cocktails to their names—but it is also the case that even this stripped-down modern version is still intense enough to benefit from being made as a scaffa.

* It is worth noting that Lautrec's actual reasoning was likely a simple aversion to taking any water while drinking. He was known for this predilection, having hosted dinner soirees with goldfish in the water pitchers to indicate that only alcohol would be available to drink. A Lautrec party was a decadent hazard.

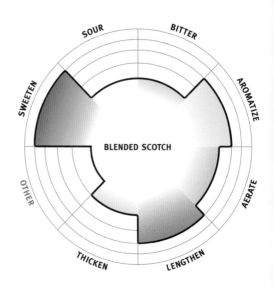

**3.24**

SOUR · BITTER · AROMATIZE · SWEETEN · BLENDED SCOTCH · OTHER · AERATE · THICKEN · LENGTHEN

**Like** the Aviation, the Blood and Sand has suffered a fall from grace with the waning of the Renaissance era, but unlike the Aviation it never had quite as far to fall in popularity. It calls to mind the Ward Eight: likewise maligned as impossible to balance thanks to its orange juice component, it can likewise be made in a way that should put such slanders to rest.

Part of the problem is that no one seems to agree on the proper proportions. Is it an equal-parts drink? Is the orange juice just a teaspoon with the others at full strength? Or is the Heering just a teaspoon? How prominent should the Scotch be? And so on.

I remain a defender of fresh orange juice in cocktails, but the trick we have often used in the past—splitting it with lemon juice to get its flavor plus adequate sourness—is not an option here. The classic texts are very consistent about what goes into a Blood and Sand, even if they can't agree on how much.

That makes the Bronx a better point of comparison than the Ward Eight, which also gives us a clue about the structure we're trying to build: this is less of a sour-wine recipe and more an orange-accented version of a liqueur-wine one. The Brainstorm or the Boulevardier should be on our minds right now.

# Blood and Sand

1¼ oz. blended Scotch

¾ oz. sweet vermouth

¾ oz. Cherry Heering

¾ oz. orange juice

Long shake with ice and double-strain into a chilled cocktail glass. Express an orange peel over the glass and discard.

I came to this recipe by iteration, beginning with the equal-parts version seen as far back as *The Savoy Cocktail Book*. To my taste, that version is ill-balanced as charged. Its middle is wanting; it has to be shaken to disperse the orange juice evenly, but this is too much dilution for the flavor profile's foundation. I compensate by dialing up the Scotch. When it reaches a relative strength sufficient to hold the center, I find the drink reading as too spiritous. And so I employ a new technique.

We have encountered the short shake in the Gimlet already, and likewise not one but two drinks that are stirred on paper but shaken in practice. Our standard stirring and shaking techniques apply for the vast majority of cocktails; that there are exceptions should not surprise us. The Blood and Sand, I find, benefits from a **long shake**, a technique that otherwise appears mostly in tropical drinks, but which is not that different from giving the Diamondback the equivalent of a "long stir" by shaking it. To achieve this, shake the Blood and Sand about half again as long as you would any other cocktail. If you like, you can think of this as making the drink with a larger proportion of lower-proof Scotch.

# 3.25

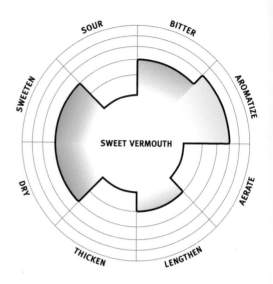

SOUR · BITTER · AROMATIZE · SWEETEN · AERATE · DRY · THICKEN · LENGTHEN

SWEET VERMOUTH

**The third** and final iteration of the Martini which we will consider in this text, the Martinez is also the oldest member of the family on record. It appears first in 1887 in *Jerry Thomas's Bar-Tender's Guide*, with its proportions given almost exactly as they are here.

Tall tales have always been popular in the barroom, and it is only natural that they should concern mixological topics from time to time. The popularity of the Martini has made it ripe for speculation, half-remembered assertions, and outright nonsense to coalesce into a rumor mill as devoid of truth as it is widespread. In this spirit, it is sometimes said that the Martini was created as a variation on the Martinez, the latter having been invented in California on such-and-such date and named after a local town. Horsecrap.

The sad, inescapable truth is this: we have no idea who invented the Martini or who gave it that name. The king of the cocktails is a foundling babe.

In point of fact, we do not know whether "Martini" is even what it was originally called. As Wondrich describes in *Imbibe!*, in those early days the Martine, Martina, Martigny, Martineau, Martena, Martini, and Martinez were *all* attested across the United States, part of a nationwide game of Telephone flavored with gin and vermouth.

# Martinez

2 oz. sweet vermouth

1 oz. Old Tom gin

1 tsp. maraschino liqueur

2 dashes Boker's Bitters or Angostura bitters

Stir with ice and strain into a chilled cocktail glass.

"Martinez" is the name that Jerry Thomas used for his recipe, and as a result it has entered contemporary usage to describe a drink in this family made along nineteenth-century lines—i.e., with sweet vermouth, Old Tom gin if possible, a more vermouth-forward balance than modern Martinis have, and ideally bitters and maraschino. The Professor's version is the best expression of this I have seen.

Note that, like the Rose, it is an upside-down cocktail, a vermouth base seasoned and dried with gin rather than the other way around. In this way, one could think of it as a variation on the Vermouth Cocktail, which may in fact be how it came about, although another version has it evolving from the Manhattan with the substitution of gin for whiskey.

It may seem depressing to think that after quite literally decades of investigation, we have if anything more questions about the Martini's origins than we did when we began and no solid answers. Take heart, though: that just means there is still room for you to make a major contribution to cocktail historiography.

SOUR · BITTER · AROMATIZE · AERATE · LENGTHEN · THICKEN · OTHER · SWEETEN

**IRISH WHISKEY & BLENDED SCOTCH**

**There is** a sense in which the Cameron's Kick is a very simple drink. It has only four ingredients, and it is built on a sour template not unlike that of the Army & Navy—it even lacks the latter's bitters, having therefore a simpler conceptual structure.

On the other hand, it is our first example of a split-base drink in which both spirits belong to the same overall class—in this case, whiskey. This technique is highly uncommon in most areas of mixology. Ordinarily, it is expected that adding a second spirit of the same type will contribute less to the drink than adding some other ingredient will, and that it is probably not worth it to go to the trouble. This is, however, not true in all cases.

Think about it this way: many distilled spirits are, in some way, blends. Distillers who bottle their own stock often combine spirits of different ages in order to achieve a particular flavor profile, while brands that source their distillates from other producers frequently combine spirits from multiple distilleries.

In this sense, we can think of the Cameron's Kick as a drink made with a blended whiskey base, in which it so happens that the blender is also the bartender and the whiskey includes components from both

# Cameron's Kick

1 oz. Irish whiskey

1 oz. blended Scotch

½ oz. lemon juice

½ oz. orgeat

Shake with ice. Strain into a chilled cocktail glass. Optionally, garnish with an orange peel.

Irish and Scottish distillers. If you combined your favorite Scotch and Irish whiskies in a decanter in equal parts, it would be easy to think of that as a homemade whiskey blend—every time you make a Cameron's Kick, you do the same thing on a smaller plan.

Single pot still Irish whiskey, which is the type I recommended when we first worked with Irish whiskey in the Tipperary, enjoys the best flavors of both malted and unmalted barley, while Scotch wraps the whole in a gossamer shroud of peat smoke. Certain single-malt Scotches could probably approximate the blend of flavors here, but could never quite attain it. Two whiskies can do what one alone could not. That said, like the Clover Club, the Cameron's Kick is not easy to pick apart on the drinking. The multiwhiskey base blends seamlessly into the orgeat, and it becomes hard to distinguish where one ingredient ends and the next begins.

As for its history, we know very little. The Cameron's Kick was first published by Harry MacElhone in *Harry of Ciro's ABC of Mixing Cocktails*, before he left Ciro's and set up shop at his eponymous New York Bar in Paris, but we have absolutely no idea why it was created, who Cameron was, or whom or what he kicked.

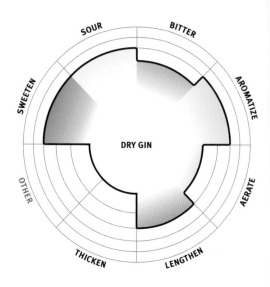

**Personally**, I have always been a sucker for drinks that don't make sense on paper. The Twentieth Century seems extraordinarily unlikely, as recipes go—it pairs chocolate with gin, of all things, which we have already panned once in our discussion of the Brandy Alexander, while the other major flavors are lemon, quinine, and white wine, none of which is thought to be buddy-buddy with cacao.

This is an opportune moment to contemplate chocolate's success. It has certain physical properties that render it convenient for confectionaries, but its flavor appears in far more applications than that. I contend that the secret to chocolate's ubiquity is in its bitterness.

I do not mean the kind of tongue-drying 137% cacao expressions preferred by aficionados, either. All chocolate is bitter, it's just that most of it is sweet as well. Our bodies condition us to like things that are sweetened, to associate those flavors with a desire to dip into that wellspring of raw energy again—but love of bitterness is something different. It represents many of the things we call "acquired tastes."

Think about it: coffee, dark chocolate, even alcohol itself—things that take multiple exposures to learn to appreciate also tend to have bitter components. Part of the attraction is the diversity of bitter flavors, with some 700-plus distinct compounds registering as bitter on

# Twentieth Century

1½ oz. London dry gin

¾ oz. Kina apéritif wine

½ oz. crème de cacao

½ oz. lemon juice

Shake with ice and strain into a chilled cocktail glass. Optionally, garnish with a lemon peel.

our taste buds while the other tastes have only a handful of chemical triggers apiece. Bitterness has simply more shades than other tastes do, which, once we overcome our instinctive aversion, means more opportunities for gastronomic variety and play within that range. This is also why people with highly overexposed palates tend to go after bitter flavors—think beer geeks with IPAs or bartenders with amari.

All this means that crème de cacao is both sweetener and bitterer in the recipes in which it appears. If we can imagine a drink like the Twentieth Century working with some other liqueur and a bitters, using a chocolate liqueur is not so different. The Scofflaw, Remember the Maine, and De La Louisiane all have elements in common with this recipe in terms of its interplay of flavors. Moreover, those bitter cacao notes pick up the cinnamon and orange flavors in the gin, two common if unexpected partners to chocolate. It is an unusual drink, to be sure, and it goes quickly awry if one mucks around with the proportions too much, but when you hit the balance right, it really sings. Ted Haigh has called it "exactly what Art Deco tastes like."

The Twentieth Century was likely named as much for the period of time as for the Twentieth Century Limited, a storied train that ran from New York to Chicago and was redesigned with a more modern look in 1937—the same year the cocktail first appears in print.

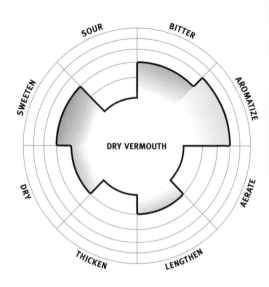

**3.28**

SOUR · BITTER · AROMATIZE · AERATE · LENGTHEN · THICKEN · DRY · SWEETEN

DRY VERMOUTH

**Described** in the *Savoy* as "well-known and very popular in the American Bar of the S.S. 'Europa'," the Chrysanthemum has percolated into general knowledge in the revival age despite never having done a stint as the "it" cocktail. The burgeoning trend for low-ABV drinks may change that, of course, but for now it is more akin to the Bamboo as something of a secret handshake.

This is another drink with a vermouth base. You will notice that, like the Rose, it calls for the dry stuff in that role. Dry vermouth is more popular than its Italian and Chamberian relations as a cocktail base, I suspect in part because its sugar content is roughly 75 percent lower, which means you have more wiggle room to incorporate sweet ingredients without the result being cloying. We see that used to great effect here, with Bénédictine and all its glorious honey making up nearly a third of the drink.

That highlights another distinguishing feature of the Chrysanthemum: where the Rose and the Martinez are upside-down drinks, still retaining a spirit element in the minority, and the Vermouth Cocktail and

# Chrysanthemum

2 oz. dry vermouth

¾ oz. Bénédictine

1 tsp. absinthe

Stir with ice and strain into a chilled cocktail glass. Express an orange peel over the glass and discard.

the Adonis make the pairing of fortified wines their centerpieces, the Chrysanthemum's anchor is its dry vermouth flying solo. It is sweetened by the Bénédictine, herbed up by that and the absinthe, and finished beautifully by an orange peel, but it is unambiguously the thing being modified, as much as the gin is in a Martini or the applejack in a Jack Rose. It is, if anything, a cousin to the Champagne Cocktail in this respect, but it has incorporated an additional century's worth of lessons in its conception of what makes a "cocktail."

**FURTHER READING**

In her book *The Art of the Shim*, Dinah Sanders proposed *shim* as a term for lower-proof drinks like this one, after the slender wedges used by carpenters to fill gaps. I wish that her suggestion had caught on more broadly. It is so much more evocative, even poetic, than the rather clinical-sounding "low-ABV cocktails" that is the current standard. Whatever you call them, they can be just as interesting as the higher-strength alternatives and are useful to have available in case one's guests (or oneself) should want to take it easy on a given night.

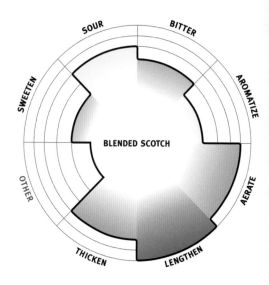

**3.29**

SOUR · BITTER · AROMATIZE · AERATE · LENGTHEN · THICKEN · OTHER · SWEETEN

BLENDED SCOTCH

**If you were** worried that all that hullabaloo about eggs in the previous chapter would not be revisited, I am pleased to dispel your concerns. After all, we have only had one fizz in this chapter, and that a partial case!

The Morning Glory Fizz has several intriguing features. It splits its citrus between lemon and lime juice, which we have seen only once before in the Ramos Gin Fizz. Where the Southside showed us orange bitters in a fizz context, the Morning Glory does the same for absinthe. And it pairs that absinthe, somewhat counterintuitively, with Scotch. We have, after all, seen absinthe combined with gin, rye, brandy, vermouth, and even Champagne so far, but Scotch? Is there not a risk of that earthy-peaty business clashing with the pungent herbs of the absinthe?

Indeed there is! Scotch can be a somewhat loud ingredient, and absinthe is a *very* loud one as we have seen. Smoke and licorice are not what we think of as a natural pairing; neither are bitter wormwood

# Morning Glory Fizz

2 oz. blended Scotch

½ oz. lemon juice

¼ oz. lime juice

1 tsp. simple syrup

½ tsp. absinthe

egg white

2–3 oz. seltzer

Shake without ice, then again with ice. Strain into a chilled highball glass.

and sour moss. Like the Twentieth Century, the Morning Glory Fizz successfully weaves together elements we would normally keep apart—even lime juice and Scotch make a rather odd pair.

The secret, you may by now be able to deduce, is the egg-fizz component. The egg white strips out some of the bitterness and muffles the boisterous flavors of the ingredients. In fact, the White Lady's lightly scented meringue effect comes into play here, the drink's texture mattering almost as much as its flavor does. It is not so much the peat and wormwood that come to the fore as the smoked malt of the barley, which takes herbs and aniseed more readily, while the absinthe's fennel notes pair off with any of the Scotch's earthiness that makes it through. Soured two ways, frothed, and fizzed up, it is complex enough to be interesting but light enough duty to be taken in the morning. Its name, while theoretically referring to the flower, also carries strong implications of being a hangover remedy, in which respect it is certainly no worse than any of the dog's other hairs.

*In this final project, you will make Amer Picon using the instructions listed here, then incorporate this novel ingredient in the Brooklyn and Creole in the following pages.*

10 oz. orange-infused grain alcohol

1 bottle Amaro Ramazotti

3 oz. Stirrings Blood Orange Bitters

1¾ cups distilled or fancy bottled water

This seminar's final assessment is more a project than a test. Periodically in the heyday of cocktail revivalism, someone would publish a list of lost ingredients that needed desperately to be revived. Invariably, absinthe and orange bitters were included. Kina Lillet and crème de violette often made the cut. We are fortunate to have all these again, as well as have Old Tom gin, Boker's bitters, and a variety of other ingredients that spent the aughts in more moderate demand. There remains, however, one glaring omission: Amer Picon.

Roughly as popular as absinthe in these enumerations of loss, Amer Picon was a bitter, orange-forward aperitif from France that popped up in several charismatic classic recipes. There is in fact still a thing called Amer Picon in production, but as happened with Kina Lillet, it was reformulated in the 1970s—an odd choice, like refinancing a mortgage when interest rates are highest—and even this diminished version is hard to come by outside its core French regions. A couple of other amari are used as substitutes in traditional Amer Picon cocktails, but people who have had the genuine article tend to pan the results. A whole industry is working blind.

I cannot fathom why it should languish still in obscurity. Fortunately, one can make a reasonable approximation at home, thanks to Jamie Boudreau of Canon in Seattle.

# FINAL PROJECT: PART 1
# Amer Picon

For the orange-infused grain alcohol, combine equal volumes of dried orange peels and grain alcohol in a sealable container, away from heat and sunlight. Let sit for 2–3 weeks, agitating occasionally.

When ready, strain out peels and add remaining ingredients in the listed order (to avoid louching when the infused-grain alcohol is mixed with water). Shake gently to combine. Let sit at least overnight so flavors can marry; it will continue to improve with age.

Boudreau had been given a bottle of Amer Picon by Last Word champion Murray Stenson and set about reverse engineering it so he could have a ready replacement when his precious supply ran out. The results were tasted against a sample of the original by an ad hoc expert panel at Tales of the Cocktail and pronounced virtually indistinguishable. The recipe presented here is my slight adaptation of his, which I find quite pleasant for cocktail use and a bit more efficient to make. If you feel ambitious, I advise you to try his original recipe, available on his website.

Your reward, after a couple of weeks, will be the ability to make Amer Picon's classic recipes, to experience them more or less as they were meant to taste. This is a good opportunity for palate expansion: smell each component of the Amer Boudreau at each stage of its development, taste the proofed-down mixture and try to imagine it in cocktails, then make the Creole and the famous Brooklyn and see how you like them. What makes them work? If you had to substitute something for your homemade amer, what would it need to be like? These are this seminar's final questions to ponder.

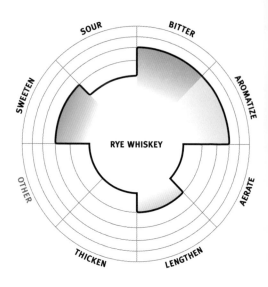

**Amer Picon's** flagship recipe, the Brooklyn, has spawned a dozen modern variations (covered in the fifth seminar), but the Brooklyn itself is rarely served, and its signature ingredient is absent from all its children. This is a sorry fate for an historic drink, all the more galling because of the prominence its namesake neighborhood has achieved in modern mixology.

In the family of New York City borough cocktails, the Manhattan has always been the favorite child, the Bronx the flamboyant one with the nontraditional career path, and the Brooklyn the contemplative wallflower. Wondrich calls it "second-string, but by no means second-rate" and credits Jack Grohusko's 1908 recipe as the first to bear the name. Fundamentally, it was an equal-parts Manhattan with dashes of maraschino and Amer Picon in lieu of the bitters. Most modern recipes derive from a later recipe by Jacques Straub (via *The Savoy Cocktail Book*), switching in dry vermouth for the sweet. Wondrich regards the sweet vermouth version as superior, but it was the slight interpolation that first captured hearts and minds during the Renaissance, and it is an estimable drink in its own right. It also places our reconstructed Amer Picon in a starring role. If you would like to make something more like Grohusko's version, trade the dry vermouth for 1 oz. of sweet, scale the Picon back to ¼ oz., and leave out the expressed lemon peel.

# FINAL PROJECT: PART 2
# Brooklyn

1 ½ oz. rye whiskey

½ oz. dry vermouth

½ oz. Amer Picon

¼ oz. maraschino liqueur

Stir with ice and strain into a chilled cocktail glass. Express a lemon peel over the glass and discard.

# Creole

1 ½ oz. rye whiskey

1 oz. sweet vermouth

½ oz. Amer Picon

¼ oz. Bénédictine

Stir with ice and strain into a chilled cocktail glass. Optionally, garnish with a lemon twist.

That said, if you're going to make an Amer Picon drink with rye and sweet vermouth, it might as well be the Creole, which lacks the tragic fame of the Brooklyn but tastes absolutely fabulous. Once again, the Picon is highlighted, but its orange is reinforced by the honey-spice of Bénédictine, and laid down in a bed of hearty grains and fruits. It is not so much a cold-weather drink as a cold*er*-weather one, something one might serve at a New Orleans Christmas dinner.*

This is also a chance to experience firsthand the thrill and the frustration of having ingredients just out of reach. You can have it, but you have to work for it. I promise, you will find the experience ultimately rewarding. Just make sure you save some Amer Boudreau for the fifth seminar—or finish it off and make a new batch, luxuriating in its being available at last. Little could be as much in the spirit of this seminar.

* Note that several very different drinks have been called the "Creole" over the years. This one is rooted in Harry Craddock's recipe from *The Savoy Cocktail Book*, sometimes called the Creole No. 2; I've adapted the proportions from Kirk Estopinal's recipe used at Cane and Table in New Orleans.

# Tropical and Tiki

**This is our** equivalent of a 400-level course, representing a specialized seminar or undergraduate capstone project. Your understanding of the art should now be sufficient to delve into advanced topics. There is no more appropriate subject for such an investigation than tiki drinks, a large corner of the mixological universe we have yet to consider.

What is *tiki*? It is a cultural movement that flourished in California in the 1930s, incorporating the aesthetics of an imagined Polynesia, American-style Chinese food, and layered elaborations on Caribbean cocktails, all seasoned liberally with escapist fantasy and delivered with masterful showmanship. When it first took off, it was as an alternative to the realities of the Depression era, but its success was goosed by the exposure of millions of Americans to actual Pacific islands during World War II, the national fanfare surrounding Hawaiian statehood in 1959, and the increasing availability of air travel.

It began in 1933 with the opening of Don's Beachcomber in Hollywood. The proprietor, born Ernest Raymond Beaumont Gantt, eventually legally changed his albatross of a name to Donn Beach. He began his working years on his grandfather's boat, island-hopping in the Caribbean and running rum back to the States during Prohibition. Beach brought his accumulated knowledge of Caribbean cocktails to his California bar, crafting an image of a charismatic layabout whose every scrap of wisdom—and every possession—had been haphazardly collected on the beaches of the Antilles.

Beach's recipes—"rum rhapsodies," he called them—were revelatory to the drinking public. Americans had just escaped the throes of the Volstead Act and were welcomed back to bibulousness with a tropical fantasia. Beach was a master of the craft, without any doubt, but the mystery and pageantry with which he surrounded his recipes enhanced their popular appeal. Had he revealed that six drops of pastis or a blend of cinnamon syrup and grapefruit juice was that tip-of-the-tongue flavor that kept patrons coming back for more—or in other words, had he brought his unknowable rhapsodies into the realm of conventional spirits and mundane grocery products—it's likely the drinkers would have awoken from the dream.

In 1937 Victor Bergeron caught wind of the fabulously trendy place in L.A. The proprietor of an Oakland bar and lunch counter called Hinky Dinks, Bergeron was first and foremost a good businessman. His one tropical drink was already a hot item, and he knew a golden goose when he saw one. He made the trip to Hollywood and studied Don's success. Soon, Hinky Dinks closed and Trader Vic's opened, with Bergeron its eponymous character.

The Beachcomber appeared to have drifted where the sea carried him, gathering lore and artifacts incidentally, but the Trader was a shrewd dealer in the mold of a Nantucket whaling captain. Bergeron added nautical paraphernalia to Beach's aesthetic—a wooden leg from a childhood injury was recast as the work of a shark—and lived up to his name by giving out drinks for decorations. A menu of tropical drinks established Bergeron as the Beachcomber's best student and most dangerous competitor.

This rivalry helped spur tiki's expansion across the country. The Trader Vic's and Don the Beachcomber chains were both highly successful. In an era when precious few advances were being made in mainstream mixology, tiki bars were where the excitement was. Chinese restaurants throughout the U.S. recognized the affinity of the drinks for their similarly made-in-America menus. Private homes soon had bamboo bars with thatched roofs built in their backyards. And enormous establishments with elaborate fire and water features teemed with glitterati in the country's major cities, taking what Donn and Vic had wrought to a level they could scarcely have imagined.

Many drinks from outside the tiki tradition were subsumed into it, including genuine Pacific drinks, like the Doctor Funk and the Singapore Sling, as well as Caribbean recipes with or without their Polynesian masks. Tiki itself has no inherent monopoly on tropical drinks, but as the standard-bearer for their inland service, it became synonymous with them in the popular consciousness, and they with it.

In the end, this was a devastating development. The secrecy surrounding tiki drinks, combined with the astronomical demand for them, led to misbegotten red mushes being served under their names in scores of bars. Most tiki drinks that were not outright forgotten suffered this fate, as did many of the fellow travelers tiki had acquired in its salad days. The deaths of the twin titans robbed the art of its most charismatic advocates and put its legacy in the hands of those who had neither known nor cared about how to make the drinks well. At the turn of the millennium, it was a shadow of itself.

The success of the Cocktail Renaissance's efforts to reestablish hospitality as a respectable field and the cocktail as an art form benefited tiki in two ways. First, those at the forefront of that charge amassed enough stature to take on riskier and more difficult rehabilitation projects. And second, they had taken cocktails so seriously for so long that they were sick of it. Tiki offered a release precisely when it was needed most.

Jeff "Beachbum" Berry, author of several essential books on tiki, was working to burnish its reputation long before the rest of us got around to it. He is responsible for piecing together the canon's great recipes, decoding the secrets of the Trader and the Beachcomber, and shepherding the revival of the style. The new millennium has brought a wave of neo-tiki and tropical bars that marshal the lessons of the Cocktail Renaissance in the service of exotic cocktails.

Rum's incredible variety has made it tiki's essential spirit. In the coming pages, I will introduce seven new types of rum beyond those we have covered already. If you prefer not to go all in just yet, you can get by with just four: a standard-proof Demerara rum, a 151-proof Demerara rum, your choice of an aged Jamaican rum or a Jamaican black rum, and your choice of a rhum agricole, other cane juice rum, or Brazilian cachaça. You can substitute one of the rums from our previous seminars in recipes that call for a lightly aged rum. If you take to this material, you will in time have a rum shelf of your very own.

We'll begin with foundational recipes that explore tropical flavors and the interplay of rum, citrus, and spice. Get a good understanding of these recipes and you will be amazed what it prepares you to do.

# A Note on Techniques

For the first time since seminar one, we are expanding our toolbox and our options for mixing cocktails beyond building, shaking, and stirring.

**Swizzling** is done by inserting a **swizzle stick** into a glass and rubbing it between the palms of your hands like an old-fashioned fire starter. We do this for built drinks, especially those with crushed ice, to ensure an even mixture of all ingredients without the aeration of shaking.

**Flash blending**, a term I borrow from Martin and Rebecca Cate's book *Smuggler's Cove,* is a much more rapid version of swizzling, which aerates drinks even *more* than shaking does. It's done with a **drink mixer**, also known as a spindle blender or a milkshake mixer. It has a rotating shaft with a sort of undulating disc at the bottom, which hangs into a mixing tin from above, and whips them effectively *without* breaking down the ice—unlike a conventional blender, which tends to pulverize ice and make the drink slushy. It's common to serve the drink using the same ice it was mixed with, topped with fresh crushed ice as needed or desired.

Roughly 40 percent of the recipes in this seminar are flash blended, so while you can get by with workarounds, I strongly advise you to invest in a drink mixer. It will improve your cocktails immensely, and make it much easier to produce them in quantity. The Hamilton Beach DrinkMaster 730C is the standard introductory-level model, usually available for $40–50.

When transferring to the serving vessel, the Cates advise to "open pour with gated finish." Many Hawthorne strainers have a thumb tab which can be used to move the perforated plate relative to the spring. Push it forward, toward the rim of the mixing tin, and less ice gets through; pull it back and more does. The *open pour* means pull it back and let everything through; the *gated finish* means that once the glass is about seven-eighths full, you should push it forward to have more control and avoid overflow—a real risk, considering tiki drinks' volumes. The Cates' technique is worth learning, but I won't require it. Tiki has many more variables than we've had to reckon with so far; I have tried to keep things relatively simple, trusting that readers who want a deeper understanding will seek out more subject-specific books.

# Ingredients for This Course

## GROCERY

| | |
|---|---|
| Angostura bitters | 3, 5, 7, 14, 15, 18, 20–22, 25 |
| cinnamon syrup* | 20 |
| condensed milk* | 10 |
| eggs | 27 |
| falernum* | 4, 5, 14, 17, 20, 22, 23, 30 |
| fassionola* | 9, 22, 27 |
| gardenia mix*† | 30 |
| ginger syrup/soda | 18, 24 |
| grapefruit | 16, 20 |
| grenadine | 6, 12, 20, 25 |
| honey/honey syrup | 14, 16, 27 |
| lemons | 9, 12, 17, 26–28 |
| lime cordial | 18 |
| limes | 1–5, 7, 8, 11–16, 19, 20, 22–25, 28–30 |
| mint | 7, 18, 20, 23, 26 |
| oranges | 14, 22, 26, 29, 30 |
| orgeat | 13, 17, 24, 26, 29 |
| passion fruit syrup* | 10, 17, 28 |
| Peychaud's Bitters | 2 |
| pineapple juice* | 6, 19, 21, 23, 25 |
| rich demerara syrup | 3, 7, 12, 19, 28, 29 |
| seltzer | 12, 16, 25 |
| sugar/simple syrup | 1, 8, 11, 15 |

## ALCOHOL

| | |
|---|---|
| absinthe | 12, 15, 20, 22, 24 |
| aged Jamaican rum* | 11, 16, 30 |
| allspice dram* | 3, 14, 21, 24 |
| apricot liqueur* | 2, 11 |
| Bénédictine | 25 |
| bourbon | 3, 27 |
| brandy | 18, 26, 29 |
| cachaça/rhum agricole* | 1, 10, 14 |
| Campari | 19 |
| Cherry Heering | 25 |
| curaçao/triple sec | 4, 8, 11, 13, 25 |
| Demerara rum* | 7, 14, 28, 30 |
| filtered lightly aged rum | 6, 8, 16 |
| Green Chartreuse | 23 |
| Jamaican black rum* | 12, 19, 20 |
| lightly aged rum* | 20, 26, 29, 30 |
| London dry gin | 2, 17, 18, 25, 26, 29 |
| maraschino | 6, 8, 28 |
| moderately aged rum | 4, 5, 9, 14 |
| 151-proof Demerara rum* | 15, 16, 20, 22, 28 |
| sherry* | 21, 26 |
| sweet vermouth | 21 |

\* indicates new ingredients

† bottled or homemade for final project

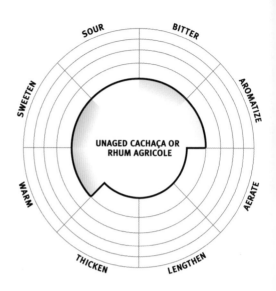

UNAGED CACHAÇA OR
RHUM AGRICOLE

(wheel labels: SOUR, BITTER, AROMATIZE, AERATE, LENGTHEN, THICKEN, WARM, SWEETEN)

**It seems** that every cane-distilling region has a signature way of combining the local spirit with lime and sugar. Cuba has the Daiquiri, Brazil the Caipirinha, Martinique the Ti' Punch—even Britain has the Grog. I have chosen this pair to drive home how much variety is found even within this trinity of flavors.

Most rum is made from molasses, which is what is left over when sugar has been refined out of the juice of the sugarcane. Sometimes, particularly in places influenced by France or Portugal, the fresh cane juice is distilled instead. This is sometimes called rhum agricole or agricultural rum, although the EU prohibits such terms for rums that are not made in French or Portuguese territories; "cane juice rum" is at least as descriptive and claimed as an exclusive term by no one. Distillates of fresh cane juice in Brazil are called cachaça, and the people who make them tend not to like it when you call their products rum. There are some peculiarities to cachaça production that are unlike those of other cane spirits, including much lower proofs of distillation and an affinity for aging in indigenous Brazilian hardwoods rather than oak, but ultimately it comes down to whether we regard *rum* as the term for all cane distillates like *whiskey* is for all grain distillates. If we do, nothing about cachaça's production makes it something other than rum, any more than Cognac having its own protected term makes it

# Caipirinha

2 oz. unaged cachaça

1 lime

2 tsp. sugar

Cut lime into quarters and muddle well with sugar in a large rocks glass. Add cachaça and ice and stir.

# Ti' Punch

2 oz. unaged Martinique rhum agricole

1 tsp. cane syrup

Combine ingredients in a rocks glass without ice and swizzle. Cut a quarter-size round from the side of a lime, including some of the flesh; squeeze 6–10 drops of lime juice into the drink to taste and drop the lime round in.

something other than brandy. If rum does not mean that, than cachaça may not be rum. I leave the question to you.

In any case, the national drink of Brazil has certain elements in common with the Daiquiri and Old Fashioned. The sugar is muddled to order, along with several wedges of lime. While you *could* swap in juice and simple syrup, Jim Meehan points out in his *Bartender Manual* that it would be contrary to the drink's rustic spirit, since *caipirinha* means "little peasant girl" in Portuguese. If the world has room for the ploughman's lunch, it has room for a muddled Caipirinha.

Martinique's favorite tipple, the Ti' Punch, takes a different approach. The rhums agricoles of Martinique are famous for vegetal, even savory characteristics, the sorts of things a gin or tequila drinker could really get behind. Cane syrup has grassy notes that pick up on similar flavors in the rum; minimally processed from fresh cane juice, it is a common all-purpose sweetener on Martinique and also in Louisiana. A small amount of lime is cut and the juice added a drop at a time, like bitters. The whole concoction is mixed together using a swizzle stick, known locally as the *bois lélé*. Place the branching end in the glass and hold the stalk between your palms, then rub it back and forth so it rotates, combining the mixture. Like the Earthquake, the Ti' Punch is traditionally served at room temperature and savored.

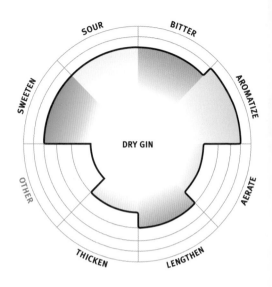

SOUR · BITTER · AROMATIZE · SWEETEN · DRY GIN · OTHER · AERATE · THICKEN · LENGTHEN

**In a chapter** that deals with the likes of Brazil, Jamaica, and Martinique, the Pendennis Club stands out as the namesake cocktail of a private social club in Louisville, Kentucky. This is one of several recipes we will consider before we get into true tiki drinks, to show how the roots of the tropical school of drink-making are planted firmly within the tradition we've been discussing so far. The Pendennis Club is a bitter-liqueur-sour cocktail, and we have seen that before in our nontropical chapters—albeit in the Pegu Club, which came out of Burma. But it also relies on an impressive ounce of apricot liqueur, which pulls it in the direction the rest of this seminar is headed.

Apricot is a delightfully odd flavor: simple and sweet and familiar enough that it can taste artificial even when it is completely natural. It appears in a great many prewar recipes, but even when made with the craft apricot liqueurs that have become available since Y2K, a good portion of those drinks come out rather cloying. It may be less bracing than kirschwasser and less pungent than absinthe, but apricot is still one of the loudest flavors we have seen. It meets its match in tiki-style drinks, where strong spices, funky rums, or simply a large volume of ingredients can keep it from overpowering the other flavors.

# Pendennis Club

2 oz. London dry gin

1 oz. apricot liqueur

¾ oz. lime juice

3 dashes Peychaud's Bitters

Shake with ice. Strain into a chilled cocktail glass.

It also works in the Pendennis Club, for the same reason the Rose can get away with a full ounce of kirschwasser: it becomes the star of the show. The healthy pour of lime juice, the three dashes of Peychaud's, and even the gin are there to dry out, counterbalance, and season the apricot. With the gin botanicals and the aniseed notes of the bitters, you end up with a spicy fruit sour that has multiple internal clusterings of complementary flavors. On a larger plan, this is precisely how a tiki drink comes together.

It is also worth noting that Peychaud's has stonefruit flavors of its own, less prominent than the licorice-y ones but very much there. In the last seminar, we discussed how recipes can slice through gin at different angles, creating unique flavor cross sections with the particular combination of scents the other ingredients reinforce. Gin, as we can see here, is not the only cocktail component that can undergo this procedure: the effectiveness of Peychaud's in the Pendennis Club depends on a similar resonance of its undertones with the apricot. Other bitters, even anise-forward ones, would not work nearly as well if they lacked those particular fruit elements. This seminar will consider many cases of such underground harmonies, which are a core component of tiki drinks' intricacies of flavor.

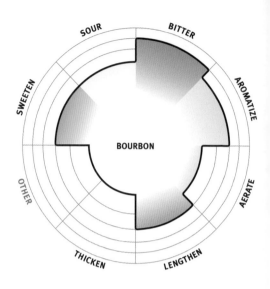

**I warned** you when we covered the Bamboo that rich demerara syrup would be a significant component of this chapter. If you have not yet bothered to prepare some, now would be a good time. (It isn't as though I'm going anywhere.)

Several pieces of the tiki tradition are present here: spices, citrus, the rich flavor of partially refined sugar. Yet despite the preponderance of rum in such cocktails, the Lion's Tail uses a bourbon base. Ted Haigh has traced the recipe as far back as 1937, to London's *Café Royal Cocktail Book*. "Twisting the lion's tail" was a colloquialism for "provoking the British," the lion having been a symbol of English monarchs for the better part of a thousand years, as part of the Angevin coat of arms and the nickname of Richard I. If that seems an odd choice for a country with no lions to speak of, remember that Scotland's national animal is the unicorn.

In its first appearance, the Lion's Tail is attributed to L. A. Clarke, of whom little else is known. It can be presumed that Clarke was a member of the UK Bartenders' Guild, whose president compiled the *Café Royal* and whose members contributed most of the original recipes. It may have been exotic to an interwar British audience in some sense, but not in the phantasmagorical way that the budding American tiki

# Lion's Tail

2 oz. bourbon

½ oz. lime juice

½ oz. allspice dram

¼ oz. rich demerara syrup

2 dashes Angostura bitters

Shake with ice. Strain into a chilled cocktail glass.

movement would later be. The Lion's Tail was a bit more like the Pegu Club, a combination of ingredients from the corners of the earth, not evoking the strange and foreign so much as the somewhat familiar of the British Empire's more distant colonies.

Its novel ingredient is pimento dram, a rum-based allspice liqueur traditionally produced in Jamaica. Modern versions are sometimes labeled as allspice dram in the interest of clarity; the pimento tree is the source of allspice berries, but that's not as widely known as it used to be. Whatever one calls it, the dram's taste is easy to get one's head around: allspice, sugar, and rum. It has a pretty potent flavor, and its appearance here in a full half ounce will be one of its most substantial uses in this book.

Interestingly, although the Lion's Tail was not part of the tiki tradition as such, it was born in a seminal year for exotic cocktails. Donn Beach had already been in business for four years, but in 1937 he opened his second bar in a larger space and continued development of his rum rhapsodies. Tiki archaeologists have done some impressive work tracing back Donn's recipes, in many cases as far as 1937 but no farther than that.

# 4.4

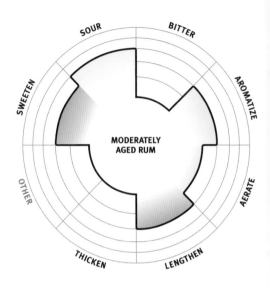

SOUR · BITTER · AROMATIZE · AERATE · LENGTHEN · THICKEN · OTHER · SWEETEN

**MODERATELY AGED RUM**

**This is our** first sighting of falernum, a low-proof Caribbean liqueur made with rum, lime, sugar, sometimes almonds, and spices, particularly ginger, clove, and nutmeg. If you can imagine drinking a molasses cookie with a side of key lime pie, you'll be in the ballpark. It delivers a lot of flavors at once, and while they're all familiar, their combination isn't to most people. The brain encodes groups of scents separately from individual ones—nutmeg, for example, smells like pine, citrus, camphor, and baking spice, but we don't parse them individually when we smell it. Hiding falernum in a drink was one of Donn Beach's favorite tricks for a taste one can't quite pin down.

Here, it appears in conjunction with orange liqueur. We know what this means: the orange liqueur is an aromatic accent, and the falernum is doing the lion's share of the work to sweeten this drink. The spice components in the falernum also do plenty of the aromatizing that allspice dram or Angostura bitters might in a different recipe. Syrups and liqueurs play a significant role in that aspect of this chapter's cocktails, both individually and in combination.

For now, though, we have a more basic template to work with: spice, orange, lime, and rum, with one ingredient for each. Getting a feel for this recipe will be good preparation for the more elaborate drinks to come.

# Royal Bermuda Yacht Club Special

2 oz. moderately aged rum

½ oz. falernum

¼ oz. curaçao

¾ oz. lime juice

Shake with ice. Strain into a chilled cocktail glass.

The Royal Bermuda Yacht Club Special appeared in *Trader Vic's Bartender's Guide*, so Vic is often credited as its inventor; however, its namesake club existed for over a century before the Trader published his book, and plenty of the recipes he included were not his inventions. My hunch is that Vic encountered the recipe in Bermuda during one of his various island trips. Vic was the consummate student, willingly crediting Donn's influence and inspiration for much of his success, but also making his own pilgrimages to the other temples of tropical cocktailery to learn as much as he could. He studied at the bars of New Orleans and made multiple forays to Cuba to watch Ribalaigua ply his craft.

There is a good lesson in this for the modern student of cocktails: however good you are, you can always keep learning, and if you want to be the best, find the people who are better than you are and learn everything you can from them. Visit good bars and see what they do. Read books that comment on and disagree with one another. Ask questions, and then ask follow-up questions. It was by this process that David Embury (an attorney!) came to write a seminal cocktail book, that Victor Bergeron built a global bar empire in a style he never claimed to have invented, and that most people who have left their mark on mixological theory or practice have acquired the skills to do so.

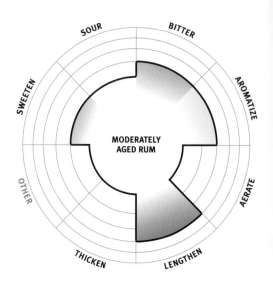

**4.5**

SOUR
BITTER
SWEETEN
AROMATIZE
OTHER
MODERATELY
AGED RUM
AERATE
THICKEN
LENGTHEN

**A common** theme in this seminar is calling for rums by the name of an island or a region. Rums from different places tend to have different characteristics—akin to the distinctions between Scotch and Irish whiskey, but often more substantial. I have limited my geographical specifications to Jamaican and Demerara rums, plus your choice of Martinique rhum agricole or Brazilian cachaça.

That said, the Corn 'n' Oil is the national drink of Barbados, and I recommend a Barbadian rum if you have one. It's also a good choice for our other moderately aged rum recipes. Some of the world's best killdevil comes from Barbados—they did invent the stuff after all!

My Barbadian sources disagreed about using lime in a Corn 'n' Oil; I've compromised with a wedge garnish, so the drinker can add juice to taste. This drink is swizzled, like the Ti' Punch, but this time we can see how that technique works with ice.

The swizzle stick opens up gaps between the pieces of crushed ice with each turn, at once combining the ingredients and helping to distribute them evenly. It's like shaking, insofar as it is kinetic enough to incorporate syrups and suchlike into the whole, but it does not aerate the drink and adds no extra dilution beyond what the crushed ice already

# Corn 'n' Oil

2 oz. moderately aged rum

½ oz. falernum

2 dashes Angostura bitters

wedge of lime

Swizzle rum, falernum, and bitters with crushed ice in a rocks glass. Squeeze lime wedge over the glass and drop it in.

provides. In a pinch, something similar can be accomplished by using a barspoon as a swizzle stick, but a genuine bois lélé works better.

Misinformed people on the internet allege that this drink is named for a float of black rum on top like an oil slick. Hogwash. As Barbadian distiller Richard Seale points out, it was originally a brandy drink, with local rum swapped in around World War I. His theory is that the name is a reference to Deuteronomy 18:4, in which the people are enjoined to reserve for the priests "the firstfruits of thy corn . . . and thine oil," as the King James Bible renders it.

Moreover, Barbados is not known for rums with the kind of visual and textural properties necessary for such an oil slick effect. I use the *Smuggler's Cove* term **black rum** to describe this type of heavily colored and often sweetened rum. Be advised that *blackstrap rum* is also commonly used for this category, but I avoid it because it has misleading implications: blackstrap molasses is a kind of molasses from which many rums are made, whether or not they have been sweetened or colored after distillation. *Black rum*, by contrast, describes the thing by its most relevant property: the heavy dose of caramel or molasses that gives the drink its color and viscosity. Any rum that is mahogany-dark is almost certainly of this type—wooden barrels just don't impart that much color, no matter how long the rum spends inside them.

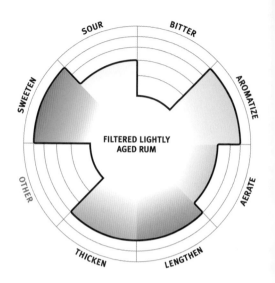

**4.6**

SOUR BITTER AROMATIZE AERATE LENGTHEN THICKEN OTHER SWEETEN

FILTERED LIGHTLY
AGED RUM

**As is the case** today, bartenders of the last two centuries named their drinks after anything attention-grabbing: places, inventions, plays, films, and even people. Mary Pickford was a famous actress and producer, one of the founders of United Artists as well as the Academy of Motion Picture Arts and Sciences. She was not the only celebrity to have a cocktail named after her, but she has one of the better ones.

Tropical drinks have two distinct difficulties with pineapple. The first is the common practice of clobbering every drink with it. Not knowing the recipes for the early, secrecy-shrouded tiki cocktails never stopped anyone from reusing their names for anything vaguely tropics-inflected, leaving the world awash in "Mai Tais" made with pineapple juice and grenadine—they contain neither—and a pseudovariety of so-called tiki drinks which were basically fruit punch mixed with rum.

In fairness, it is very easy for a pineapple juice recipe to end up tasting mostly like pineapple. Subtleties are easily lost underneath its weight, which leaves few options other than to accept the new recipe as a juice drink and focus on accenting the pineapple. This is also a template that masks harsh flavors well and can therefore accommodate base spirits of arbitrarily low quality.

# Mary Pickford

2 oz. filtered lightly aged rum

1 oz. pineapple juice

½ oz. maraschino liqueur

½ oz. grenadine

Shake with ice. Strain into a rocks glass with fresh ice.

I share all this to set up the contrast with the Mary Pickford, which uses pineapple juice *well*. It pairs it with maraschino, a heavyweight ingredient that draws unexpected flavors out of the pineapple. Pineapple has a diversity of aromas in its juice, and some of them are relatively floral. These are easily missed when the rest are grabbing your attention, but maraschino's own flowery notes pull them into the open. If you want to triple down on this, add some orange flower water when making your grenadine; it's a reasonably traditional accent to the syrup and a marvelous addition here. What you expect to be a fruit-forward and cloyingly sweet drink is instead blossomy, slightly earthy, with fruit elements that add at least as much tartness as sugar, and drier than you would think. We moderate the drink's punchiest flavors by adding some extra dilution, both shaking the drink and serving it on the rocks, fix-style—we'll pull that lever again and again in this seminar.

As noted in seminar one, most white rums are aged and filtered rather than unaged. There are pungent unaged overproof rums from Jamaica and rhums agricoles from Martinique, but all-purpose mixing rums of this type are uncommon. If, however, you have the good fortune to have access to them, I find them an improvement in this recipe— and indeed in many white rum recipes. For whatever reason, general-purpose unaged rums are disproportionally made these days by small U.S. distillers, and I know of several in New England alone.

## 4.7

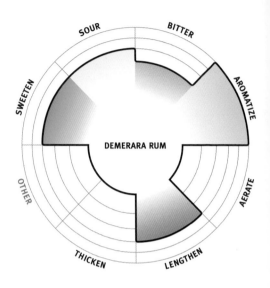

SOUR · BITTER · AROMATIZE · AERATE · LENGTHEN · THICKEN · OTHER · SWEETEN

DEMERARA RUM

**In the days** of steamer travel, a port's marquee hotel would sometimes have a signature cocktail, doled out to guests upon arrival. In Trinidad, the Queens Park Hotel was the best game in town, and its namesake swizzle showed off the island's most famous product—not rum, but Angostura bitters, produced there since the 1870s.

There is Trinidadian rum today, some made by the House of Angostura, but at the time of the Queens Park Swizzle's invention, the local rum industry was not nearly as robust as that in neighboring Guyana. This is therefore an apt occasion to introduce our first geographically specified variety of rum, namely **Demerara rum**.

The name comes ultimately from the Demerara River in Guyana via the region of the same name, where substantial sugar and rum production took place. The demerara sugar we have been using is not necessarily from Guyana; the name has come to refer to a particular kind of semiprocessed sugar by association with the Guyanese product.*

Demerara rums are known for an almost smoky, burnt-sugar character. Guyanese rums often have some added sugar, a practice that is

---

* If you've ever served turkey on fine china, you've experienced a similar transformation of place name into generic product name.

# Queens Park Swizzle

2 oz. Demerara rum

¾ oz. lime juice

½ oz. rich demerara syrup

3 dashes Angostura bitters

4–6 mint sprigs

Gently muddle 2–3 mint sprigs with lime juice, demerara syrup, and bitters in a highball glass. Add rum and crushed ice and swizzle. Garnish with 2–3 additional mint sprigs.

anathema in certain places (e.g., Cuba, Barbados, Martinique), occasionally practiced in others (Jamaica, the U.S.), and readily embraced in still others (Guatemala, Venezuela, India). Rum is often considered sweet because it is distilled from sugarcane products, but that isn't how distillation works. Sugars are used up in making ethanol during fermentation; if any remain, they will be too heavy to pass through the still during distillation. If your bottle tastes sweet, sugar has probably been added. This can be done unscrupulously, to mask the taste of inferior distillates (especially when they are priced as "premium" products). But it's also done honestly, and rums with a beefier mouthfeel from added sugar are often intended for cocktails.

We needn't worry too much about the sugar content of the rum here; any Demerara rum will do, in part because we are reinforcing it with some sugar of our own. This is balanced by souring, sweetening, and aromatizing with bitters and mint. Remember from the first seminar that we never want to crush the mint leaves so much as gently bruise them with the muddler, releasing the oils without also getting the enzymes to break them down. Note also that the crushed ice serves as a lengthener, diluting the mixture and elongating the drinking period. Eagle-eyed observers will spot certain commonalities with the Mojito, the popularity of which facilitated the Queens Park Swizzle's early embrace by the Cocktail Renaissance.

# 4.8

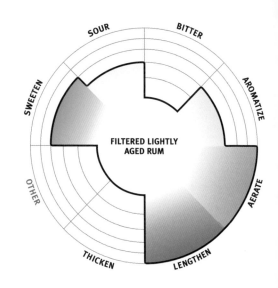

SOUR · BITTER · AROMATIZE · SWEETEN · AERATE · OTHER · THICKEN · LENGTHEN

**FILTERED LIGHTLY AGED RUM**

**This recipe** for the Beachcomber is based on one in the 1972 edition of *Trader Vic's Bartender's Guide*—ironically, it has nothing to do with Donn Beach. It is a straightforward enough variation on the Daiquiri, experimenting with floral-citrus synergies much as the Royal Bermuda Yacht Club Special does for citrus-spice ones. Although it is often a shaken drink, and is quite pleasant in that form, I have included it here as our introduction to **blending**, which is the way Vic called for it to be prepared.

Specifically, we will be employing the **flash blending** technique discussed in this seminar's introduction and at length in *Smuggler's Cove*. Combine all ingredients in the mixing tin with about a cup of crushed ice and run your spindle blender for 4–5 seconds. This will combine, chill, and dilute very efficiently. You can pour the finished drink into the glass unstrained or control how much ice you allow through by using your Hawthorne strainer. Either way, you may want to top the drink off with fresh crushed ice before serving, for both aesthetic and thermal reasons.

The reason conventional blending does not work as well here is that it tends to break the ice down. We don't want to pulverize our crushed ice, we simply want to get the liquid evenly into all the little spaces in

# Beachcomber

2 oz. filtered lightly aged rum

½ oz. orange liqueur

½ oz. lime juice

¼ oz. simple syrup

1 tsp. maraschino

Flash blend with crushed ice for 5 seconds. Pour unstrained into a highball glass, or open pour with gated finish, depending on the size of the glass.

between the pieces. In this respect, flash blending is more like swizzling than it is like conventional blending.

That said, flash blending also aerates the mixture, as shaking and conventional blending do. This is in contrast to swizzling, where all of the mixing action takes place below the surface of the liquid and virtually no air will be introduced however vigorous the action.

If you're hesitant to invest in the equipment without trying the cocktail first, you can shake this one vigorously with one large ice cube and then strain over crushed ice. This will be an acceptable substitute for all flash blended drinks in this section unless otherwise specified. But as someone who went many years without making the leap, I assure you that you'll be happy you did.

### FURTHER READING

Trader Vic took detailed notes on Ribalaigua's Daiquiris. We know from other sources that many of them were blended and served frappé and that Ribalaigua used a spindle blender for years before the introduction of the Waring Blendor, the template for the standard blender today. To recreate Ribalaigua's Daiquiri, flash blend 2 oz. of filtered lightly aged rum, 1 tsp. sugar, and the juice of half a lime. Vic says to juice it with your fingers to get the most oil and the least pith!

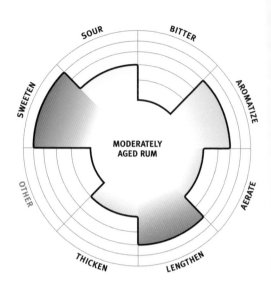

SOUR · BITTER · AROMATIZE · AERATE · LENGTHEN · THICKEN · OTHER · SWEETEN

**MODERATELY AGED RUM**

**Last seminar's lost ingredients** have nothing on fassionola. Every aspect of it has been disputed, from how it tastes to which drinks should be made with it and even whether or not it's still available. It deserves a monograph of its own, but I will do my best to summarize.*

Fassionola is a passion fruit syrup with other fruit flavorings. According to historian Martin Lindsay, it was made in the San Diego area under the name *passionola* as early as 1916 and marketed to drugstores for use in soft drinks and atop ice cream sundaes. Red, gold, and green varieties have been made, each with its own flavor, but unless otherwise specified fassionola usually refers to red fassionola, which has the character of fruit punch. The product's name was changed from passionola in the 1960s.

Production has passed through several hands, but lies today with the Jonathan English Company, which makes the syrups primarily for the Southern California market. Multiple times over the last thirty years, it has been reported, concluded, or otherwise believed that Jonathan English had ceased operations or was no longer making fassionola. On no occasion has either been true, but the difficulty of obtaining

---

* For this historical discussion, I am indebted to Dan Huntley at Jonathan English as well as to Martin Lindsay, who has a forthcoming book about fassionola's history.

# Hurricane

1½ oz. moderately aged rum

¾ oz. fassionola

½ oz. lemon juice

Shake with ice. Strain into a rocks glass with fresh ice. Garnish with a lime wheel.

the stuff has encouraged tikiphiles to reverse-engineer it. A mixture of passion fruit syrup and grenadine has been proposed in some quarters; Matt Pietrek of *Cocktail Wonk* has published a more appealing recipe for a homemade version, and both BG Reynolds and Cocktail & Sons have products that compete with Jonathan English's.

The Hurricane is fassionola's best-known recipe. Its birthplace, Pat O'Brien's in the French Quarter, makes it today using a proprietary red mix with a fruit punch flavor; but this is not so great a leap.† Some modern attempts to restore the original 1940s recipe use plain passion fruit syrup—a different approximation of fassionola.

In any case, the Hurricane made as described here is fabulous: sweet, tart, and accessible as a boat drink, with all the refinement and subtlety of a classic cocktail. Jonathan English still makes the original, but if you can't get it, I think the BG Reynolds version, which blends cherry and mango with passion fruit, hits most of the right notes. And the baroque, nontraditional Cocktail & Sons version with hibiscus and fresh Louisiana strawberries makes an unparalleled Hurricane.

† Chloe Frechette, writing about the Hurricane for *Punch*, says it's "best described as 'red-flavored'," while Jeff Berry says of Pat O'Brien's in *Beachbum Berry Remixed*, "Go for the lovely patio garden, but order a beer." The Hurricane's birthplace could use a little rehabilitating of its own.

# 4.10

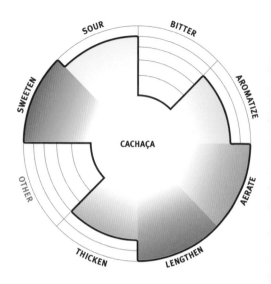

SOUR · BITTER · AROMATIZE · AERATE · LENGTHEN · THICKEN · OTHER · SWEETEN

CACHAÇA

## SOLUTION

Condensed milk adds texture and fattiness to a cocktail. It is also sweetened, so in this recipe we're dealing with extra sugar. This is one reason we might prefer the pulverizing action of a conventional blender to the turboswizzling of the drink mixer: a slushy drink is just about as cold and diluted as one can get, both of which qualities will reduce its sweetness.

My description of passion fruit syrup should have sent you reaching back to seminar one for the Gimlet's lime cordial, our original sour-sweet syrup. Even with the consistency and appearance of a boozy milkshake, the Batida has a bit of acidity to it—we want that to be part of the drink's balance, rather than having it read as an off note in our sweetener.

Another popular Batida uses coconut milk or coconut cream, either in addition to passion fruit syrup or in place of it. But the sky is the limit—try it with your favorite fruit syrup! Tart sweeteners like lime cordial or raspberry syrup will change the drink's structure least of all. You can also replace your condensed milk with a combination of evaporated milk and sugar to have more control over the sweetness. 1½ oz. sugar and 1¼ oz. evaporated milk will be roughly equivalent to 2 oz. condensed milk.

2 oz. cachaça or cane juice rum

2 oz. passion fruit syrup

2 oz. condensed milk

Combine in a conventional blender and blend until smooth. Pour unstrained into a highball glass and serve with a straw.

# EXERCISE
# Batida

cachaça or rhum agricole

passion fruit syrup

condensed milk

*Using the given ingredients, determine the proportions of the Batida and its method of preparation.*

**Conventional blenders** are generally used when ice is meant to be pulverized for a texture that is more a thick, semifrozen liquid than a flowing one with solid bits of ice in it. This approach was common among the boat drinks that displaced tiki as the popular archetype of the tropical cocktail. Martin Cate has called such creatures "slushy Visigoths laying waste to the already wounded and failing tiki bar," and identified the Piña Colada as their warlord. Now, I have enjoyed a Piña Colada or two in my day, but this seems an appropriate time to highlight a more interesting alternative from Brazil.

The Batida (bah–CHEE–dah in Brazilian Portuguese) is probably the second most popular use of cachaça after the Caipirinha. A frozen blended drink, it is sweet without being cloying, refreshing but deadly, and readily available from street vendors. If you like the Piña Colada, you'll enjoy this one even more.

Batidas come in many flavors. Specifically, the subject of this exercise is the Batida de Maracujá, which uses sweet, tart, and aromatic passion fruit syrup. It also incorporates sweetened condensed milk. Think about these ingredients, reflect on the properties of conventional blending, and see if you can work out how they translate into the recipe. Remember: it should be accessible enough to be a giant country's number two drink!

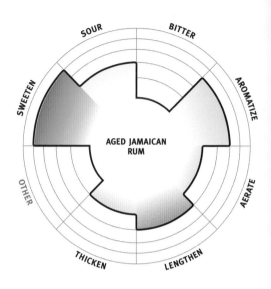

**AGED JAMAICAN RUM**

SOUR · BITTER · AROMATIZE · AERATE · LENGTHEN · THICKEN · OTHER · SWEETEN

**Jamaica** is one of the most highly regarded rum-producing countries, its rums known for a distinctive flavor that is hard to describe. The terms *funk* and *hogo* are often used, the latter derived from the French *haut gout*, which was historically a reference to aged game meats.

This signature "funk" often comes from using *muck*, a cultivated fermentation starter not unlike a sour mash in principle, but far more disturbing to the nose in practice—rum writer Matt Pietrek has called the smell "off-the-chart malevolent." This acidic microbial soup kickstarts the fermentation's flavor-production process. Acids react with alcohols to form esters: fragrant, fruity, but above all *pleasant*-scented chemicals that are especially concentrated in Jamaican rums. This results in big flavors of banana, overripe fruit, and scores of other scents that collectively come under the umbrella of hogo or funk.

The modern Periodista was invented by a Cambridge bartender named Joe McGuirk in the 1990s, when he swapped a Jamaican rum into an obscure and forgettable white rum recipe. He later brought his creation to the B-Side Lounge, where many of the future leaders of Boston's Cocktail Renaissance learned the trade. Through them, the Periodista became the city's accidental signature: everyone in town knew it, but an hour away nobody had heard of it. Locally, it was even assumed to be a classic! McGuirk's occasional assertions that he had invented

# Periodista

1½ oz. aged Jamaican rum

¾ oz. apricot liqueur

½ oz. orange liqueur

½ oz. lime juice

1 tsp. simple syrup

Shake with ice and strain into a chilled cocktail glass. Garnish with a lime wheel.

it were usually waved off with a laugh until 2010, when a Boston University videographer named Devin Hahn set out to find the recipe's true origins and vindicated him as its creator.*

McGuirk's key insight was that the rum needed to contribute more. When a filtered rum is the Periodista's base spirit, it's overwhelmed by the apricot. It becomes more like vodka, contributing dryness but not flavor; the result is a sweet, fruit-forward ethanol sour, the kind of cruise ship fare that sooner stirs the stomach than the soul.

A funky Jamaican rum, on the other hand, is an able match, because of its robust flavor *and* because its intricate palate contains a number of fruit notes consonant with orange and apricot. The fruitiness of the drink no longer suggests sweetness, but enhances its rumminess.

McGuirk used a Jamaican black rum, but I've followed Brother Cleve and suggest a moderately aged one instead. Its contrapuntal flavors of vanilla and wood further diversify the palate and divert a portion of our attention away from the punchiest ingredient. But try it both ways—a black rum's resonant molasses works very well in this drink, too!

* I highly recommend Hahn's twenty-two-part blog series, "Periodista Tales," which provides a start-to-finish account of his investigation.

# 4.12

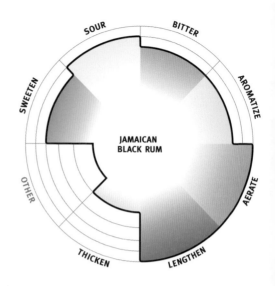

SOUR  BITTER  AROMATIZE  SWEETEN  AERATE  OTHER  THICKEN  LENGTHEN

JAMAICAN
BLACK RUM

**It is worth** reiterating that tiki flavors are more Caribbean than Polynesian in origin and the drinks themselves overwhelmingly hail from the United States. The genuine article—cocktails first compounded in the South Seas—is a rarity. Consequently any drinks that *can* claim a legitimately Pacific origin are eagerly embraced and enfolded into the canon, in much the same way that everyone crowds around an actual Irish person in a bar on St. Patrick's Day.

The Doctor Funk is the first such drink we'll see—but not the last. Its namesake was a German doctor, Bernhard Funk, who practiced medicine in Samoa, palled around with Robert Louis Stevenson, and published a Samoan grammar and dictionary in German. The precise circumstances of the drink's creation are murky, but the version that made the rounds in the Pacific was a sort of long absinthe sour, augmented in some variations with grenadine. Vic and Donn both put rum-spiked versions on their menus, and dozens of later tiki bars followed suit, with names like Doctor Funk's Son, Doctor Fong, Doctor Wong, and so on.

With all these variations, the Doctor Funk presents a problem for cocktail archaeologists: if there is no clear consensus or original version, how do we determine whether we're making it "right"? This is the bane of tiki in general, and an issue we will run into again and again.

# Doctor Funk

2¼ oz. Jamaican black rum

½ oz. lemon juice

½ oz. lime juice

½ oz. rich demerara syrup

¼ oz. absinthe

¼ oz. grenadine

1 oz. seltzer

Pour seltzer into a chilled highball glass. Flash blend remaining ingredients with crushed ice for 5 seconds and pour unstrained into the same glass; or shake with ice and strain into the same glass, then top with fresh crushed ice.

The best answer I have is that we must look at the whole of the tradition for the drink, identify common elements, and give extra weight to contemporaneous sources and the opinions of tiki authorities (Donn, Vic, Jeff Berry, Martin Cate). Treat each cocktail as a canon unto itself and attempt by that method to understand the unchanging essence of the mutable recipe. Then, before we veer too far into phenomenology, we taste the resulting recipe and see if it's any good.

This version of the Doctor Funk closely tracks Martin Cate's in *Smuggler's Cove*, an invaluable resource for the tikiphile. Cate contends that the absinthe shining through is the essential feature of this drink. The rum, while not to my knowledge attested in any version of the Doctor Funk that Dr. Funk might have recognized, is a definite improvement in terms of flavor, yielding a drink that is more cocktail and less bracing medicinal tonic. I recommend a pungent, viscous Jamaican black rum as the ideal base, largely in line with Cate's specifications. It fills in the center of the sip, stands up to the absinthe, and is apt for a drink with "funk" right there in the name.

The Doctor Funk is a good introduction to the herbal/hogo pairing, which we'll be using a lot. It's also a sort of tiki twist on a fizz, shaken and topped with seltzer but served on the rocks for extra dilution.

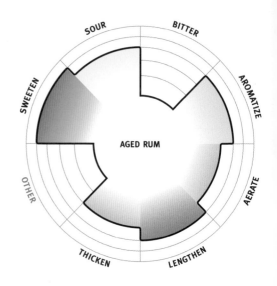

SOUR · BITTER · AROMATIZE · AERATE · LENGTHEN · THICKEN · OTHER · SWEETEN

**AGED RUM**

**The Mai Tai is,** to paraphrase Martin Cate, a rum-delivery system second only to the Daiquiri in its perfection. It has also suffered more indignities from both its foes and its champions than most other recipes—even by tiki standards. It was definitely invented by Trader Vic, probably in 1944. The official story is that he created it for Ham and Carrie Guild, friends of his who were in from Tahiti. Upon tasting it, Carrie exclaimed "*maita'i roe a'e!*" which is Tahitian for "out of this world—the best!" True or not, Vic went to court to defend this story. According to Beachbum Berry, the Sun-Vac corporation was promoting a bottled Mai Tai as a Beachcomber invention, under a license from Donn's company; Vic sued and received an out-of-court settlement. Other attempts to lay claim to the Mai Tai royally annoyed him for the rest of his life—in his 1972 cocktail guide, he wrote, "Anybody who says I didn't create this drink is a dirty stinker."

The '44 Mai Tai was a four-ingredient drink, anchored by a 17-year-old expression of J. Wray & Nephew Jamaican rum, the world's supply of which was swiftly exhausted. Vic initially substituted J. Wray's still-available 15-year-old expression. By the 1950s, that was running low, too, and Vic began splitting it with two younger Jamaican black rums to achieve the same overall character. When it ran out entirely, Vic bottled his own 15-year-old and 8-year-old Jamaican rums, and supplemented them with a Martinique rum.

# Mai Tai

2 oz. aged rum
¾ oz. lime juice
½ oz. curaçao or triple sec
½ oz. orgeat

Long shake, double-strain into a rocks glass filled with crushed ice. Optionally, garnish with a spent lime shell and a sprig of mint.

Many recent books interpret that as a rhum agricole. But when Vic wanted a rhum agricole, he called for rhum agricole, not Martinique rum. Cate offers compelling evidence that his Mai Tai blend used rhum *traditionnel*, a heavily colored molasses distillate sometimes even blended with Jamaican rum. The characteristics Vic enumerates—nutty, snappy, pungent, the color of coffee—also sound more like a traditionnel.

Absent a 17-year-old Jamaican rum, we must do as Vic did and blend several together. It cannot be overstated how unusual this is. So far only the Cameron's Kick has mixed spirits within a single class. We have not had bourbon-rye drinks or Cognac-Armagnac drinks or drinks that called for three kinds of gin. Intra-spirit blending is the core contribution of tiki to mixological theory, and rum is the spirit class best suited to the technique. As Donn Beach famously said, "What one rum can't do, four rums can." Blending rums is the beating heart of this seminar and of tiki.

The Mai Tai benefits from dilution, but it isn't a long drink per se. Some recipes say to shake with crushed ice; one can shake with regular ice for 1.5–2x the usual time—sometimes called a **long shake**.

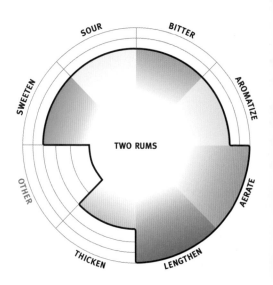

**4.14**

SOUR     BITTER

SWEETEN     AROMATIZE

TWO RUMS

OTHER     AERATE

THICKEN     LENGTHEN

**The Three Dots** and a Dash is a World War II–era Beachcomber creation. Its name refers to the Morse Code for the letter "V," a common shorthand for "Victory."

It is also a vindication of rhum agricole in multi-rum cocktails. It should be avoided in the Mai Tai because it does not provide the nutty "snap" that Vic was after in replacing the 17-year-old Wray & Nephew. Here, however, it works, because the drink is designed around the distinctive vegetal notes it offers.

A small amount of Demerara rum is blended in to add depth and help the agricole get along with others. The agricole remains star of the show, its grassiness enhanced by the freshness of the honey-citrus combination and held in counterpoint to a robust spice blend from the falernum, bitters, *and* allspice dram, which all appear in the same recipe for the first time. Structurally, we end up with two relatively assertive camps, the fresh-agricole and the brown sugar-spice, mediated by the orange juice and mellowed by the lengthening and diluting effects of the crushed ice. It ends up being refreshing; the spices recede into seasoning because the aggressive flavor of the rhum agricole is adequately tempered.

# Three Dots and a Dash

1½ oz. aged rhum agricole or cachaça

½ oz. Demerara rum

¼ oz. allspice dram

¼ oz. falernum

½ oz. lime juice

½ oz. orange juice

⅓ oz. honey

1 dash Angostura bitters

Flash blend with crushed ice for 5 seconds and pour unstrained into a rocks glass, or shake vigorously and strain into a rocks glass filled with crushed ice. Garnish with three cherries and a chunk of pineapple on a skewer.

You have the option to substitute another cane juice rum or a cachaça for the agricole. While there are differences, they are similar enough for cocktail purposes that it is not necessary to have each type on hand at all times. Pick the one you prefer, and make your Three Dots and a Dash accordingly.

We know that honey can be uncooperative in the shaker when it's cold. This is even truer in the flash blender. If your honey is on the thick side, this is a good time to make a honey syrup. Mix three parts honey and one part warm water until well combined, then bottle until you're ready to use. If taking this route, use ½ oz. of syrup instead of ⅓ oz. of honey. Alternatively, you could dry shake the mixture before blending or warm the honey before use.

The elaborate garnishes and drinking vessels for which tiki is famous are part of the aesthetic experience of the drinks, but they are often also symbolic. Tiki art historians make note of the lime shell and mint leaf atop the Mai Tai, for example, as depicting a small island and a single palm tree. Feel free to riff on symbolic garnishes in ways that capture the same meaning with a different presentation. Traditionally, the Three Dots and a Dash is garnished with three cherries and a cube of pineapple on a skewer, spelling out its namesake Morse code, but anything you can use to say "... —" will work just as well!

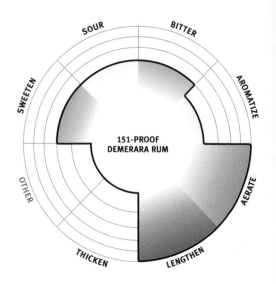

**A Don the Beachcomber** recipe that inspired many imitations, the 151 Swizzle is in one regard an exceedingly simple drink. Like the Queens Park Swizzle, it's a lengthened bitter-sour drink with a Demerara rum base. Although it's generally flash blended, it has the feel of a swizzle, as the stirred Sazerac has the sense of an Old Fashioned. Its most novel aspect is the use of 151-proof Demerara rum. We'll begin there.

Why this instead of the Demerara rum we have already dealt with? Moreover, what reason could we have to need a rum that is more than three-quarters alcohol by volume? The proof of it, certainly, is one piece. You can dry out a drink much more per unit of volume with a 151-proof rum than with a standard 80-proof spirit. This is part of the way we can balance these drinks, especially ones that are mostly crushed ice by volume and in danger of being overlengthened.

Another reason, going back to one of our earliest lessons, is that alcohol is a fabulous vector for flavor chemicals. That is not to say that alcoholic *drinks* are, per se; distilled spirits contain water as well as ethanol and other substances in varying quantities. If ethanol is the best of those at carrying flavors, it stands to reason that higher-proof spirits can be more concentrated and toothsome than lower-proof ones. We have seen this with absinthe and Chartreuse, both of which

# 151 Swizzle

1½ oz. 151-proof Demerara rum

½ oz. lime juice

½ oz. simple syrup

1 dash Angostura bitters

6 drops absinthe

Flash blend with crushed ice for 5 seconds. Pour unstrained into a flared metal swizzle cup, adding more crushed ice to fill. Dust with nutmeg. Garnish with a cinnamon stick, flamed if desired.

get their character from the herbs infused into them. But it works that way for unflavored liquors as well.

Most spirits come off the still at a strength much closer to 151 than to 80 proof. They are then diluted with water before aging in oak barrels, and again before bottling. Each step makes the drinks more potable but reduces the concentration of those flavors produced during fermentation or distillation. A dose of high-proof rum can therefore deliver a bigger flavorful punch than the standard Demerara rums.

The 151 Swizzle uses these characteristics to great effect. It squares that concentrated burnt sugar off against a load of crushed ice, the overproof facing down the overlengthening. Its closest counterpart would be neither a 151 drink nor a swizzle, but a bittered Daiquiri with a regular demerara base, achieving a similar ratio of flavor-carrying ethanol to water but on a shorter plan. This longer version is more refreshing, even with a higher octane base spirit. It also shows off a Donn Beach signature: aromatizing the cocktail not only with bitters but also with six drops of absinthe. (At the time, it would have been six drops of pastis, but pastis mostly made its way into cocktails as a substitute for absinthe, so I've swapped the latter in for the convenience of your wallet and bar.)

# 4.16

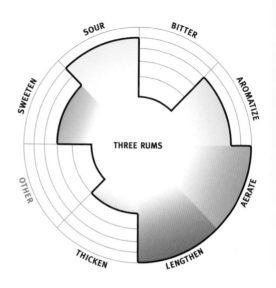

SOUR · BITTER · AROMATIZE · AERATE · LENGTHEN · THICKEN · OTHER · SWEETEN

THREE RUMS

**The Navy Grog** was an olive branch from the Beachcomber to bargoers too macho to drink anything called a "rhapsody": a triple serving of rum (one of them overproof) that bellows over the other ingredients, advertising the cocktail's strength where his other offerings were quieter about it. The result is still plenty delicious, but just as the Rickey caters to an audience that likes things on the sour side, the Navy Grog is for drinkers who want cocktails to both be *and* taste highly spiritous.

This is our first recipe with more than two types of rum, but each is doing something we've seen before: the one without strong country-specific flavors serves as the glue, another gives us an extra high concentration of ethanol and toasted caramel flavor, while the last provides Jamaican hogo and a bit of much-needed sweetness. The remaining ingredients are simple and familiar, augmenting the spirits without distracting from them; the blend of rums is not only the core of the drink but the majority component of its flavor.

Adding seltzer at the mixing stage is another Beachcomber signature, although we saw in seminar two that it goes back to the nineteenth century. In the blender, seltzer helps the mixture foam up and enhances aeration, a useful trick for lightening a spirit-heavy cocktail.

# Navy Grog

1 oz. filtered lightly aged rum

1 oz. aged Jamaican rum

1 oz. 151-proof Demerara rum

¾ oz. lime juice

¾ oz. grapefruit juice

¾ oz. seltzer

½ oz. honey

Flash blend with crushed ice for 5 seconds. Pour unstrained into a rocks glass, or strain into a rocks glass and garnish with an ice cone.

For a similar reason, Donn's Navy Grog was traditionally served with an ice cone, our first encounter with what can best be described as an ice garnish. You can buy ice cone molds on the internet, but the easiest way to make one is to fill a tapered beer glass with shaved ice—or the finest ice you have access to—stick a chopstick or a metal straw down the center to create a hole, and then put the whole apparatus into the freezer until the ice solidifies. You can then insert it broad side–down into the rocks glass you're serving your Navy Grog in, and feed a straw through the hole in the cone. In addition to being visually impressive, it will help to chill and dilute the drink as ice normally does while making sure that each sip is as cold as possible by the time it leaves the straw.

Trader Vic has a Navy Grog as well. I give the Beachcomber's recipe because I think it is the better drink, but the Trader's can boast a certain notoriety. Richard Nixon was a known fan, and according to Henry Kissinger, the president would occasionally drag cabinet secretaries along to the DC Trader Vic's. Allegedly, he kept going there during the Watergate hearings—after-hours and through a back entrance—so he could knock back a couple of Navy Grogs and tell his troubles to the bartender. To make Vic's version, cut the honey and seltzer and add in ¼ oz. each of rich demerara syrup and allspice dram.

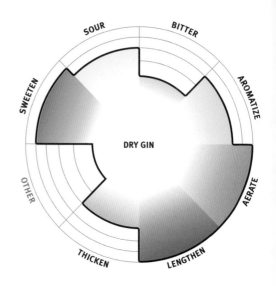

**Each of the last** thirteen cocktails has had a rum base, and I have already lauded that spirit for its versatility and centrality to the tiki style. However, its preeminence does not amount to a monopoly, and several tiki classics use other bases.

The Saturn is frequently presented as the exemplar of gin-based tiki drinks. It combines several of the classic ingredients, blends them with citrus, and ends up with a tart-fruit-spice-nut flavor that is clearly of the genre.

How it gets there, though, is rather interesting. In most of our recipes thus far, we use bitters or syrups for spice, while our base spirit provides deep, rich, rummy flavors with aromatics appropriate to its country of origin. The Saturn turns this on its head. The *gin* is the source of a lot of the spice, drawn out by similar notes in the falernum. The orgeat does the same for the gin's floral qualities, as we saw in the Army & Navy. And both the rumminess of the falernum and the nuttiness of the orgeat contribute the kind of low tones to the drink that we normally derive from the rum. Despite being gin-based, all that syrup makes this a heavier-bodied drink than it might appear on paper. It does not feel heavy in the sense of a rich dessert, though, the tartness of lemon and passion fruit amply compensating for the sugars and the orgeat's fattiness.

# Saturn

1½ oz. London dry gin

½ oz. lemon juice

½ oz. orgeat

¼ oz. passion fruit syrup

¼ oz. falernum

Flash blend with crushed ice for 5 seconds and pour unstrained into a rocks glass, or shake vigorously and strain into a rocks glass filled with fresh crushed ice. Top with fresh crushed ice as needed. Garnish with a long, thin twist of lime wrapped around a cherry on a skewer.

The Saturn was invented by J. "Popo" Galsini in the 1960s and has become a favorite offbeat recipe of the tiki revival as a standard-bearer for exotic gin drinks. Galsini was revered by his fellow midcentury tiki bartenders—Jeff Berry reports that "they speak of him in hushed tones to this day"—and had a perfectionist streak that served him well.

Galsini's drink reintroduces plain passion fruit syrup as distinct from fassionola. Passion fruit is what "tropical" most tastes like. Where pineapple and coconut taste like pineapple and coconut, passion fruit is the thing you mix into a fruit punch to make it *tropical* fruit punch. Sweet, tart, juicy, bright, with some subtle hints of fruit blossoms, it is hard to pin down but immensely familiar even if you have never tried it on its own before. The Saturn uses it almost as an aromatic extension of the citrus juice and does something similar with the falernum and orgeat. The fruit-spice-citrus triad is strongly present, and the gin is able to pick up elements of all of them.

This is another good opportunity for a symbolic garnish, like the one recommended by Martin Cate: cut a very long, thin strip of citrus peel, preferably lime, then form it into a circle around a cherry and spear both with a skewer. The result should look like a ringed planet— be sure to leave enough space between the peel and the cherry so that it does!

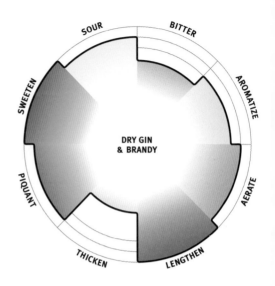

**4.18**

SOUR · BITTER · AROMATIZE · AERATE · LENGTHEN · THICKEN · PIQUANT · SWEETEN

**DRY GIN & BRANDY**

**Tropical cocktails** are necessarily an intercontinental phenomenon. The Suffering Bastard holds the distinction of being the highest-profile cocktail invented in Africa—at least, for now.

It was created in 1942 by Joe Scialom at Shepheard's Hotel in Cairo and served to Allied troops between bouts with Rommel. A folk etymology holds that it was originally the Suffering Bar-Steward and was corrupted into Suffering Bastard by either an honest mishearing or the vulgar tongues of battle-hardened soldiers. This, as those soldiers might have said, is nonsense. Scialom named it the Suffering Bastard, and "Suffering Bar-Steward" was a later bowdlerization.

We know all this from Jeff Berry's work unearthing the original recipe, and also because of Scialom's later variations, the Dying Bastard and the Dead Bastard, which he popularized during his later years as a globe-trotting bar consultant. With the help of Scialom's daughter Colette and his personal archives, Berry also confirmed that the original recipe used a split base of gin and brandy rather than gin and whiskey as is sometimes alleged, and that, like the Gimlet, it used lime cordial rather than lime juice.* If you have been looking for a

* Berry also alleges that it was not until the 1970s that Rose's, the original lime cordial, became the disappointingly artificial product it is today.

# Suffering Bastard

1 oz. London dry gin

1 oz. brandy

½ oz. lime cordial

2 dashes Angostura bitters

4 oz. ginger beer

Shake all but the ginger beer. Pour unstrained into a highball glass and fill with ginger beer. Garnish with a sprig of mint and an orange slice.

second use for your bottle of lime cordial since the first seminar, your wait, at last, is over.

Understanding the Gimlet also gives us a window into this drink. Much as we might like to build it, as we would a Moscow Mule, lime cordial is too heavy for that, so we shake it first even though we'll be serving it on the rocks, just as we do with the Mojito. We know the lime cordial is robust enough to handle the dilution, and we help the Angostura do the same by giving it two healthy dashes. The drink is spicy and spice-y, from the ginger beer and the bitters, layered through citrus and gin botanicals to the warm, welcoming vanilla-raisin of brandy. As ginger beer drinks go, it tilts relatively more toward complex and away from refreshing, but it remains mostly the latter.

Note that while the Suffering Bastard is a tropical drink, it is not a tiki drink. It does not come from either the Californian mixological school of Donn and Vic or even its antecedents in the Caribbean cocktail tradition. It was, however, rapidly welcomed onto menus at American tiki bars, much as the earlier cocktails from the East and West Indies had been. If it helps, think of the true tiki drinks as the ones created as part of the island fantasia of twentieth-century Polynesian pop, while those created earlier or outside of that cultural context are not.

# 4.19

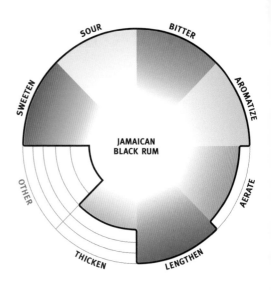

SOUR · BITTER · AROMATIZE · AERATE · LENGTHEN · THICKEN · OTHER · SWEETEN

JAMAICAN
BLACK RUM

**Invented by** Jeffrey Ong Swee Teik in 1973, the Jungle Bird was originally a welcome cocktail at the Kuala Lumpur Hilton, which had a bar called the Aviary and a netted area full of colorful birds the patrons could watch. It did not initially achieve widespread fame, but it was noteworthy enough to appear in the *New American Bartender's Guide*, where Jeff Berry found it about twenty years ago. He almost passed over it, but decided that its use of Campari was too interesting not to include in *Intoxica*; from there, it rocketed to success in a mixological era awash in amari and fascinated by the forgotten. Giuseppe Gonzalez's tweaking of the base to a Jamaican black rum was widely embraced, and the Jungle Bird swiftly established it as a standard.

In addition to Berry, credit is due to Kim Choong, who traced the drink's history back to its origins and was the first to conclusively determine its inventor. Her research, published in *ThirstMag*, is my source for much of the above. Her efforts also helped make Ong into a celebrity in Malaysia, and upon his death in 2019 he was eulogized in the national press as the Jungle Bird's creator. The drink remains a point of pride for Malaysian mixologists, and justly so.

Let us consider again that use of Campari, the thing that enabled the Jungle Bird to achieve global fame and spawn a thousand variations

# Jungle Bird

2 oz. Jamaican black rum

¾ oz. Campari

½ oz. lime juice

1 tsp. rich demerara syrup

2 oz. pineapple juice

Shake with ice until foamy. Strain into a rocks glass with fresh ice. Optionally, garnish with a wedge of pineapple.

while most other hotel drinks from the 1970s have been forgotten. Like pineapple juice, Campari is a very loud ingredient. This is a drink that works by balancing them against each other, a technique we have seen many times. The bold, tart fruit of pineapple and the bitter astringency of Campari are well-matched contrasts. They both add sugar, and pineapple adds acidity, but we want a bit more of each than they provide without amplifying their voices any further—thus the demerara syrup and lime juice. The funky Jamaican rum plays off the floral notes in the pineapple and the Campari's herbaceousness as it did in the Doctor Funk, while the Campari's orange element resonates with similar pitches hit by the pineapple. There is a lot going on here, and it gives one the scent-sense of being in tall grasses with fresh plants, blooming flowers, and dewey soils all around.

As if that were not enough, it is also a texturally interesting drink: pineapple foams up when shaken, especially if a decent quantity of it is used. It also does so without the need for a dry shake, which we'll continue to take advantage of throughout the remainder of this seminar.

# 4.20

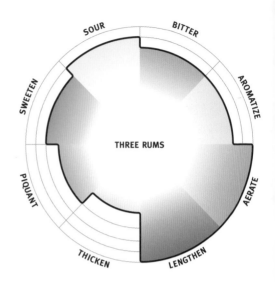

SOUR · BITTER · AROMATIZE · AERATE · LENGTHEN · THICKEN · PIQUANT · SWEETEN

THREE RUMS

## SOLUTION

We have three rums, matching the Navy Grog's in proof and style: a lightly aged rum as glue, Jamaican black rum for funk and molasses, and overproof Demerara for extra ethanol and a full spread of toasted sugar and soil.

Without question, this drink needs dilution, so we flash blend it with crushed ice. The mixer's vigor also helps integrate its numerous and somewhat viscous ingredients. There are multiple sweeteners, multiple citrus juices, and multiple aromatic finishers—Donn's signature pairing of Angostura with six drops of absinthe—all comingled in the more-is-more style typical of tiki.

1½ oz. lightly aged rum
1½ oz. Jamaican black rum
1 oz. 151-proof Demerara rum
¾ oz. lime juice
½ oz. falernum
⅓ oz. grapefruit juice
1 tsp. cinnamon simple syrup
1 tsp. grenadine
6 drops absinthe
1 dash Angostura bitters

Shake vigorously and strain into a Zombie glass or Collins glass filled with crushed ice, or flash blend with crushed ice and pour unstrained into a Zombie glass. Top with fresh crushed ice as needed. Garnish with a sprig of mint.

# EXERCISE
# Zombie

lightly aged rum

Jamaican black rum

151-proof Demerara rum

lime juice

falernum

grapefruit juice

cinnamon simple syrup

grenadine

absinthe

Angostura bitters

Using the given ingredients, determine the proportions of the Zombie and its method of preparation.

**The Zombie** is easily Donn Beach's most famous creation. Indeed, it was the most famous tiki drink until Vic's Mai Tai came along, known for an oft-repeated limit of two per customer which invariably made people want to get three. It was a tough nut for historians to crack—no single person knew the Zombie's true composition for decades after Beach's death. It took tiki historian Jeff Berry more than eleven years to track down the coded recipe and figure out how to translate it. The hardest ingredient to identify was "Don's Mix #2," a 2:1 combination of grapefruit juice with "Spices #4," which in turn was a cinnamon simple syrup. This was the Beachcomber at his finest, upping the ante on intricacy and making the familiar taste foreign. Nobody else could have engendered decades of speculation with something as simple as grapefruit and cinnamon.

This is also our first recipe to use **lightly aged rum**, an unfiltered rum aged one to four years. A popular ingredient in triple-base cocktails, its properties lie between those of filtered rums and moderately aged ones, and either can substitute in a pinch.

Remember, the Zombie is meant to be potent enough to justify the menu's warning. Consider how to layer these ingredients to achieve that effect, and then read on!

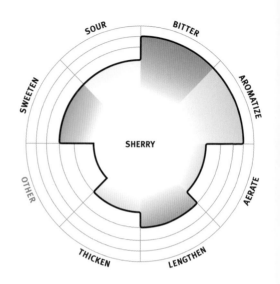

**4.21**

SOUR BITTER AROMATIZE SWEETEN SHERRY AERATE OTHER THICKEN LENGTHEN

**If you've been** missing fortified wines for the last twenty drinks, here's a bit of good news for you. Tiki drinks didn't use them much in their heyday—in Embury's classification system, they were ordinarily sour- rather than aromatic-type—but their aromatic density can play well in the genre, much as Campari's did in the Jungle Bird. From an Adonis-like starting point of vermouth, sherry, and bitters, the U.S.S. Wondrich takes a hard turn into the tropical by being shaken with pineapple juice. This is not unlike the citrus-soured wine cocktails we have seen before, although this application may be less intuitive.

While we have discussed Jeff "Beachbum" Berry chiefly as an historian of tiki drinks, he also created many of his own while working on his books. Cocktail historians must have a firm grasp of mixological practice in order to ply their trade. This is not how all historians operate—some political historians have been world leaders, but most aren't—and what sets the field apart even more is that it is the *norm* for students of this history to make significant contributions to current practice as well.

The Beachbum has parlayed his study of exotic drinks into the proprietorship of a modern tiki bar in New Orleans called Latitude 29. His

# U.S.S. Wondrich

1½ oz. sherry

¾ oz. pineapple juice

¾ oz. sweet vermouth

½ oz. allspice dram

1 dash Angostura bitters

Shake with ice and strain into a chilled cocktail glass. Garnish with a wedge of pineapple.

U.S.S. Wondrich is named after—who else?—cocktail historian David Wondrich, the first person to ask for a sherry cocktail at Berry's bar. While it was first made with a chocolate-orange liqueur, every printed recipe I have seen allows for the substitution of allspice dram, and the resulting drink is excellent. I have never tasted the original, and I do not feel deprived. (If you do, try to get your hands on a bottle of Sabra or something similar, and swap ¾ oz. of it in for the dram in this recipe.)

Fittingly, Berry envisions this as an "intermission drink," a concept of which Wondrich has been a great proponent: a low-ABV cocktail meant to be taken between more spirit-forward offerings. It serves a similar role in our lesson plan, immediately following the limit-two-per-customer Zombie and providing some respite after we've gone two-thirds of a seminar with mostly very rum-forward drinks. It also sets the tone for the final third, with its unexpected callbacks and innovative adaptations of familiar techniques. We have quite a bit of both to come.

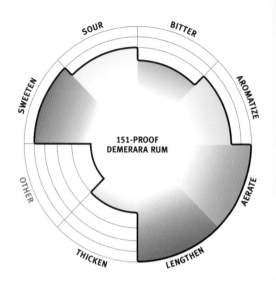

SOUR · BITTER · AROMATIZE · AERATE · LENGTHEN · THICKEN · OTHER · SWEETEN

**151-PROOF DEMERARA RUM**

**A Beachcomber drink** from the 1930s, the Cobra's Fang is the second most famous fassionola cocktail—but also may never have been one in the first place. Such is the tiki revival's trouble with fassionola.

Mysterious in its past and composition, obscure and unavailable in the present, fassionola has become the Oak Island treasure of neo-tiki circles. Depending on whom one asks, there has either been fruitful modern work restoring it to its proper place in the canon or an avalanche of ahistorical uses in drinks where it never belonged.

The elusive syrup appears in cocktail books published by Donn's widow, Phoebe Beach, many years after his death, but in no earlier sources that I know of. In fairness, it's not as though we have a lot of those—the Beachcomber never did like to share his recipes.

Berry has collected the wisdom of Donn's bartenders from their notebooks and, where possible, interviews. Dick Santiago's 1937 notes on the Cobra's Fang call for plain passion fruit syrup, and Berry hasn't found evidence of fassionola in any early Beachcomber recipe.

Mrs. Beach's books may have reflected later versions. Her recipes are often entirely unlike what we see in other sources. But other than the choice of syrup, her Cobra's Fang is remarkably close to Santiago's.

# Cobra's Fang

1½ oz. 151-proof Demerara rum

½ oz. lime juice

½ oz. orange juice

½ oz. fassionola or passion fruit syrup

¼ oz. falernum

1 dash Angostura bitters

6 drops absinthe or pastis

Flash blend with crushed ice for 5 seconds and pour unstrained into a highball glass. Top with fresh crushed ice as needed.

It makes one wonder. Passion fruit was relatively new to the U.S. when fassionola was first produced. Called *passionola* in the 1930s, it was, like Donn's bar, a creature of Southern California. Trader Vic describes it in his cocktail guide as "a nonalcoholic syrup made from passion fruit," but why he does so is a mystery tikiphiles are still working to address: Vic doesn't use it in a single recipe. One could imagine a world in which the passion fruit syrup Donn had readiest access to was passionola, and its commonness or use by his competitor motivated Vic to mention it in his book.

Beachbum Berry might say this is grasping at straws to fit fassionola into tiki before it was there. Perhaps it is. The definitive book on fassionola's history is still being written. And being unsure whether it belongs in your drink is a quintessential experience of the tiki revival.

The Cobra's Fang is superb either way, layering intricate flavors into its overproof Demerara rum base. Where the 151 Swizzle is content with Daiquiri fixings and Donn's absinthe-Angostura finisher, this drink splits the sweetener between a syrup and falernum, working in both tropical fruit and Caribbean spice, and uses orange and lime to keep all its moving parts well lubricated. This version follows Santiago's recipe, with the possible substitution of fassionola.

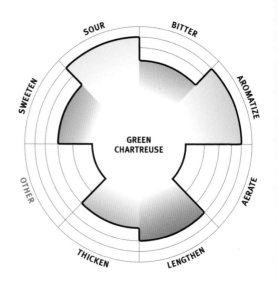

**4.23**

SOUR · BITTER · AROMATIZE · AERATE · LENGTHEN · THICKEN · OTHER · SWEETEN

GREEN
CHARTREUSE

**As exotic drinks** were being revived, new recipes in the style were also being created. Although I have devoted the fifth seminar to topics in contemporary mixology, I have found it useful to put the tiki-style modern drinks here, particularly where they reveal something about the genre.

The Chartreuse Swizzle is one of the tikiest there is, hitting hallmark after hallmark of the style's post-Donn-and-Vic evolution. Use of a deceptively high-proof base spirit? Check. Combination of pineapple with something equally loud? Check. Unexpected combination of herbaceous ingredient with citrus and spice? Check and check.

The drink's inventor, Marcovaldo Dionysos, has never to the best of my knowledge described his creation as "a Jungle Bird on steroids," but one can see the family resemblance. Green Chartreuse clocks in at 55% ABV, so rum would be somewhat superfluous here, particularly with half an ounce of rum-based falernum to ground it. As with the

# Chartreuse Swizzle

1½ oz. Green Chartreuse

1 oz. pineapple juice

¾ oz. lime juice

½ oz. falernum

Swizzle with crushed ice in a highball glass. Garnish with a sprig of mint and a sprinkle of grated nutmeg.

Jungle Bird, we add a second tart element to the pineapple juice to stand up to the sugars in the Chartreuse and the falernum. And we swizzle the mixture, lengthening it and dialing back each of its fairly assertive ingredients while keeping the whole in balance. The garnish is easy to forget after all that, but it is essential to finish the cocktail—the grated nutmeg, in particular, which has affinities for all of the other ingredients with its citrus, spice, and pine components.

The Chartreuse Swizzle is also interesting because you are very unlikely to see it in a bar. It made appearances on a few cocktail menus after its creation, but in the grand scheme of things, Chartreuse is expensive, and bars don't want to have to list a cocktail at the price they'd have to charge to justify using an ounce and a half of the stuff. A good contemporary tiki bar will be able to whip one up for you, of course, but this is a particularly good recipe to make at home. A $70 bottle of Green Chartreuse will make you sixteen of them at about $4.25 a serving.

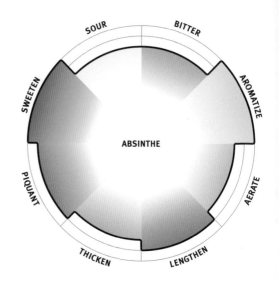

**Another** contemporary recipe, less explicitly in the tiki tradition than the Chartreuse Swizzle but manifestly tikier than the Suffering Bastard, the Dead Man's Mule is the best single way I know to make a dent in your absinthe bottle.

One can think of it as an elaboration on the themes of both drinks. Like the Suffering Bastard, it takes the buck or mule template and adds complexity with spices, allspice dram in this case, and a syrup, orgeat. Like the Chartreuse Swizzle—and, indeed, the 151 Swizzle—it is a long drink with a high-proof and full-flavored base spirit, something we're used to seeing in much smaller doses, which we can work with here only because it is appropriately contrasted and diluted.

At a cool 70% ABV or so, absinthe definitely packs a wallop. It needs the sugars of that full ounce of orgeat to keep it from drying out the cocktail entirely. The syrup, in turn, is soured by the lime and bittered by the allspice to keep it from oversweetening things, and the ginger beer lengthens the mixture enough that all the flavors get some room to breathe. Most importantly, though, that punch of spicy ginger is the biggest thing holding the absinthe in check. When it's finished, the Dead Man's Mule should almost taste like a ginger beer drink with a lot of spiced modifiers rather than an absinthe drink. It should be difficult

# Dead Man's Mule

1 oz. absinthe

1 oz. orgeat

½ oz. lime juice

½ oz. allspice dram/pimento dram

2 oz. ginger beer to fill

Shake all nonsoda ingredients with ice. Serve on the rocks and top with ginger beer.

to tell where one ingredient ends and the other begins and to pick out the absinthe from the mixture. This is in contrast to the Doctor Funk, which uses less absinthe but also does less to bury it. It is also very much in the spirit of tiki: a recipe that cannot easily be parsed, that tastes more like an experience than individual ingredients.

This version is a slight modification from the original recipe, which cropped up in Europe sometime after the absinthe bans began to be lifted. Back in 2010, a group of Danish tourists requested a round at Drink, a Cocktail Renaissance bar in Boston that famously has neither a menu nor any visible bottles on the backbar, so that each order is either a canonical cocktail or the result of a conversation with the bartender, rather than being cued by a familiar brand name. The Copenhagen version used Goldschläger, a cinnamon schnapps that Drink did not carry, so manager John Gertsen and bartender Joe Staropoli devised a variation with allspice dram in its place.* If you have Goldschläger, by all means try both, but I find the Drink version more than satisfactory.

* The core of the recipe and the history here were recorded by Fred Yarm, the scribe of Boston's cocktail scene for the last decade or so, who has written two books documenting the city's contemporary creations.

# 4.25

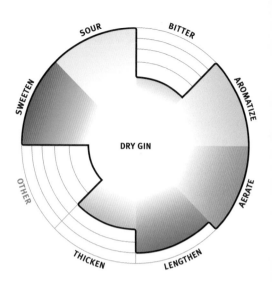

SOUR · BITTER · AROMATIZE · AERATE · LENGTHEN · THICKEN · OTHER · SWEETEN

DRY GIN

**The Singapore Sling**, Mai Tai, and Zombie constitute the triple crown of tiki cocktails—though the upstart Jungle Bird is gaining on them. The Mai Tai is Vic's ode to complex flavors from simple preparations, the Zombie Donn's rhapsody of excess in combining rums and spices, and the Singapore Sling the somehow-subtle pineapple fizz with a legitimate Pacific pedigree.

The Singapore Sling is often said to have been invented at the Raffles Hotel in 1915 by a Hainanese bartender named Ngiam Tong Boon. The date, at least, is unlikely, given that Mr. Ngiam died that year. Moreover, slings of various types had already been popular in Singapore for years. Wondrich has found pink ones as early as 1903, which suggests that modern attempts to restore the original recipe by reading "cherry brandy" as "kirschwasser" rather than a brandy-based liqueur like Cherry Heering are overcorrections.*

A picture begins to form of Singapore as a sling-drinking town, with a couple of decades of ferment beginning in the 1890s, culminating

* Singapore's National Library created a searchable archive of the city-state's newspapers circa 2010—presumably for reasons other than cocktail archaeology, but it was a godsend for sling research. Previously, the only Singaporean sources on it were from much later; its earliest attestations were in 1920s European or American cocktail guides, all of which differed about what went into it.

# Singapore Sling

1½ oz. London dry gin

¾ oz. Cherry Heering

¼ oz. Bénédictine

¼ oz. curaçao or triple sec

½ oz. lime juice

¼ oz. grenadine

1 dash Angostura bitters

2 oz. pineapple juice

½ oz. seltzer

Pour seltzer into the bottom of a Collins glass. Shake remaining ingredients with ice until foamy, then strain into glass and add ice to fill. Garnish with a cherry and a slice of pineapple.

in no single recipe for a Singapore Sling because there were dozens of versions in circulation. Wondrich cites a *Singapore Weekly Sun* article from 1913 that gives an approximate version of equal parts gin, cherry brandy, Bénédictine, and lime juice, with ice, water, and bitters, which gives us a sense of the core of the drink.

Ngiam probably created a popular version, but his long shadow at the Raffles—and his descendants' tendency to work there—helped elevate his reputation as a slingmaker. According to Theodora Sutcliffe, who interviewed many of the Ngiams for *Difford's Guide*, orange had made its way into the drink by at least midcentury. The Ngiams also report that pineapple gradually displaced it, oranges being an expensive import in Singapore. Seltzer is a wise alternative to the *Weekly Sun*'s plain water, especially when there is pineapple juice to foam up.

The Singapore Sling, you may have noticed, is hardly a sling in the nineteenth-century sense of a mere sweetened spirit. It looks more like a fizz, with pineapple rather than egg as a foaming agent. It isn't quite a fizz, of course, because it's served on ice; however, in my experience this does not prevent its being drunk as quickly as a fizz. This version is my own attempt to weave together the Singapore Sling's various threads, from the modern Raffles recipe to the inverse-fizz technique used at PDT for this and the Ramos Gin Fizz.

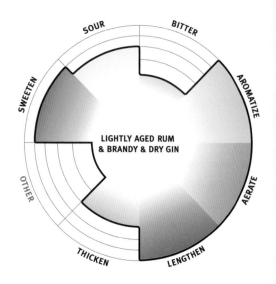

**4.26**

SOUR · BITTER · AROMATIZE · AERATE · LENGTHEN · THICKEN · OTHER · SWEETEN

LIGHTLY AGED RUM
& BRANDY & DRY GIN

**Donn and Vic** had distinct styles for their exotic elixirs, to the point that one can examine a classic tiki recipe and deduce which of the two invented it—assuming one of them did—just by looking through the ingredients. The Angostura-absinthe combination we've already seen is classic Beachcomber, for example.

One of the Trader's hallmarks is the use of non-rum spirits, often blended together with some type of rum to ground the recipe. Gin and brandy are popular selections, but whiskey, pisco, and tequila all show up in *Trader Vic's Bartender's Guide*. You'll also notice that Vic recipes are less likely to be particular about their rums than Donn ones. Both were seeking a certain level of complexity in the spirit element of their cocktails. Donn achieved it primarily by using depth within the rum category; Vic was more likely to get there via breadth across different classes of spirit.

Once we understand this, the Fog Cutter begins to look more straightforward. It is a three-base cocktail, not unlike the Zombie or the Navy Grog; it just uses bases other than rum. This should remind us of the Twelve-Mile Limit as well, and it shares something else with that drink: having divvied up the base spirits three ways, it doesn't overdo it in its sweet or sour elements. Granted, the standards for "overdoing

# Fog Cutter

1½ oz. lightly aged rum

½ oz. brandy

½ oz. London dry gin

1½ oz. orange juice

½ oz. lemon juice

½ oz. orgeat

½ oz. sherry

Flash blend all but the sherry with crushed ice and pour unstrained into a Collins glass. Top with fresh crushed ice as needed and float sherry on top. Garnish with a sprig of mint and drink through a straw.

it" are a bit more generous in a tiki cocktail, but still: We have only one sweetener, orgeat, with which we are by now very familiar. We have two citrus juices, which we know from elsewhere pair well together—but in this case, their usual proportions are reversed. Think about the orange/lemon pairing less in terms of the Ward Eight and more in terms of the pineapple/lime pairing in the Jungle Bird. The lemon is now the accent, the thing that adds enough acidity that we no longer have to worry about the other's sugar content. The orange can be there for flavor, for texture, and in this case for length as well. Incidentally, this is another Vic signature: Donn used orange sparingly and lemon basically not at all.

In the meantime, we come to the final aspect of the Fog Cutter and its most interesting single element: the sherry. Its flavors of oxidation, dried fruit, and the slight piquancy of a soft cheese hit the right blend of familiar and unfamiliar, exotic and evocative. Here we see it used as an aromatic float, accompanied by a garnish of mint. The Fog Cutter should, if at all possible, be served with a straw not much taller than the mug, so that the drinker gets a noseful of sherry and mint with every sip—appropriate, considering the Sherry Cobbler's role in popularizing the straw in the first place.

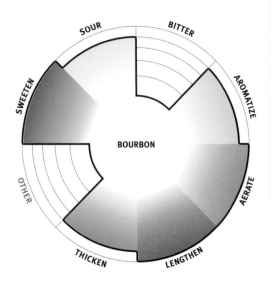

# 4.27

BITTER

SOUR

AROMATIZE

SWEETEN

BOURBON

OTHER

AERATE

THICKEN

LENGTHEN

**The tiki canon** is given to iterative riffing, an evolutionary process that has made sussing out its history a massively complicated undertaking. This entry on the Port Light may confuse things even further.

There are two extant versions of the Port Light. Both are whiskey-based, with one originating at Trader Vic's and one at the Kahiki in Columbus, Ohio.

Vic's lends itself to the more interesting technique. His recipe is an egg sour with a bourbon base, sweetened with honey and passion fruit syrup. I take a cue from *Smuggler's Cove* on this one and shirr it all up in the drink mixer—without ice. The principles of dry shaking apply equally well to **dry flash blending**. Whirr for a bit without ice to unfold the egg proteins, then add ice and flash blend as usual. We don't need to spend much time dry flash blending to get to the desired fluffiness; 2–3 seconds is plenty. Any longer and we risk overwhipping the egg whites and turning the entire drink into foam. (Egg whites also like to spatter when the blender first turns on, so watch out!)

This technique is neat, but Vic's recipe is somewhat underwhelming. After all the hullabaloo to prepare it, one hopes to have something that tastes a bit more elaborate than a Silver Fizz.

# Larboard Light, alias Port Light

2½ oz. bourbon

1 oz. lemon juice

⅔ oz. fassionola

½ oz. honey (or ¾ oz. honey syrup)

egg white

Dry flash blend for 2–3 seconds, then add crushed ice and flash blend for 5 seconds. Pour unstrained into a highball glass.

The Kahiki version skips the egg white for a bourbon sour with passion fruit syrup and grenadine. As many fassionola revivalists have done before, I say we swap those both out for the elusive red syrup of legend. Another advantage of the Kahiki's version is that it is actually red, the color of port lights on ships and airplanes (starboard lights are green). Trader Vic's version comes out more of a pale yellow-cream; his restaurants compensated for this by serving it in a vessel that looked like a nautical light, complete with red glass to mark it for the port side.

I have elected to run the two versions together. Starting with Trader Vic's template, we dial up the bourbon to ensure it is detected under the egg white. The honey and lemon common to both drinks can stay. For the passion fruit syrup, we substitute the bigger flavor and aptly colored fassionola, inspired by the Kahiki's passion fruit–grenadine axis.

The drink retains the fluffy-meringue character of heavily agitated egg sours, punched through by tart-tropical fassionola and the vanilla and tannins of the bourbon. Everything below the foam will look appropriately rosy-red.

To minimize confusion for future readers interested in the history of the *actual* Trader Vic's and Kahiki Port Lights, I have dubbed this hybrid the Larboard Light, using an old synonym for "port."

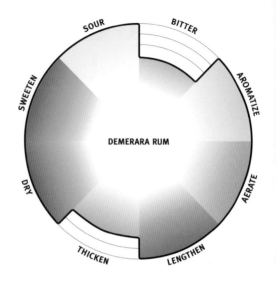

**4.28**

SOUR · BITTER · AROMATIZE · AERATE · LENGTHEN · THICKEN · DRY · SWEETEN

DEMERARA RUM

**The spirit of tiki**—and the tiki revival—is throwing out the rule book and making drinks that work anyway. To whatever extent this chapter has created a new, tiki-specific set of rules, the Demerara Dry Float violates those, too.

Two ounces of citrus juice, plus a teaspoon? An ounce and a half of syrup? What kind of drink has *lime juice* as its base spirit?

It is possible to think of the Demerara Dry Float as a juice drink, rendered elaborate at Don the Beachcomber's, or as an extra-intricate rum sour. But does either approach get us to a better understanding of the drink?

Let's begin with its most unusual elements and work from there. Lime juice makes up the bulk of the recipe. It is seasoned by a small amount of lemon juice, which keeps the acidity from dissipating too quickly, lime having a faster-decaying blend of acids than lemon. It needs a substantial serving of sweetener to counterbalance all that acidity, but passion fruit has a bit of tartness as well, so its presence also assists the lemon in maintaining a baseline of sourness throughout the sip. Like pineapple, passion fruit has a distinct floral component once you get past the sweet and the sour, which is buttressed and enhanced by that of the maraschino. The earthy caramel character of the demerara

# Demerara Dry Float

1½ oz. Demerara rum

2 oz. lime juice

1 tsp. lemon juice

1½ oz. passion fruit syrup

¼ oz. rich demerara syrup

¼ oz. maraschino

¾ oz. 151-proof Demerara rum

Flash blend all but the 151-proof rum with crushed ice. Pour unstrained into a highball glass and top with fresh crushed ice as needed. Serve the 151-proof rum in a separate small glass so it can be stirred in to the extent desired.

sugar and Demerara rum stretches out the experience of the sip across a wider range of flavors, notes of various heights and depths working in concert and in contrast. It starts from a very different place and follows no easily identifiable structure, but the Demerara Dry Float does hew to the iron law of balances, that each ingredient must serve to complement or counterbalance the others.

Its greatest violation is its ambivalence to the amount of rum used. Traditionally, the Demerara Dry Float is "served with a side of danger," by which is meant a sidecar of 151-proof Demerara rum. The drinker can then add it to the mix to suit their own tastes. Many will dump the whole thing in right away, some will pour it in periodically as their ice melts to maintain a roughly consistent proof, some will find their sweet spot and leave the rest in the glass, and others will add a bit at a time to see how it changes. While we have yet to encounter a recipe that used a spirit in this way, we *have* seen ones that allow the drinker to adjust them to taste. Normally this takes the form of a citrus wedge garnish, squeezed as desired; but we have seen it as well in floats, as with the Irish Coffee and the New York Sour. The eponymous float of overproof rum works similarly in this case—although as with the 151 Swizzle, the name is a slight misnomer, the drink being far better if the rum is stirred in rather than floated on top of it.

# 4.29

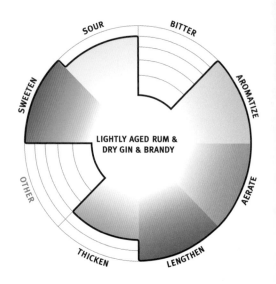

SOUR · BITTER · AROMATIZE · AERATE · LENGTHEN · THICKEN · OTHER · SWEETEN

**LIGHTLY AGED RUM & DRY GIN & BRANDY**

**After the Mai Tai,** the Scorpion is probably Trader Vic's most famous creation. In most versions it is less a cocktail than a punch: proportioned for 2–3 people, it is served in ceramic bowls with long straws and drunk communally, a presentation for which Vic was inspired by the Polynesian kava bowl tradition. In many places, any drink served in this way is called a "scorpion bowl," as is the vessel itself; all of these ultimately derive their names from Vic's Scorpion.

Credit for the drink's fame is due in part to the third man of tiki, Steve Crane, a penniless Hoosier who moved to California and bluffed his way into a successful career as a nightclub impresario and a marriage to Lana Turner. His place, the Luau, was the "it" bar in Beverly Hills in the 1950s and probably the pinnacle of tiki showmanship. A variation on the Pearl Diver came with an actual pearl that would be set into an earring or necklace before you left. Crane boasted about a (fictitious) resident bar genius who had supposedly worked for both Donn and Vic and set the standard for future establishments that would steal—er, adapt—drinks from both.

He carried it off well: the Luau's Scorpion looks even more like a Trader Vic drink than Vic's original, which omits the gin. It also has a lot in common with the Fog Cutter. Its base is a blend of multiple non-rum spirits. It makes good use of orgeat—Vic's favorite syrup,

# Scorpion (Bowl)

2 oz. lightly aged rum

2 oz. London dry gin

1½ oz. brandy

2 oz. orange juice

⅔ oz. orgeat

½ oz. lime juice

½ oz. rich demerara syrup

Roll between two mixing tins without ice, then divide evenly between two tins. Flash blend each with crushed ice for 3 seconds, then pour into a ceramic Scorpion bowl or other communal vessel and drink with long straws. Serves 2–3 people.

appearing in three of his drinks in this seminar. It takes a heavy pour of orange juice, reinforced by other, more acidic citrus. Add a bit of simple syrup, blend, and we're off to the races.

The comparison with the Fog Cutter helps us understand large-format drinks. An aromatic float and garnish won't work here because no one's face will be close enough to the surface to experience them. To compensate for the lost aroma, we dial up the other spirits. Ditching the float also makes the drink less liable to change over time, so that everyone has more or less the same experience.

To prepare the Scorpion, I recommend another technique from Martin Cate: first, **dry roll** it to jump-start the work of integrating this large volume of ingredients without adding dilution. Then split it in half, flash blend each portion with crushed ice, and recombine in your serving vessel. This ensures the punch is consistent and well-mixed even though we're using a blender designed for much smaller drinks.

Fire garnishes are common in tiki and appropriate here. The ceramic bowls designed for the Scorpion usually have a raised area in the center, often shaped like a volcano. You can pour some 151-proof rum into the caldera and light it on fire or soak a crouton in high-proof spirit and do the same. Presentation, as Steve Crane knew, is everything.

# 4.30

*In this final project you will make gardenia mix, a novel and multilayered ingredient, and then incorporate it in the Pearl Diver Punch in the following pages.*

**Perhaps the most** maddening experience for the tiki archaeologist is coming to the end of a long journey to unearth the true composition of a coded Donn Beach ingredient, finding its recipe, and discovering that one of *its* ingredients is also written in code. That we have the recipe for the Zombie at all is a testament to Beachbum Berry's capacity for disappointment.

It would be poetic for this seminar's final examination to require you to go on such a journey, but as much time as we've spent on history, the purpose of this course is mixological *practice*. So we'll be doing the next best thing: a final project with several subrecipes.

Gardenia mix has a reputation as Donn's *other* mix, less important than the cinnamon-grapefruit one that is the key to the Zombie. But for my money it's the more impressive invention, devised by Donn to capture the essence of a colonial-era Hot Buttered Rum in an iced drink like the Pearl Diver Punch. Of course, melting butter into alcohol is one thing—getting it into a cold drink is something else entirely.

Before preparing our gardenia mix, we have to make two of its components: cinnamon syrup and vanilla syrup. If you have some cinnamon syrup left over from the Zombie, that will work as well here. For vanilla syrup, I recommend Berry's recipe: get two whole vanilla beans, split

# FINAL PROJECT: PART 1
# Gardenia Mix

*(scale up as needed)*

1 oz. softened, unsalted butter

1 oz. honey

1 tsp. cinnamon syrup

½ tsp. vanilla syrup

½ tsp. allspice dram

Cream butter with other ingredients in a bowl. Use at room temperature and refrigerate any excess.

them in half the long way, and scrape out the pulp. Combine the pulp and the beans with a cup of water and a cup and a half of sugar. Bring that mixture to a boil, stirring until the sugar is dissolved, then reduce heat and simmer covered for two minutes. Take the pot off the heat and let it sit for at least two hours, although more wouldn't hurt. Strain into a bottle when ready and refrigerate afterward. Whatever you do, do not try to substitute vanilla extract for whole beans. Don't get me wrong, vanilla extract tastes just fine, but vanilla beans are breathtaking. Split one open and you'll understand why they're the second-most expensive spice on earth.

It wouldn't hurt to leave your butter out while doing all that, so it can come to room temperature and soften up. Once your vanilla syrup is ready, cream the butter with it and the other listed ingredients. Creaming, in this context, means mixing them thoroughly and aerating them a bit, as when we made the whipped cream for the Irish Coffee. If your gardenia mix is fluffy, that's a good sign, but don't worry too much if it isn't, as long as the ingredients are well combined.

Give some thought to our chemistry lessons from previous units, and this seminar's novel mixing methods. If the gardenia mix is a sort of batter, what roles is it fulfilling in the recipe that it might not have to in a hot drink?

# 4.30

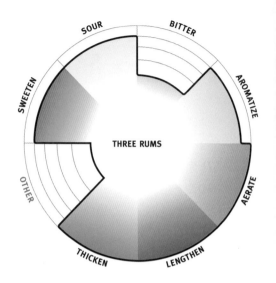

SOUR · BITTER · AROMATIZE · AERATE · LENGTHEN · THICKEN · OTHER · SWEETEN

**THREE RUMS**

**If you go** looking for a Pearl Diver recipe, you'll find a few different ones in circulation. This is not just because people imitated the Beachcomber, but also because he revised his recipes over time—usually in the direction of simplicity. So we have two-rum Pearl Divers with Angostura, as well as the three-rum Pearl Diver Punch with falernum. The latter has my endorsement.

It seems only fair to warn you that gardenia mix can be fickle. People sometimes report having trouble with it one day but not the next, and not knowing what made the difference: A change in the humidity? A slight difference in whipping technique? A misalignment of the stars?

I don't mean to overstate the difficulty. It's also common to get it right on your first try. I just want to prepare you for the possibility that you won't. Truth be told, gardenia mix cocktails are harder to learn from a book than any of our previous final examination recipes—and that's saying something. There are simply too many variables between my kitchen and yours. This is a wild horse that only you can break.

Working with gardenia mix is like working with other fats: easier at room temperature. You won't want to shake it, because a slippery ingredient in a cocktail shaker is the enemy of dry clothes and a clean workspace. Besides, its thickness calls for something with a bit more vigor.

# FINAL PROJECT: PART 2
# Pearl Diver Punch

1½ oz. lightly aged rum

¾ oz. Demerara rum

½ oz. aged Jamaican rum

¾ oz. lime juice

1 oz. orange juice

¾ oz. gardenia mix

1 tsp. falernum

Combine in mixing tin with crushed ice, adding gardenia mix near the end to keep it from sticking. Flash blend for 15 seconds and pour unstrained into a Pearl Diver glass, topping with fresh crushed ice as needed. Garnish with a purple orchid, pineapple frond, or the food-safe flora of your choice. Note that there should not be solid residue from the gardenia mix, but if there is, fine strain the mixture and fill the glass with fresh crushed ice instead.

Combine the ingredients in the milkshake mixer with crushed ice. Run the blender about three times longer than you normally would, on the order of 15 seconds—the gardenia mix is heavy, and you want to make sure it gets fully integrated. Then pour the whole beautiful mess into your favorite decorative vessel and top with fresh crushed ice.

The traditional Pearl Diver glass is sort of like a ribbed highball glass that opens into a shallow dish at the top. Smoke 'em if you got 'em. Otherwise, go for whatever seems fittingly elaborate.

The gardenia mix is doing a lot of the flavor work in this recipe, unsurprisingly. Granted, there are three rums, including the crown jewels from Jamaica and Guyana, but the recipe's principal conversation is between its base rum blend and the gardenia mix, with the falernum and juices in supporting roles.

If it takes you a couple of tries to get the Pearl Diver Punch right, don't worry about it. You'll have plenty of vanilla syrup to work with if you used the recipe I gave you. And even if you got it on the first go, I encourage you to take some time to practice it. Don't rely on beginner's luck. You've come to the end of a long, intense study of rums and densely packed flavor; savor the meditativeness of getting this right. Take your time.

# Topics in Contemporary Mixology

**We have** now arrived at the final chapter of our journey together, a review of the modern—and in some cases the postmodern—state of the art of the cocktail. This seminar will be presented in the style of a 500-level university course, which is to say one intended for the most advanced undergraduates or first-year graduate students. Instruction at this level presumes a firm understanding of the basics, some exposure to specialty subtopics, and a certain amount of experience in formulating original answers to important questions in the field.

You should by now have sufficient grounding to meet that standard. The previous seminars have prepared you to deal thoughtfully with new ingredients, find balance within mixological structures of arbitrary complexity, and discerningly consider situations without a single right answer.

My confidence in your abilities at this stage means this seminar will be a little different from the previous ones. First, I have added more recipes for Further Reading. In many previous cases I have separated recipes that had subtle distinctions between them. At this point in your study of the cocktail, I assume that doing so is no longer necessary and you can recognize when drinks work for similar reasons. I have also increased the assessments from three to five, enabling us to consider more novel ingredients than we otherwise could; this permits the inclusion of a higher proportion of significant modern drinks than our ordinary recipe restrictions would allow. It's not so much that one-off ingredients are especially popular today, as that we have not yet had enough time for the Cocktail Renaissance's creative dust to settle and the era's true staples to become apparent.

In the ensuing pages, I will bring us as near to the cutting edge of the present as we can get. We will consider the uses of unfamiliar ingredients in modern recipes that employ classical techniques and balances and then swiftly dispense with them to investigate ever more baroque preparations.

Our theme for this unit is, at last, the Cocktail Renaissance period itself, which first began to bubble up in the late twentieth century, when Dale Degroff was tending bar at the Rainbow Room and the first wave of organic growers and microbreweries was lapping at the public's consciousness. It gained steam in the 1990s, abetted as we have previously discussed by everything from internet forums to the same nostalgia that drove the swing revival. Seminal texts were published at the turn of the millennium, and in the aughts the spark of the cocktail met the tinder of hipster retrophilia and the sturdy logs of renewed public interest in all things craft. It was the era of *The Omnivore's Dilemma*, of vinyl and vintage, of a newfound market for the local and the handmade. It was a boom time for serious cocktail programs.

I've touched on all this earlier in the context of revitalizing older cocktails. But the spirit of revival was never the only thing: it coincided with a burst of inventiveness by those simultaneously wringing the past dry of its wisdom. The best programs tended to do both at once—and over time, as the water level fell lower in the well of history, serious bartenders focused more and more on the new and exciting. In time, this would beget the glittering Cocktail Baroque Period, but for the better part of thirty years it was an instrument for restoring respectability to the mixological arts, working in tandem with the revival of classic recipes toward the same goals.

As with previous eras, there are some recurring themes among the ingredients that became prominent in this period. The spirits of Mexico were big winners, with first tequila and later mezcal becoming staples at cocktail bars the world over. Bitter amari and fortified wines won the hearts of bartenders, with Aperol, Cynar, and Punt e Mes making frequent appearances. Spicy, savory, salty, and smoky flavors that previously had little business behind the bar were becoming stars in their own right. Fresh fruits and lush natural sweeteners like agave nectar and maple syrup were revelatory after decades of prepackaged corn syrup mixes. And no single ingredient more effectively conquered both high and low mixology than elderflower liqueur, a new creation realized by Ron Cooper in 2007.

These new ingredients emerged alongside new techniques. The dry shake, introduced way back in seminar two, was a creation of the

Renaissance period. Some places began smoking their cocktails; others would "wash" their ingredients with fats to extract flavor or infuse them with tea and spices to impart it. Small barrels made their way behind the bar for multiweek cocktail aging experiments. Dave Arnold, not to be outdone, got himself a rotary evaporator to make house extracts and eventually began selling a countertop centrifuge cheap enough for other bars to use.

Our work thus far culminates in this. Like the pioneers of the cocktail's future have done, we will test the boundaries of the mixological rules established in our study to date. We now know enough to begin to break them.

# Ingredients for This Course

## GROCERY

| | |
|---|---|
| agave nectar* | **1, 15** |
| Angostura bitters | **2, 15, 18, 24, 29, 30** |
| cucumbers* | **18** |
| eggs | **2, 24** |
| falernum | **28** |
| ginger syrup/soda | **20, 22** |
| grapefruit | **26** |
| honey/honey syrup | **22** |
| lemons | **2, 3, 5–7, 11, 13, 14, 17, 19, 21–25, 29** |
| limes | **1, 8, 18, 20, 26, 27** |

| | |
|---|---|
| maple syrup* | **2, 19, 30** |
| mint | **3, 18, 20, 27** |
| orange bitters | **7, 11, 13, 23** |
| oranges | **4, 15, 16, 30** |
| orgeat | **29** |
| peach bitters* | **12** |
| Peychaud's Bitters | **16, 19, 28** |
| pineapple juice | **25** |
| rich demerara syrup | **24, 27** |
| rose water* | **18** |
| seltzer | **4, 17** |
| sugar/simple syrup | **3, 6, 17, 18, 20, 25** |

\* indicates new ingredients

† bottled or homemade for final project

# ALCOHOL

| | |
|---|---|
| aged Jamaican rum | 19 |
| amaretto* | 24 |
| Amaro Nonino* | 14, 16 |
| Amer Picon | 28 |
| Aperol* | 4, 8, 14 |
| apple brandy | 16, 25 |
| aquavit* | 12 |
| blanc vermouth | 17 |
| blended Scotch | 22 |
| bourbon | 3, 14, 30 |
| brandy | 25 |
| cachaça/rhum agricole | 17 |
| Campari | 5 |
| cask-strength bourbon* | 24 |
| crème de mûre* | 6 |
| crème de violette | 7, 17 |
| curaçao/triple sec | 5, 25 |
| Cynar/carciofo* | 9, 12, 23, 27 |
| elderflower liqueur* | 11, 13, 21, 26 |
| fat-washed spirit(s)*† | 30 |
| filtered lightly aged rum | 27 |
| Green Chartreuse | 25, 27, 28 |
| high-proof rye whiskey | 9, 29 |
| Irish whiskey | 13 |
| Islay Scotch* | 13, 22 |
| Kina apéritif wine | 7 |
| London dry gin | 5–7, 18, 20, 26 |
| maraschino | 8, 10 |
| mezcal* | 8, 15, 21 |
| moderately aged rum | 28 |
| 151-proof Demerara rum | 19 |
| Punt e Mes* | 10, 21 |
| rye whiskey | 2, 10, 16 |
| sherry | 12 |
| sparkling wine/Champagne | 4 |
| sweet vermouth | 9, 16, 23 |
| tequila | 1, 11, 15 |
| Yellow Chartreuse | 11, 26 |

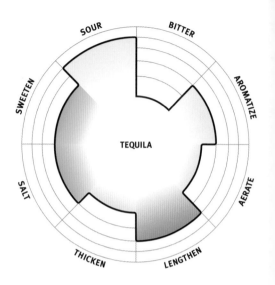

SOUR BITTER AROMATIZE AERATE LENGTHEN THICKEN SALT SWEETEN

**TEQUILA**

**Agave is the name** for a whole family of succulents—not cacti, as is sometimes said—found in Mexico and parts of Central America and the U.S. Tequila is made from blue agave specifically, in the Mexican states of Guanajuato, Michoacán, Nayarit, or Jalisco, with production concentrated in the last.

Just as one must make wine to make brandy, tequila production begins by fermenting the juice of the agave plant into pulque. The plants have long, beautiful, pointed fronds radiating out from a central core which, when denuded of them, looks something like a pineapple. For this reason, the cores are referred to as *piñas*. They are cooked to break their complex molecules down into sugar, then crushed or shredded to extract the juice, which is allowed to ferment.

The resulting pulque may be drunk as is or distilled into tequila, a spirit known for a certain vegetal savoriness that places it in an entirely different sandbox of flavor than most other spirits, Martinique rhums agricoles and certain gins excluded.

Julio Bermejo invented this Margarita variation at Tommy's Mexican Restaurant, his family's place in Richmond, California. At a time when mixto (i.e., blended) tequila was the standard, Bermejo's first taste of a 100 percent agave product was a revelation. He revamped

# Tommy's Margarita

Salt half the rim of a rocks glass and fill with ice. Shake with ice and strain into glass. Garnish with a wedge of lime.

2 oz. reposado tequila

1 oz. lime juice

½ oz. agave nectar

*Adapted from a recipe by Julio Bermejo, Tommy's Mexican Restaurant, San Francisco*

the bar's Margarita with it, also cutting the sour mix and eventually the curaçao; the latter he replaced with agave syrup to highlight and reinforce his base spirit's flavor.

We may consider this an example of the West Coast approach to reviving the art of the cocktail. Bartenders working in the Pacific states drew inspiration from the farm-to-table restaurants that were the region's driving culinary force. Fresh herbs, citrus juiced to order, and adjusting recipes to accommodate the idiosyncrasies of the day's produce were common features. Agave syrup—the boiled, concentrated juice of the agave plant—fits within this tradition as well. Less refined than cane sugar, more agricultural than a liqueur, and close to the same land from which the spirit came, its use makes the Tommy's Margarita a sort of tequila analogue to the Ti' Punch. To keep it from overthickening the drink—and to hold all that lime juice in check—we revisit our fix-style technique of shaking and serving on the rocks. We'll see that repeatedly in this seminar.

The Tommy's has become so popular it rivals the original Margarita. It even masquerades under that name on cocktail menus around the globe. Some split the difference and use both agave and orange liqueur. After trying the Tommy's, I encourage you to experiment and find your own house version, as Bermejo did.

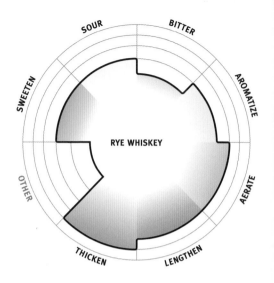

**The Filibuster** is another California recipe that turns on a natural sweetener, in this case maple syrup. Recall from our discussions of rich demerara syrup that it has roughly the same density of sugars per unit of volume as maple syrup; they can therefore be conveniently substituted for each other. However, they also each have unique aromatic components, so although they will tend in similar flavor directions, such substitutions still result in cocktails with noticeably different profiles.

Contemporary bartenders often want more than just sweetness from their sweeteners. Table sugar does a perfectly fine job introducing glucose and viscosity, but other ingredients can make aromatic contributions as well. Maple syrup had appeared here and there in recipe guides over the years, but in the farmer's market–friendly environment of the Cocktail Renaissance it won a permanent place behind the bar. Agave syrup did the same as a complete newcomer.

Dry shaken because of the egg white and sweetened using a natural syrup, the Filibuster echoes honey drinks as well as egg sours. It is the first drink we have seen to bridge this gap. The depth of the maple gives it an almost fliplike quality as well, even absent the fatty substrate of the yolk and despite the presence of bright citrus. If the flip is a particularly wintry drink, the Filibuster is an egg sour for all seasons.

# Filibuster

2 oz. rye whiskey

½ oz. lemon juice

½ oz. maple syrup

egg white

3–5 drops Angostura bitters

Shake all but the bitters without ice, then again with ice. Strain into a chilled cocktail glass and decorate with bitters.

*Adapted from a recipe by Eric Adkins, Trick Dog, San Francisco*

There is one additional novelty to its preparation: using bitters as an aromatic garnish. We have not yet dealt with bitters in egg drinks, but that description should tell you everything you need to know. Like a sprinkle of nutmeg or a sprig of mint, it needs to be positioned where its scent will contribute to each sip. Rather than mixing it in and running the risk that it will get lost under the egg foam or stripped out by it, we add a few drops on top—"decorating" our cocktail. Because the foam itself is not all that aromatic, some bartenders make a habit of decorating *all* of their egg cocktails this way, or at least incorporating some other aromatic element in its place.

We use the terms *garnish* and *decorate* because the bitters provides visual interest as well. They top the foam in a few artistically spaced drops, sometimes formed into shooting stars or other designs with a toothpick. This flourish takes some cues from the latte art that hit the mainstream concurrently with the cocktail revival. Try it for yourself: simple designs are quite easy to learn, but never fail to impress.

### FURTHER READING

The Santiago Flip applies these principles to whole-egg drinks: combine 1½ oz. reposado tequila and ½ oz. agave nectar with a whole egg, dry shake, wet shake, then strain into a cocktail glass. Decorate with five drops of chocolate mole bitters and a sprinkle of cinnamon.

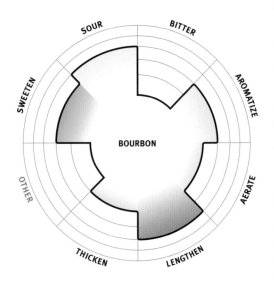

**More than** any person, Dale Degroff deserves credit for jump-starting the Cocktail Renaissance. In the late 1980s, when Joe Baum was re-opening the Rainbow Room, a storied 1930s establishment atop Rockefeller Center, he tapped Degroff to create a top-notch bar program to match the venue's grandeur. He had the right man.

Degroff had come up in a hospitality industry to which the classic cocktail canon was as the ruins of a Roman city to medieval Europeans: evidence of prior achievements was everywhere, even mundane in the eyes of most, but very few people cared to recreate or sustain them. As Robert Simonson put it, "At a time when bartenders largely winged it, he chose to give a damn."

Now, he was reviving those old drinks and techniques, juicing fresh citrus, flaming orange peels—even stirring rather than shaking a Manhattan attracted notice at the time. And he was doing all of this at the hottest spot in New York City, under the spotlight of the world.

Degroff invented plenty of drinks during his tenure, carried to the world by his fame and that of his disciples—Saunders, Reiner, and Petraske among them. Perhaps the cocktail for which he is best known, though, was one he revived: the Whiskey Smash.

# Whiskey Smash

2 oz. bourbon

¾ oz. simple syrup

½ lemon, quartered

1–2 sprigs of mint

In a cocktail shaker, muddle the lemon with the mint and simple syrup. Add whiskey and ice and shake. Strain into a rocks glass filled with ice and garnish with a fresh sprig of mint.

*Adapted from a recipe by Dale Degroff in* The New Craft of the Cocktail

It's a simple drink at first blush, a permutation of the Whiskey Sour, but in the Rainbow Room era it was a revelation. Fresh groceries in a cocktail, the old tools dusted off for use again, a recipe that took time and skill—these were not the hallmarks of just any bar in the 1980s. The agreeable taste of the drink didn't hurt, either.

As with the Caipirinha, the citrus is juiced by muddling, giving us a nice, pulpy preparation with plenty of oil from the peel. This is followed by a regal shake, doubling down on our extraction of flavors from the fresh ingredients and adding a good bit of dilution. This helps avoid the issue I have warned about previously in overmuddled drinks of exposing the scent chemicals to enzymes that render them less wholesome to the senses. That and the potential for getting the bitterness from the lemon pith are held to acceptable levels by the recipe's water content. And like the foregoing Californian recipes, the smash as a style has a certain rusticity. It's meant to highlight the freshness of one's ingredients and the slow-food attitude of one's cocktail program. Slight imperfections are part of the charm.

**FURTHER READING**

For Hamburg bartender Jörg Meyer's Gin Basil Smash, exchange this recipe's whiskey for gin, swap the muddled lemons with 1 oz. of lemon juice, and muddle a fistful of fresh basil rather than 1–2 sprigs of mint.

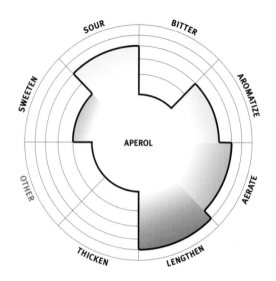

## 5.4

**When the prestige** drama producers of the future get around to setting films or television shows in the late Cocktail Renaissance, they will use the Spritz as shorthand for the cocktail culture of the period, much as we do with the Scotch and Soda for the 1950s. It has won the hearts and minds of an era, converting professionals in hospitality and amateurs at brunch alike.

Ironically, nothing about it is particularly new. Understood as simply a combination of soda, bitter liqueur, and sparkling wine, the Spritz has been around for ages, principally in Italy and especially in the Veneto region where it originated. It could be made with any amaro, but Campari was often the only option in other countries.

The Spritz benefited from the early twenty-first century explosion in interest in amari and wisely hitched its wagon to Aperol, the category's breakout spirit. Much like Campari, Aperol is bittersweet, citrusy, and more or less fire engine red. But compared with Campari, it is less sweet, less bitter, and less spiritous, clocking in at a refreshing 11% ABV as opposed to 24%. While the Negroni had made great strides converting the world to red Italian bitters, Campari was still challenging to most palates. Aperol, while Campari-like enough to interest maturing taste buds, is more accessible to the general public.

# (Aperol) Spritz

3 oz. sparkling wine

2 oz. Aperol

1 oz. seltzer

Combine ingredients in a wine glass with ice and stir. Garnish with a large wedge of orange.

*Adapted from traditional Italian recipes*

Mixed into a Spritz, it becomes downright quaffable. The cocktail is "juicy" in the same way that an IPA or a fresh peach can be juicy. It makes the mouth water, while pricking up our senses with inoffensive levels of sweet, tart, and bitter. This effect is enhanced by its usual garnish: a big wedge of orange, not juiced into the mixture but allowed to aromatize each sip. It is ordinarily eaten after the drink is finished, when it has absorbed some of the Spritz.

The Aperol Spritz is often served in a stemmed glass with ice and a straw, a preparation we have not previously encountered. While in general I advise serving iced drinks in stemless glasses and reserving stemware for shaken or stirred recipes, we have already seen that this is not a hard-and-fast rule (e.g., with the Sazerac).

Serving the Aperol Spritz down and on the rocks would fit our expectations for built drinks. But we also want to be careful to avoid melting the ice too quickly—the spirits are low in proof and already diluted by the seltzer, so we have little room for dilution. We could shake or stir the drink, to cap the amount of added water, but we would lose more effervescence with either method than we would by building it. The alternative is to move the whole apparatus—ice, vessel, and cocktail—away from the warm, ice-melting influence of the hand. Thus, we end up serving our cocktail on the rocks in a wineglass.

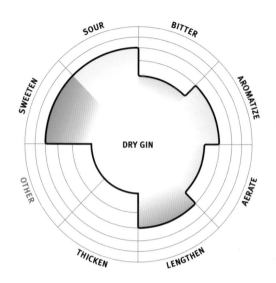

**For the most part,** the recipes in this seminar use new ingredients, novel techniques, or both, but the Renaissance has also produced its share of drinks that require neither. As practitioners reintroduced elements from the golden age of cocktailery, they could experiment with them, often coming up with winning combinations which had been overlooked in the past. There is something to be said for fresh eyes, after all: the Gold Rush fits this mold, as does the Jasmine.

Its creator, Paul Harrington, was a bartender at Townhouse in Emeryville, California, in the 1990s. He was also part of the vanguard trying to dethrone vodka and restore gin to its proper place in the public consciousness. He would regularly suggest the Pegu Club, of which he was a fan, to those open to expanding their palates.

These days, if you walk into a bar and ask the bartender to create something new for you on the spot, you're more likely to annoy than to inspire them. But in the early Renaissance, when craft cocktails were still a niche interest and knowledge flowed freely across the bar in both directions, it could be a fun challenge on a slow night, something that built bonds between bartenders and their regulars and kept skills sharp.

# Jasmine

1½ oz. London dry gin

¾ oz. lemon juice

¼ oz. Campari

¼ oz. curaçao or triple sec

Shake with ice. Strain into a chilled cocktail glass.

*Adapted from a recipe by Paul Harrington, Townhouse, Emeryville, California*

So it came to pass that Harrington's friend Matt Jasmin waltzed in one night asking for something new and Harrington obliged, whipping up a drink with structural similarities to the Pegu Club but with Campari doing the job of the latter's simple syrup and bitters. Jasmin informed him that he had invented grapefruit juice. Harrington named the drink after the man who had induced him to create it, realizing only years later that he had been misspelling his last name.

The drink made it past Townhouse's doors and out of Emeryville in part because Harrington published one of the first bar guides of the Renaissance, the aptly titled *Cocktail: The Drinks Bible for the 21st Century* in 1998. From there, it got picked up by everyone from Paul Clarke of *The Cocktail Chronicles* to the Bellagio in Las Vegas and was swiftly established as a modern standard. That it had the same rosy blush as the Cosmo—a well-made one, anyhow—did not hurt its popularity or endear it less to the growing cocktail community, who could now with a wink and a nod have something more interesting that looked just like what everyone else was drinking.

**FURTHER READING**

For Katie Stipe's Siesta, another Campari-kissed sour, combine 1½ oz. blanco tequila with ¾ oz. simple syrup, ½ oz. each of grapefruit and lime juice, and ¼ oz. Campari. Shake, strain, and serve up.

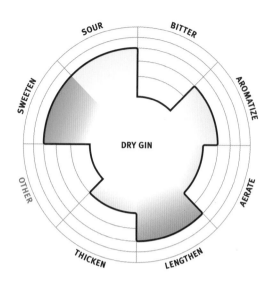

SOUR · BITTER · AROMATIZE · AERATE · LENGTHEN · THICKEN · OTHER · SWEETEN

DRY GIN

# SOLUTION

I know it's been a while, but think back to seminar one. Crème liqueurs are required to have a high sugar content, which makes them viscous and creamy. That tells us everything we need to understand this recipe.

We want it to be fruity without being cloying. That means we want to maximize aroma without adding too much unanswered sugar. Bradsell's solution to the latter problem is to serve this fix-style, both shaken and on the rocks. Keep your eye on that shaken-rocks technique: it will crop up a lot this seminar.

Dilution answers the sugar, but it's only half the battle. To maximize aroma per unit of crème de mûre, we **drizzle** it over the top of the finished drink. This is similar to floating, but done with heavier ingredients that we expect to sink. Drizzling makes the most sense when there's something to impede that process—a pulpy juice, crushed ice, etc. It also preserves the rusticity of the drink, ensuring that each sip is a little different.

1/2 oz. crème de mûre

1/2 oz. simple syrup

3/4 oz. lemon juice

2 oz. London dry gin

Shake all but crème de mûre with ice. Strain into a rocks glass filled with fresh ice and drizzle crème de mûre on top. Garnish with a slice of lemon and 1–2 blackberries speared on a toothpick.

*Adapted from a recipe by Dick Bradsell, Fred's Club, London*

# EXERCISE
# Bramble

London dry gin

lemon juice

simple syrup

crème de mûre

*Using the given ingredients, determine the proportions of the Bramble and its method of preparation.*

**I use** "West Coast" to describe the close-to-the-earth style of the last few drinks, but geography is not destiny. Dick Bradsell's Bramble fits the type just as well—despite hailing from the United Kingdom.

What Dale Degroff was to New York, Bradsell was to London. The bar that bore his name would remain an essential training ground for the British Cocktail Renaissance even after his departure. His impressive roster of original recipes includes the Vodka Espresso, more commonly—if improperly—called the Espresso Martini.

The Bramble is right up there with it in popularity, particularly in the UK. Today, its most noteworthy ingredient is crème de mûre, a French blackberry liqueur—but while this was unheard of in the early 1990s, the choice to use gin as a base spirit was only slightly less offbeat. Bradsell was inspired by the aroma of the crème de mûre, which transported him to a blackberry patch from his childhood on the Isle of Wight, and created a drink that was thoroughly British. That it ignored the cocktail fashions of the day was immaterial; it was a hit.

Consider the crème liqueurs we have worked with previously and how one might integrate them into a cocktail in the farm-fresh West Coast style. Make sure the crème de mûre really sings—we want the drinker to end up in that Isle of Wight blackberry patch, too!

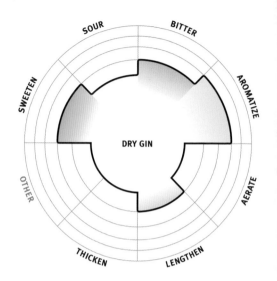

SOUR BITTER AROMATIZE SWEETEN DRY GIN OTHER AERATE THICKEN LENGTHEN

**If Harrington's** Jasmine shows us the archetype of making the new from the old, the Deep Blue Sea is an example of making the new with the new-again. Two of its ingredients were successfully revived; it could more easily have been invented in 1930 than in 1990. It shares elements with both the Martini and the Yale, but its flavor axis involves bright citrus and bitter quinine as well as delicate violet. It is emblematic of the Milk & Honey house style, in which one mastered the classics first and innovated only gradually, informed by traditional recipe structures.

I have mentioned Milk & Honey and its founder, Sasha Petraske, in prior seminars. "The Bar Heard Round the World," as it was called in *Punch*, had an incalculable influence on the trajectory of the Cocktail Renaissance after opening in 1999. Petraske was more an enthusiast than a bartender at the outset, a man with very strong convictions about craft and hospitality who built a bar in a former mah-jongg parlor with neither money nor expertise. His list of house rules was not ironic; he expected guests to behave at a time when bars were known for quite the opposite. Mandatory reservations and a frequently changing phone number came about at least in part because Petraske was committed to being a good neighbor in a mostly residential neighborhood and wanted to avoid rowdy would-be patrons lining up at the door. He disliked press coverage even when it was positive, and

# Deep Blue Sea

2 oz. London dry gin

¾ oz. Kina apéritif wine

¼ oz. crème de violette

2 dashes orange bitters

Stir with ice and strain into a chilled cocktail glass. Express a lemon peel over the glass and discard.

*Adapted from a recipe by Michael Madrusan, Milk & Honey, New York*

would probably have been displeased to be a topic in this book.* Nevertheless, his influence on the field is undeniable.

It is well established that Petraske drew inspiration from the civilized drinking experience he had at a Japanese bar called Angel's Share, but it was through Milk & Honey that that approach to drinking reached the rest of the world.† Petraske fostered strong loyalties among his employees and partnered with many of them to open a slew of influential bars. He also cofounded the San Antonio Cocktail Conference, unique among major cocktail conventions in donating its proceeds to charity.

* Sadly, Petraske did not live long enough to experience that annoyance. He died of a heart attack in 2015 at the age of forty-two. He had already turned Milk & Honey over to his employees Sam Ross and Michael McIlroy, whose bar Attaboy still occupies the space. He had also begun work on a cocktail book. His wife, Georgette Moger-Petraske, collected his writings as well as recipes and reflections from bartenders in the Milk & Honey family into the posthumously published *Regarding Cocktails*.

† Or the rest of the Western world, at least. The Japanese bar tradition has been increasingly recognized in recent years for its unwavering commitment to craft, detail, and guest experience. Japan's cocktail culture has also placed far less of a premium on novelty than its Western counterparts over the decades, and as a result has been able to refine itself without undergoing cyclical complete transformations. In the United States, Milk & Honey was the apogee of one of those cycles; in Japan, bars like Angel's Share are the norm.

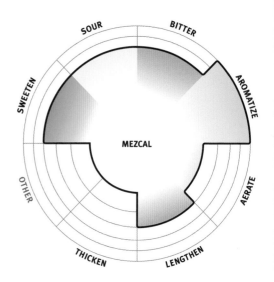

SOUR · BITTER · AROMATIZE · AERATE · LENGTHEN · THICKEN · OTHER · SWEETEN

MEZCAL

**If Mexican spirits** were underrated outside their home country before, the Cocktail Renaissance made amends and then some. Mezcal has undergone the most dramatic rehabilitation: dozens of estate expressions are now available, coveted and priced like rare bottles of Scotch or Cognac, while having a basic mixing mezcal has become a necessity for a serious cocktail program.

By law, mezcal can be made in nine Mexican states, from any sort of agave. This includes blue agave, but if the product is made from blue agave in a state where it *could* be labeled tequila, it *must* be labeled tequila rather than mezcal. Essentially, Mexico has defined the two to be mutually exclusive. The general term *agave spirits* has entered common parlance to refer to the overall category.

Another significant difference is in the production process. In the case of mezcal, the agave *piñas* are traditionally cooked in a covered pit for days, infusing a smoky flavor into the raw material before the fermentation or distillation even takes place. That smokiness carries through to the distillate and is a signature element of its flavor.

Mezcal is also known for the savory and plantlike characteristics it shares with tequila. Because mezcals are mostly unaged, there is no vanilla oakiness to them, and the flavors contributed by the agave plants

# Division Bell

1 oz. mezcal

¾ oz. Aperol

¾ oz. lime juice

½ oz. maraschino

Shake with ice. Strain into a chilled cocktail glass. Optionally, garnish with an orange or grapefruit peel.

*Adapted from a recipe by Phil Ward, Death & Co., New York*

are not stripped out by adsorption. Fresh and even flowery aspects can make it through the still. It's common to label mezcal by the specific agave varietal used, reflecting the diversity of options available and the significant flavor distinctions among them. Espadin is the most common varietal, especially at a cocktail-friendly price point.

Like tequila, mezcal has inspired mixological experimentation in the realms of taste outside the sweet, sour, and bitter that have historically been cocktails' bread and butter. In the Division Bell, the freshness of the lime and Aperol and the floweriness of the maraschino pick up on the elements of mezcal that are most like an unaged tequila or most governed by the varietal being used. The deeper, more brooding aspect of the smokiness is set off against the stonefruit-pit nuttiness of the liqueur and the bitter orange of the Aperol, while the savoriness of the mezcal is clarified by the sourness of the lime.

The result is a harmonious encapsulation of the contemporary cocktail zeitgeist, employing period signatures like mezcal, Aperol, and the unexpected with equal deftness. It has been called a should-be classic by Robert Simonson and a future classic by Simon Difford; if anything, I think those assessments are too conservative. I first made it when testing recipes for my last book, and after tasting it, I neither felt the need to tweak it nor had any doubts about its inclusion.

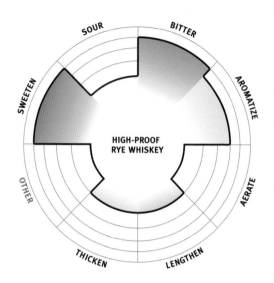

**In addition to** fresh ingredients and all things Mexican, the Cocktail Renaissance has firmly enshrined amari as necessities behind the bar. *Amaro* is the Italian word for "bitter," and the term is used for a variety of herbal liqueurs with pronounced bitter notes. We have seen a few already: Campari, of course, and now Aperol, as well as Amaro Ramazzotti when making Amer Picon back in seminar three.

Classifying amari is a tricky business. There are so many subtle distinctions—proof, sugar content, bitterness, herbs used—that they are ordinarily referred to by brand rather than category. Where it is possible to put them into a taxonomy, it is most often due to a signature ingredient, like rhubarb in rabarbaro or arugula in rucolino.*

Of these, carciofo has attained the greatest success in modern cocktails, represented in most cases—and in most recipe books—by the venerable Italian brand Cynar. I have stuck to the convention of using Cynar as a metonym for all carciofi in this section, on the grounds that it will be the only option available in many places. If, however, you have access to another one, you should feel free to substitute.

---

* Amari of this type generally share names with the plants that distinguish them— e.g., *carciofo* is the Italian word for "artichoke," while *rucolino* is a diminutive of the word for "arugula."

# Little Italy

2 oz. high-proof rye whiskey

¾ oz. sweet vermouth

½ oz. Cynar

Stir with ice. Strain into a chilled cocktail glass and garnish with three brandied or maraschino cherries on a toothpick.

*Adapted from a recipe by Audrey Saunders, Pegu Club, New York*

The success of carciofo speaks to the tastes of the times: novel, herbal, bitter, savory but not overly so, above all an enticing opportunity for experimentation. Audrey Saunders, who already had a reputation as a cocktail creator when she opened Pegu Club in 2005, invented the Little Italy to mark the occasion. It harmonizes elements from both her prior experience and the neighborhood that was welcoming her new venture.

A popular application of amari has been to replace some portion of the vermouth and bitters in a Manhattan-style preparation. This is possible because amari do similar things to spirits: sweeten, bitter, and intensely aromatize, all without overly attenuating the strength of the drink. In some cases, this has gone as far as preparing Manhattan-like cocktails with no vermouth whatsoever.

I think Saunders's recipe takes a more compelling route. Retaining the vermouth preserves a rich texture that's more difficult to replicate with an amaro. The savoriness of the carciofo is subtle, its bitter herbaceousness more prominent—akin in some ways to adding a rinse of Chartreuse or absinthe to one's Manhattan. In this respect it has elements in common with the Remember the Maine, but skewed in a more vegetal direction.

**Another way** to work amaro into a vermouth cocktail is to put some of it *into* the vermouth. This is the approach taken by Punt e Mes, a venerable product and contemporary success story consisting of two parts vermouth and one part amaro bottled together. This style is more generally known as *vermouth con bitter*, but here again, Punt e Mes will be the only game in town in most places outside Italy. You can generally substitute another vermouth con bitter if you can find one; you can also make your own approximation by combining two parts of sweet vermouth with one part amaro; I find Cynar works quite well.

In a world awash in amari and everything "stirred, bitter, and boozy," Punt e Mes found a natural home in places where unbittered vermouths were not enough for the bitter-tilted balance then ascendant. It also endeared itself to bartenders looking to adapt rather than replicate the classics.

Such is the case with the Red Hook, one of many responses to the artistic and existential crisis of the Brooklyn Cocktail in the Renaissance era. The borough on the bleeding edge of modern mixology had an ancestral namesake cocktail, but it could not be made without taking great pains to acquire—or substitute for—Amer Picon. Manhattan, the Bronx, and even Queens could drink their hometown classics whenever they liked, but Brooklyn could not.

# Red Hook

2 oz. rye whiskey

½ oz. maraschino

½ oz. Punt e Mes

Stir with ice. Strain into a chilled cocktail glass.

*Adapted from a recipe by Vincenzo Errico, Milk & Honey, New York*

Enterprising barkeeps responded by inventing a slew of Brooklyn-*inspired* recipes, all named after the borough's neighborhoods. Vincenzo Errico's Red Hook is the simplest and most enduring, hewing close to the style of its forebear. If we break down the Punt e Mes for our analysis, we have rye, maraschino, sweet vermouth, and amaro, the last being the only real departure from the Brooklyn—although the linguistically inclined reader may note that the *amer* in Amer Picon is cognate with *amaro*, correctly inferring this is a product in the same general class.

**FURTHER READING**

Too much talk about New York neighborhoods, not enough about Boston bartenders. The 1910 elaborates on the Red Hook's techniques by splitting the bases and adding bitters back in. It was created by Ezra Star during her time at the helm of Drink, where a rum-and-whiskey drink called the 1919 is a house specialty. The 1919 is named in honor of the Great Molasses Flood, Star's variation for the year of the Mexican Revolution that brought down the regime of Porfirio Díaz. To make it, combine ¾ oz. each mezcal and brandy, ½ oz. maraschino, 1 oz. Punt e Mes, and 2 dashes Peychaud's. Stir, strain, serve up; express an orange peel over the top and discard.

# 5.11

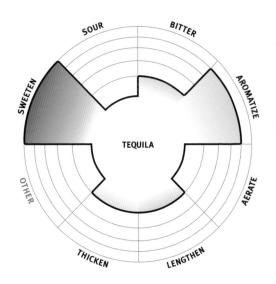

**In 2007**, Robert Cooper secured his legacy on every backbar in the United States with the release of St.-Germain. As a flavor, elderflower had been known for centuries in Europe. There were elderflower cordials, nonalcoholic syrups used for soft drinks and confectionaries, but until Cooper there was no significant elderflower liqueur category. You will find it conspicuously absent from pre-Renaissance bar guides.

Cooper had liqueurs in his blood: his family had produced crème de violette's more intricate doppelgänger, Creme Yvette.* St.-Germain's international success was such that he could revive the heirloom liqueur decades after it had ceased production. While the Creme Yvette of the third millennium has remained a relatively niche product, St.-Germain became so popular it was nicknamed "bartender's ketchup"—i.e., you could put that stuff on anything.

Several newly successful modern cocktail ingredients do not have recognized canonical recipes, often because not enough time has passed to learn which drinks have staying power. With St.-Germain, *all* of its recipes have staying power. Once you taste it, you can guess

---

* Cooper was working for the family liqueur business when he left to start St.-Germain. His father somewhat famously offered to hire him back in a year, expecting the elderflower liqueur to be unsuccessful; instead, his son created a global sensation and sold the brand to Bacardi for an undisclosed sum.

# Yellow Jacket

2 oz. reposado tequila

1 oz. elderflower liqueur

¾ oz. Yellow Chartreuse

1 dash orange bitters

Stir with ice and strain into a chilled cocktail glass. Express a lemon peel over the glass and discard.

*Adapted from a recipe by Jason Kosmas and Dushan Zaric, Employees Only, New York*

its most popular preparations—in a sour, with sparkling wine, etc. Those drinks have been invented independently many times, making them hard to attribute and harder to conclusively name. I will stick to recipes that have some measure of individual renown—or that I think ought to—which use elderflower liqueur in interesting, less obvious ways.

Structurally, the Yellow Jacket splits the difference between the Alaska and a true duo in the Reganian sense. The base spirit anchoring a drink aromatically dominated by its sweeteners, the complex and spirited Chartreuse and the crowd-pleasing elderflower liqueur. This is a heavy dose of liqueur, and both the bitters and the lemon peel are necessary to keep all that sugar in check. What is remarkable is that no more is necessary: the Chartreuse is dry enough and the tequila robust enough that balance can be achieved with relatively subtle adjustments in the directions of bitter and bright.

The source of this recipe is *Speakeasy* by Jason Kosmas and Dushan Zaric, the house cocktail book of Employees Only and one of the earliest twenty-first-century coffee-table recipe books put out by bars of stature. It was the first good cocktail guide I owned, given to me before the first meeting of MIX110b, and it undoubtedly had a major impact upon that course and the trajectory of my mixological thought.

# 5.12

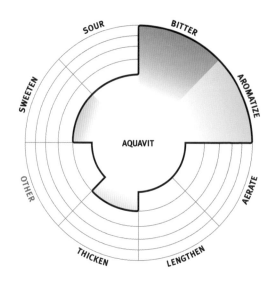

Around the wheel: SOUR · BITTER · AROMATIZE · AERATE · LENGTHEN · THICKEN · OTHER · SWEETEN

AQUAVIT

## SOLUTION

Hess has described the Trident as a Negroni in which he switched out each of the ingredients for something more obscure. Structurally, it works for all the same reasons. Like gin, aquavit holds its weight deceptively well against forceful ingredients. Sherry is aromatically intricate and strong in a supporting role. Cynar is bitter and herbal and hits your palate like a cinder block.

Peach bitters date back to the nineteenth century, but by the early Cocktail Renaissance it was more of a novelty, made only by the stalwart Fee Brothers of upstate New York. Hess has written that he was motivated to include it in part because so few recipes did. It fills in gaps in cocktails like mortar, just as orange bitters does—Hess recommends trying the Trident with one dash of each.

It is strange now to think about a globally successful recipe coming from a nonprofessional, but it was possible in the early Renaissance, when enthusiasm and expertise were in short supply and anyone with a little of both could make a significant contribution. Hess would go on to write a cocktail book of his own and cofound the Museum of the American Cocktail.

1 oz. aquavit
1 oz. sherry
1 oz. Cynar
2 dashes peach bitters

Combine ingredients in a rocks glass with ice and stir.

*Adapted from a recipe by Robert Hess, DrinkBoy, Seattle*

# EXERCISE
# Trident

aquavit

sherry

Cynar

peach bitters

*Using the given ingredients, determine the proportions of the Trident and its method of preparation.*

**The Trident** may be the most successful modern drink invented by an enthusiast rather than a bartender. Robert Hess was working at Microsoft when he developed an interest in cocktails. He was an autodidact, but he had exacting standards; Murray Stenson remembers him bringing his own bitters into the bars he patronized.

The cocktail's gravity well never pulled Hess into a bartending career, but he did end up in a tidally locked orbit. In 1998, he launched a website called DrinkBoy, where he gathered information about cocktails as well as fellow lovers of the art—among them Haigh, Saunders, Regan, and Degroff. His site filled a need for connection among people with an interest in, as Hess puts it, "cocktails as a cuisine instead of just an alcohol delivery vehicle." Others like it would soon follow.

Hess shared the Trident recipe on DrinkBoy, and his audience brought it to bars from coast to coast. It was built for success: each ingredient was unusual and packed with complexity. In addition to Cynar and sherry, it used aquavit—Scandinavia's answer to gin, with dill and caraway as its predominant flavors. It called for peach bitters at a time when the less obscure orange bitters had yet to be fully revived.

It may not be obvious, but the Trident is structurally very similar to another recipe we've seen. Consider which one it is, and then read on!

# 5.13

**A lot of people** have contributed to the contemporary cocktail canon, and this seminar necessarily presents an idiosyncratic snapshot of that rogues' gallery. Dick Bradsell and Julie Reiner are underrepresented, their recipes tending to use at least one ingredient I could not easily work in. Not appearing much in these pages should therefore not be taken as a sign of casting only a short shadow over the industry.

That said, appearing frequently does tend to signify a major role. Phil Ward, the author of the Division Bell, is responsible for three of the thirty recipes in this seminar, tying him with Saunders for first place.

In the tight community of New York City bartending, Ward had worked for both Reiner and Saunders before being hired by the founders of Death & Co. to serve as its first head bartender. St.-Germain launched the same year and found a ready audience.

Like Employees Only and many others, Death & Co. would eventually put out an official bar book. In theirs, the Cooper Union is in the Sazerac section, a parallel not immediately apparent but impossible to forget once revealed. A highly aromatic spirit rinses a glass, while another base spirit is stirred with bitters and sweetener and then poured into it, served in a rocks glass even though it is stirred rather than built, because it is too much like an Old Fashioned to have on a stem.

# Cooper Union

2 oz. Irish whiskey

½ oz. elderflower liqueur

1 dash orange bitters

¼ oz. Islay Scotch (rinse)

Stir Irish whiskey, elderflower liqueur, and bitters with ice. Strain into a rocks glass rinsed with Islay Scotch. Express a lemon peel over the glass and discard.

*Adapted from a recipe by Phil Ward, Death & Co., New York*

All our Scotch recipes to date have relied upon blended whiskies, the ingenious creation of Scottish distillers to make their most pungent products palatable for foreign audiences. Single malts have seldom been called for—in this book or in cocktails in general—but in a time when mezcal, flamed orange peels, and literal smoke found favor as cocktail ingredients, the smokiest of Islay Scotches found its way into mixed drinks as well. Like absinthe, it appears most commonly as a rinse or otherwise in small doses.* That said, if you enjoy the flavor and would like to drink more of it, feel free to experiment with single-malt versions of our earlier Scotch cocktails.

To me, the most interesting thing about this recipe is how the elder-flower draws out the green notes of the unmalted barley in the single pot still Irish whiskey. A single malt would not work nearly as well here. The liqueur is then tempered by the orange bitters and the whole thing wrapped up in a whispered cloud of peat smoke. One could say the Cooper Union has the flavor of an autumn snowstorm.

---

* You could transfer some of the Scotch into a small spray bottle called an **atomizer**.

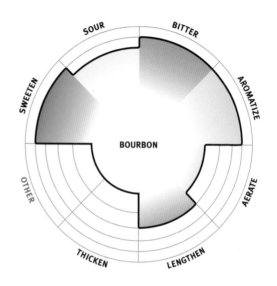

**When Murray Stenson** dusted the obscurity off the Last Word, he helped catalyze an interest in equal-parts cocktails that animates bartenders to this day. The elegant simplicity—to say nothing of the professional challenge—of finding a set of four evenly matched components is naturally attractive.

Sam Ross's Paper Plane is easily the most successful modern equal-parts cocktail, the sort of drink one might now see listed under "classics" on a bar menu without further qualification. As amari of all types have reached the backbars of the world, Amaro Nonino has emerged as a mandatory selection. The Paper Plane has forever inscribed its creator's name in the Book of Cocktails.

It is a tad ironic, then, that Ross created it for a bar where he never worked. Chicago's great temple of modern high mixology, The Violet Hour, opened in 2007, while Ross was tending bar eight hundred miles away at Milk & Honey. But its proprietor, Toby Maloney, was a friend of his and had asked him to contribute something for the opening menu. Ross dutifully obliged.

The original recipe called for Campari rather than Aperol, a substitution Ross made almost immediately and to great effect. Campari

# Paper Plane

¾ oz. bourbon

¾ oz. Aperol

¾ oz. Amaro Nonino

¾ oz. lemon juice

Shake with ice. Strain into a chilled cocktail glass.

*Adapted from a recipe by Sam Ross, Milk & Honey, New York (for The Violet Hour, Chicago)*

makes a much heavier drink; with Aperol, it has zip befitting its name. Although he shared his revision with his Windy City counterparts, the Campari version had already made its debut, and there are Violet Hour regulars to this day who prefer the original spec.

No matter. Simultaneous with its emergence in Chicago—facilitated by The Violet Hour's place at the vanguard of the city's cocktail revival—the Paper Plane was being served at the groundbreaking bar where Ross actually worked. Having two influential bases to expand from helped the Paper Plane take off. By 2014, it had been adopted by the bartenders of Toronto as a local specialty. It gave its name to a bar in San Jose the same year—an honor otherwise reserved for recipes like the Clover Club that have a patina of age.

Amaro Nonino, the unfamiliar ingredient in this recipe, hails from Friuli, a region in northeastern Italy. It is made with a grappa base and bottled at a relatively potent 70% ABV; this gives it a low viscosity by amaro standards, which, when coupled with its carefully moderated bitterness and sugar level, means it presents well with light ingredients in light-bodied cocktails. This, in turn, means that Ross was right about his switch to Aperol.

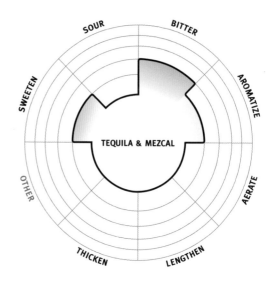

**This is our third** recipe by Phil Ward, enough to begin seeing recurring themes as we did with Donn and Vic. A Ward drink is disproportionately likely to use something smoky, have a "green"-tasting or vegetal component, and incorporate agave in some way. The Oaxaca Old Fashioned, Ward's most famous creation, checks all these boxes.

As its name suggests, it riffs on the original "cock-tail" described by Harry Croswell in 1806. Short built drinks à la the Old Fashioned were created more often in the Renaissance than in most prior eras, reflecting a renewed interest in history, bitters, and spirit-forward preparations. This is not even the only Old Fashioned in this seminar!

Ward's otherwise-classical formulation unites three of the Mexican ingredients we are still learning to use, with one or two additional flourishes. Agave nectar takes the place of plain sugar or simple syrup—an immediate signal that we want the savory and plantlike characteristics of the spirits to come through. Two distillates within the same broad class are united, the smoke and specificity of mezcal blending with the more generalist tequila to form the backbone of the drink. The wood and vanilla notes from the reposado's aging process drop the pitch of the drink down a third or so, where it can resonate with the spices in the bitters and the burnt orange oil.

# Oaxaca Old Fashioned

1½ oz. reposado tequila

½ oz. mezcal

1 tsp. agave nectar

2 dashes Angostura bitters

Combine ingredients in a rocks glass with ice and stir. Flame an orange peel over the glass and drop it in.

*Adapted from a recipe by Phil Ward, Death & Co., New York*

"What do you mean, burnt orange oil?" The Oaxaca Old Fashioned goes a step beyond the expressed citrus peel we have seen before and is instead garnished with a *flamed* orange peel. The same principle applies: cut a swathe of peel, aim it at the glass, and give it a pinch to spray the oils across the surface. The only change is that you hold a lit match between the peel and the drink. The spray of oil passes through the flame, getting toasted and smoked en route. This is even more effective if the peel has been warmed beforehand—pass it briefly over the match before expressing the oils for best results.

Flamed orange peels add a smoky note—or reinforce one—and also contribute an element of caramelized citrus that plays nicely with aged spirits. This is not a new technique, but flaming peels instead of merely expressing them was a mark of attention to craft in the Early Renaissance—and Degroff's trademark at the Rainbow Room. To the generation of bartenders that followed, what had been something of a parlor trick came into its own as a mixological technique.

That said, the theatricality of the flamed peel is undeniable. Done correctly, it creates a flash and a whoosh as the oils ignite, followed by an aroma of smoke wafting gradually throughout the room. It is an excellent promoter of a drink: everyone who sees, hears, or smells it will want to know more.

# 5.16

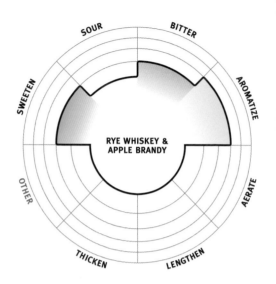

**RYE WHISKEY & APPLE BRANDY**

SOUR · BITTER · AROMATIZE · AERATE · LENGTHEN · THICKEN · OTHER · SWEETEN

**If the Cooper Union** was a stirred drink that presented like a built drink, the Fallback is its inverse. This is our first recipe to use vermouth in a built drink while incorporating spirits at all. We have tended to use fortified wines as bases in their own right or as modifiers in stirred drinks; the Fallback shows us the arbitrariness of that distinction.

It is also unusual, even among the recipes published in *Regarding Cocktails*, for being a Petraske original. Milk & Honey's bread and butter was always the classics, or slight variations thereon. Innovation was fine but not the point; the Petraske school taught discipline, tradition, and mastery of the craft as it was. The leader of this movement was also its exemplar, and most of the new recipes to emerge from Milk & Honey or its offshoots were the inventions of Petraske's bartenders, not his own.

It is particularly ironic, then, that his sole original recipe in this book is included specifically because of its innovative touches. One can parse the Fallback as a built drink that employs a combination of spirited sweeteners in lieu of sugar or simple syrup, having the same structural relationship to the Old Fashioned that the Sidecar has to the Daiquiri. This is perfectly correct—and probably how Petraske would have thought of it.

# Fallback

1 oz. rye whiskey

1 oz. apple brandy

½ oz. sweet vermouth

½ oz. Amaro Nonino

2 dashes Peychaud's Bitters

Combine in a rocks glass with a large ice cube and stir for 10 seconds or until sufficiently chilled. Garnish with an orange twist.

*Adapted from a recipe by Sasha Petraske, Milk & Honey, New York (for the John Dory Oyster Bar, New York)*

Another way to think about it, though, more in keeping with our studies in this seminar, is as a cousin to the fix. It is stirred, not briefly to combine its ingredients, as built drinks are, but so it is fully chilled *before* being served with ice. It's even included in the stirred drinks section of Petraske's posthumous book, rather than the built drinks one, giving further credence to this interpretation. And if it's a stirred-rocks drink, that tells us it is intended to have a relatively high water content. It is meant to be easy drinking, its challenges readily overcome—more Sunday afternoon than Saturday night, if you will.

This is facilitated by the comforting complexities of Amaro Nonino. Giving tasting notes for amari is always dangerous, the things in them being so numerous, and the likelihood of any two people picking out the same flavors being so low. That disclaimed, I would describe its flavor as a honey-orange peel axis that resolves into a blend of alpine herbs on the swallow, with pronounced notes of saffron and thyme and subtler echoes of rhubarb and gentian along the way. Cinnamon is another common note, but I only taste it on the finish. I recommend writing down your own tasting notes before comparing your experience with anyone else's. Palate education is about experience, but it's also about discovering the knowledge you already have. Don't be afraid to give odd tasting notes—that's a sign that your sense memory is good and your ability to pick out specific flavors improving.

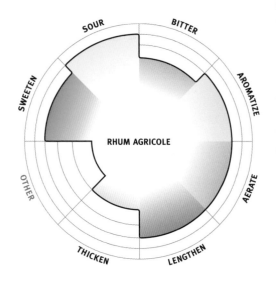

**To avoid getting** too comfortable with any one method of interpretation, let us double back on our analysis of the Fallback as a fix and consider another built recipe using both spirits and vermouth. This one takes things a step further and makes a Collins out of them. For all my gushing about the fizz these past few hundred pages, I cannot deny that there are other innovative long drinks.

This one originated at the Hawthorne in Boston's Kenmore Square, a creation of second-generation Renaissance bartender Jared Sadoian. Like Milk & Honey, the Hawthorne has had a predilection for coming up with new crème de violette cocktails. In this case, the floral liqueur is paired with several unexpectedly excellent partners. The blanc vermouth, for a start, has a highly complementary blend of alpine botanicals to back up the violet fragrance.

The rhum agricole will also have pungent fermentation flavors at the high end of the volatility spectrum, where fruity and floral notes tend to reside. This puts the liqueur in a chorus of friendly voices. Note also that this recipe is flexible enough to accommodate the same substitutions among cane juice spirits discussed in seminar four. I have, for instance, made it with an aged cachaça and still found it excellent.

# Crème de Canne Collins

1 oz. unaged rhum agricole or cachaça

1 oz. blanc vermouth

¾ oz. lemon juice

½ oz. simple syrup

1 tsp. crème de violette

~2 oz. seltzer

Combine ingredients in a Collins glass with ice and stir to combine.

*Adapted from a recipe by Jared Sadoian, The Hawthorne, Boston*

Finally, we have the seltzer, a great friend to crème de violette if ever there was one. Dilution and that slight snap of carbonic acid are powerful tools in preventing the violette from predominating. This would be true even if the drink used ¾ oz. of it; at a mere teaspoon, it becomes almost an ethereal accent, taking on a role more like a Scotch or absinthe rinse in a short drink. Make no mistake, though, it is the linchpin, the aromatic finish that draws the other ingredients together into a single, internally complete synthesis.

From a technique perspective, note that this does not have nearly the volume we would otherwise expect of a Collins. It is closer to a fizz or a highball in size, similar to the former in that its carbonated mixer makes up less than half the volume, to the latter in that it is served iced. We can triangulate it based on these comparisons: meant to be drunk slowly, not at cocktail speed; nevertheless expected to be finished sooner than a full-sized Collins would be; and bolder in flavor than the average highball. One could choose to interpret the Crème de Canne Collins as containing a step in which a violet-lemonade soda is created, and then mixing that with vermouth and rum at proportions slightly altered from those of the standard highball to account for the lower proof of the wine. The usefulness of that reading will vary from drinker to drinker—I present it in case it is helpful in understanding why this recipe works despite breaking with these established forms.

# 5.18

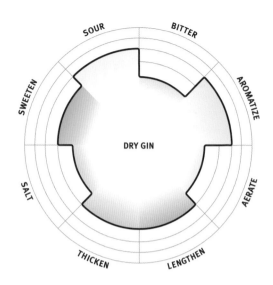

SOUR · BITTER · AROMATIZE · AERATE · LENGTHEN · THICKEN · SALT · SWEETEN

**DRY GIN**

## SOLUTION

In cocktails, the adage is that sugar is the bartender's salt, but among modern mixologists there's a growing interest in making *salt* the bartender's salt. The Juliet & Romeo relies on subtle ingredients with evanescent flavors. The salt keeps them on our radar until we finish the drink.

It also draws water out of the cucumber while muddling, even as its being crushed to dissolve more easily. We regal shake our juiced produce with some fresh herbs, double-straining the pulp out before serving.

2 oz. London dry gin

¾ oz. lime juice

¾ oz. simple syrup

4 drops rose water

3 drops Angostura bitters

3 slices cucumber

1 sprig mint

1 pinch salt

In a cocktail shaker, muddle cucumber slices and salt. Add gin, mint, lime juice, simple syrup, 3 drops of rose water, and ice. Shake, then double-strain into a chilled cocktail glass. Float a mint leaf on the cocktail's surface; top it with 1 drop of rose water and surround it with 3 drops of Angostura.

*Adapted from a recipe by Toby Maloney, The Violet Hour, Chicago*

# EXERCISE
# Juliet & Romeo

London dry gin

lime juice

simple syrup

rose water

Angostura bitters

cucumber

mint

salt

*Using the given ingredients, determine the proportions of the Juliet & Romeo and its method of preparation.*

**A house specialty** at The Violet Hour in Chicago, part-birthplace of the Paper Plane and leading light of the Windy City's Cocktail Renaissance, the Juliet & Romeo is a study in delicacy. I would go so far as to say that if you're a few drinks in already, you should come back to this one tomorrow, when it can be your first drink of the evening.

As befits a Great Lakes recipe, it strikes a balance between the coastal approaches, leveraging the farm-fresh West Coast style for something more refined than rustic, decorated with gently intricate aromatic elements layered in gossamer atop the drink.

Cucumbers have a high water content, pulp rather easily, and frequently appear in drinks that are meant to be refreshing. They have been popular in an era interested in fresh, green, and vegetal flavors. Rose water, meanwhile, is our second hydrosol after orange flower water. It is a solution of the water-soluble aromatic chemicals from the rose—a different subset than would be found in an oil or ethanol infusion.

And finally, we have salt. Unlike in our tequila drinks, it would be detrimental to actually taste the salt here. Think about what its purpose could be, and how it relates to the other ingredients.

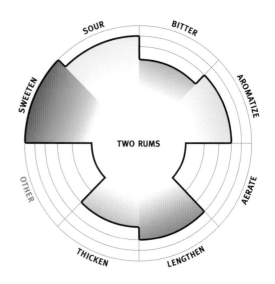

SOUR · BITTER · AROMATIZE · AERATE · LENGTHEN · THICKEN · OTHER · SWEETEN

TWO RUMS

**We've already** covered some of the tikiest contemporary recipes, but the techniques of tropical and exotic cocktails have also found their way back into mainstream modern mixology. The Red Maple Swizzle belongs to Jackson Cannon, one of the major figures who drove the Cocktail Renaissance in Boston.

I have taken one liberty with his recipe. Cannon calls for Smith & Cross, a 114-proof Jamaican rum that will open your eyes and your nostrils to what *hogo* can really mean. It has no counterparts of the same proof and style, and so like Bénédictine it's called for by its brand name—and fairly often in modern recipes at that. However, I cannot in good conscience ask you to purchase yet *another* rum to complete this course, so I've used the last seminar's lessons to devise a substitute.

An equal mixture of 151-proof Demerara rum and standard-proof Jamaican rum is 115.5-proof, on the same order as Smith & Cross. If you have an appropriately fragrant Jamaican rum, you will get some of the characteristics the drink was designed around. You lose a certain amount of funk-bomb-iness with this substitution, but the smoked-soil quality of the Demerara will resonate with the maple syrup and hold the drink together—a tiki solution to a mainstream problem.

# Red Maple Swizzle

2 oz. Smith & Cross Jamaican rum, or 1 oz. each aged Jamaican rum and 151-proof Demerara rum

1 oz. lemon juice

1 oz. maple syrup

2 dashes Peychaud's Bitters

Combine ingredients in a highball glass with crushed ice and swizzle. Add crushed ice as needed to fill. Serve with a straw.

*Adapted from a recipe by Jackson Cannon, Eastern Standard, Boston*

Retaining the Smith & Cross is also fairly tiki: using a highly pungent overproof rum as a base spirit in its own right. The Red Maple Swizzle blurs these genres, equally at home in a neo-speakeasy or a temple of the tiki revival. It's in either case a long drink, a crushed-ice sipper, aromatized chiefly by its rum and secondarily by its bitters, sweetened and soured in such a way as to let the base spirit(s) shine.

The thematic lesson to take from this is that mixological schools can and should inform one another. We have the Manhattan because someone tried crossing a Whiskey Cocktail with a Vermouth Cocktail, the Corpse Reviver No. 2 because people got curious about blending the sour with wine-driven recipes, and the Red Maple Swizzle because the tools of Donn's rum rhapsodies have crossed the rattan line and left their mark on drinks outside the tiki tradition. Even disco drinks can be rehabilitated—well, some of them—as we will see a few pages hence, by smashing one together with some revival-era techniques.

### FURTHER READING

Cannon's Les Sablons is similarly genre-bending. Combine 1½ oz. vodka with ¾ oz. lemon juice, ½ oz. each sherry and Bénédictine, and ¼ oz. simple syrup. Shake, strain, and serve up.

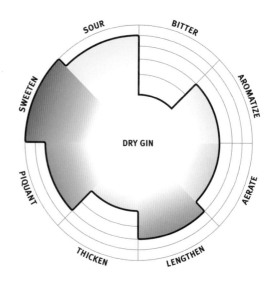

**I have mentioned** that gin's reputation needed help in the nineties and aughts. It is hard to imagine, given its preponderance in classic recipes, that gin's fortunes were at a nadir in the late twentieth century. Its renewed omnipresence is a testament to a generation of bartenders who recognized its value and found ways to evangelize on its behalf. Audrey Saunders was among its greatest promoters.

A protégé of Renaissance godfather Dale Degroff, Saunders made a name for herself reestablishing the storied bar at Bemelmans as a cocktail destination. When she opened Pegu Club in 2005, high cocktailery and mainstream consumption collided at full speed.

The Gin-Gin Mule runs together two ginless recipes which were riding high around the turn of the millennium: the Mojito and the Moscow Mule. Saunders pulled elements from each and added a bit of mother's ruin to convert the drinking public to gin.

You will notice that the Gin-Gin Mule uses a lot less of its lengthener than either of its antecedents. Partially, this is because Saunders's recipe uses a homemade ginger beer with a healthy kick, and a little goes a long way. Partially, it reflects that this is meant to be a gin vehicle rather than a ginger one; the Moscow Mule uses its base spirit only for drying, but we want to taste it here.

# Gin-Gin Mule

1½ oz. London dry gin

1 oz. simple syrup

¾ oz. lime juice

~12 mint leaves

1 oz. ginger beer

Shake all but the ginger beer. Strain into a chilled Collins glass with fresh ice and top with ginger beer. Garnish with a sprig of mint.

*Adapted from a recipe by Audrey Saunders, Pegu Club, New York*

In fact, in the original recipe, the ginger beer is uncarbonated and shaken with the drink. If you've been using homemade ginger syrup to make your ginger sodas, you can swap out the seltzer in the ginger beer recipe for plain water to make something a bit more like Saunders's.

I find it more convenient to make as written here, a Saunders-approved alternative published in the *Washington Post*. While it is somewhat fizzlike—and can be made as a fizz to great effect—the Gin-Gin Mule draws on most of the structural elements we've encountered, from the smash to the semipartial highball state of the Crème de Canne Collins.

It also makes use of a flavored mixer, a trick we have seen in semishort drinks only when fizzed up with sparkling wine. It is worth remembering that you can lengthen and embubble a drink with anything carbonated. Sparkling cider, Moxie, Russian Imperial stout—the world is your fizzy oyster.

### FURTHER READING

For the subtly innovative Old Cuban, Saunders's other alt-fizz, shake 1½ oz. moderately aged rum with 1 oz. simple syrup, ¾ oz. lime juice, 2 dashes Angostura, 6 mint leaves, and ice. Strain into a chilled cocktail glass and top with 2 oz. sparkling wine.

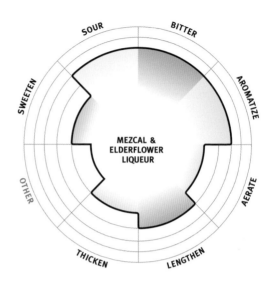

SOUR · BITTER · AROMATIZE · AERATE · LENGTHEN · THICKEN · OTHER · SWEETEN

MEZCAL &
ELDERFLOWER
LIQUEUR

**We are now** in the final leg of our course of study, considering recipes that are especially advanced, elaborate, or unlikely. I have tried to avoid overusing the words *baroque* and *rulebreaker*, apt as they are. If you take nothing else from this last section of our journey together, be firmly and forever convinced that cocktail structures recur at most incidentally and much wonderful mixological work can be done outside their bounds.

This shining example of that truth is another Boston cocktail, perhaps the city's most famous modern contribution and fittingly the last to appear in this book. It was invented by Misty Kalkofen, who in addition to her contributions to the revival of cocktails in the Cradle of Liberty has made a profound impact as an evangelist for mezcal.

The cocktail—affectionately nicknamed the Max. Affair in its native city—originated at a Cambridge bar called Green Street when mezcal cocktails were still quite new. Kalkofen whipped it up for Ron Cooper of Del Maguey when he brought her a sample bottle of mezcal; she had enough left over to enter the drink in a St.-Germain recipe contest. It was picked up for *Food & Wine*'s annual cocktail book in 2009 and then for Eric Felten's article in the *Wall Street Journal* hailing the declining popularity of vodka. The Maximilian Affair had gone from sudden inspiration to interstate sensation virtually overnight.

# Maximilian Affair

1 oz. mezcal

1 oz. elderflower liqueur

½ oz. Punt e Mes

½ oz. lemon juice

Shake with ice. Strain into a chilled cocktail glass.

*Adapted from a recipe by Misty Kalkofen, Green Street, Cambridge, Massachusetts*

It isn't intuitive. To parse it, we have to think in terms of a split-base cocktail, albeit one that divides its foundation between a spirit and a liqueur. This is unusual, but not as strange as it may seem.

Consider how much elderflower liqueur we've been using per drink. Agreeable as it may be, it isn't cloying—and this is not specific to one brand, but seems to remain true even when a nonalcoholic elder-flower cordial is substituted. The aroma of elderflower is delicate, juicy, and floral all at once. It is subtler than it appears, and it does not telegraph sweetness as much as other fruits and flowers do. We can blend it with the more forceful mezcal in equal parts and not worry about losing either.

Additionally, as it did with the Irish whiskey in the Cooper Union, it draws out the vegetation in its base spirit. That bundle of sweet, smoky plants then gets the bitter-sour-wine treatment we have seen before, the first and third both being supplied by the Punt e Mes.

Kalkofen eventually went to work for Del Maguey, which more than any other company has cemented mezcal's status behind the bar. She has coauthored a cocktail book called *Drinking Like Ladies* with Kitty Amann; the recipes are inspired by women throughout history and each one is the handiwork of a contemporary female bartender.

# 5.22

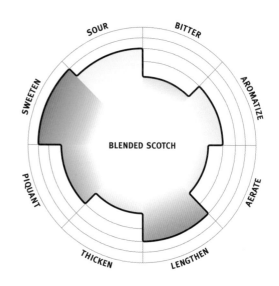

SOUR  BITTER  AROMATIZE

SWEETEN

**BLENDED SCOTCH**

PIQUANT  AERATE

THICKEN  LENGTHEN

**Sam Ross** places a respectable third behind Ward and Saunders for most recipes in this seminar. Those recipes are the Paper Plane and Penicillin, two of the most iconic modern classics, known internationally and listed on menus alongside the most venerable of cocktails. That is to say, he's doing just fine.

The Penicillin began its life as Ross's riff on the Gold Rush. As Milk & Honey's bartenders moved to other cities to open their own places—with Petraske's blessing and encouragement—the recipes went too. In 2007, the Penicillin accompanied the Gold Rush to L.A., when Ross was tapped to train the opening bar staff at David Myers's Comme Ça. It spread from there, building a following among Angeleños while it was gaining notoriety back in New York.

Interestingly, the Penicillin makes use of two spirits even closer to one another than those in the Cooper Union: not only are they both whisky, they're both *Scotch* whisky, just two different types of it. If our encounters with Scotch-Irish recipes have been analogous to using both Jamaican and Demerara rum in the same tiki drink, this is more like combining standard- and 151-proof Demerara rum in the same drink or Jamaican black rum with Jamaican rum that's aged and unsweetened. There is a granularity to this kind of blending that goes beyond anything we have seen outside seminar four.

# Penicillin

2 oz. blended Scotch

¾ oz. lemon juice

⅜ oz. ginger syrup

⅜ oz. honey

¼ oz. smoky Islay Scotch

Shake all by the Islay Scotch and strain into a rocks glass with fresh ice. Float Islay Scotch on top and garnish with a piece of candied ginger.

*Adapted from a recipe by Sam Ross, Milk & Honey, New York*

The original Penicillin also made use of a honey-ginger syrup. You can certainly go this route, but most recipes, including the one in *Regarding Cocktails*, break that down into its components for convenience. We have been working with both ginger syrup and honey since the first seminar, so I have elected to follow the trend. Note, though, that Ross's recipe calls for ¾ oz. of the combined syrup, so splitting it up would necessitate using ⅜ oz. of each to retain the intended balance. This is another feature of contemporary mixology: old recipe books often do not even use ounces, just proportions as in the *Savoy*, or a couple of standard measures, e.g., wineglass, pony, etc., in *The Bon-Vivant's Companion*. They admit a certain amount of approximation and do not expect precision. Not so the modern bar; ⅜ oz. isn't even the finnickiest measurement we will encounter in this seminar.

If you do not have access to an eighth-ounce measure, there are a few alternatives. One is to make a combined honey-ginger syrup and use ¾ oz. of it, as Ross intended. Another is to make a double, which would let you use both the honey and ginger a more convenient ¾ oz. at a time. In a pinch, the third option is to use ⅓ oz., which differs from ⅜ oz. by less than a twentieth of an ounce. For the honey, you can use syrup to make shaking easier—or you can dry shake the honey as we did in seminar two. The choice is entirely yours!

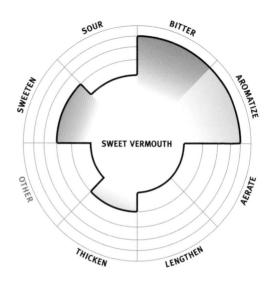

## 5.23

SOUR · BITTER · AROMATIZE · AERATE · LENGTHEN · THICKEN · OTHER · SWEETEN

SWEET VERMOUTH

**Here we see** carciofo making another appearance, this time in more of a starring role. Given the uses that we have put amari to already, it was perhaps inevitable that we would end up here. The Bitter Giuseppe is a bit like a double-wine or upside-down cocktail, blending a healthy pour of vermouth with something else more often found modifying spirits. If we wish to, we can identify traces of the Adonis, with the sherry exchanged for the more forceful Cynar.

It gets even more interesting when we get to the garnish. This application of lemon most resembles that of the lime in the Ti' Punch: a combination of oil and a *bit* of juice added to taste by the user. We have not tended to see that technique employed in wine-based drinks, and this being our first amaro-wine recipe, we have no precedent to examine there either. The closest counterpart—the wedge garnish—has appeared most often in longer built drinks, the imbiber's capacity for stretching out sourness with a periodic squeeze of the lemon or lime serving to counteract the inevitable dilution of a tall iced cocktail. The lemon in this drink also shows us how the central axes of cocktails adapted to recent tastes: it is not there so much to counteract sweetness as to balance savoriness from the carciofo, much as one might add a bit of lemon juice when cooking vegetables.

# Bitter Giuseppe

Combine ingredients in a rocks glass with ice and stir. Cut a quarter-size round from the side of a lemon, including some of the flesh; squeeze 8–12 drops of lemon juice into the drink to taste and drop the lemon round in.

*Adapted from a recipe by Stephen Cole, The Violet Hour, Chicago*

2 oz. sweet vermouth

¾ oz. Cynar

2 dashes orange bitters

More peculiar still for a drink of such recent vintage is the fact that multiple and rather different recipes exist. Other versions tend to make the following changes: first, the orange bitters is tripled; second, the Cynar is dialed up, often to the point of trading places with the vermouth in terms of volume; and third, the slightly tricky garnish is replaced with lemon in some other form, potentially an expressed peel combined with a slice garnish or else a wedge squeezed for just a few drops. I am content with the balance of the recipe here—besides which, its unusual garnish technique is part of what got the Bitter Giuseppe onto our lesson plan!

This is another Violet Hour original, although unlike the Paper Plane it was actually invented on-site. They seem to have a fondness for double-take recipes. The Bitter Giuseppe's reputation outside Chicago was bolstered by its inclusion in *beta cocktails* by Kirk Estopinal and Maksym Pazuniak, both of Cure in New Orleans. Part recipe book and part manifesto-by-doing, *beta cocktails* made the case against the trend of recipes with subrecipes—e.g., "before we make this drink, you'll need to make this vanilla-chai vermouth infusion that you won't use for any other cocktails in this book"—that was marching toward dominance when it came out. It pushed instead a collection of modern drinks that limited their set of ingredients to ones more available and more versatile, but combined in innovative ways.

# 5.24

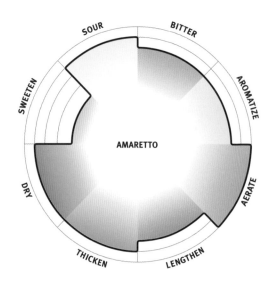

SOUR • BITTER • AROMATIZE • AERATE • LENGTHEN • THICKEN • DRY • SWEETEN

AMARETTO

## SOLUTION

We mustn't be tempted to make the bourbon the base, which would fashion this as something other than an Amaretto Sour. Spiritually, this has to be a liqueur-driven drink. Amaretto is a reasonable foundation: it's a little bitter—that is, in fact, the meaning of the name—with many of the warm phenolic compounds that give aged spirits their flavor. The cask-strength bourbon is the accent; clocking in around 55%–60% ABV, it's enough to calibrate the drink's core to appeal to people without a sweet tooth.

Texturally, Morgenthaler likes to whip these with an immersion blender before shaking. Giving it a quick dry flash blend, as we did for the Larboard Light, will achieve the same effect: a fluffy, frothy drink, with an aromatic garnish of bitters topping off the nutty-spicy-vanilla palate.

1½ oz. amaretto

¾ oz. cask-strength bourbon

1 oz. lemon juice

1 tsp. rich demerara syrup

egg white

3–5 drops Angostura bitters

Flash blend for 2–3 seconds without ice, then shake with ice. Strain into a chilled cocktail glass and decorate with 3–5 drops of Angostura bitters.

*Adapted from a recipe by Jeffrey Morgenthaler, Pepé Le Moko, Portland, Oregon*

# EXERCISE
# Morgenthaler Amaretto Sour

amaretto

cask-strength bourbon

lemon juice

rich demerara syrup

egg white

Angostura bitters

*Using the given ingredients, determine the proportions of the Morgenthaler Amaretto Sour and its method of preparation.*

**I did promise** that we'd rehabilitate a disco drink. Contemporary bartender Jeffrey Morgenthaler claims to make the best Amaretto Sour in the world, and I have yet to try a better one.

As much as it was a romantic revivalist movement, the early Renaissance was also a revolt against the style of drinking immediately preceding it: chemical mixes, sickly sweet liqueur drinks, the twin base-spirit tyrants of flavorless vodka and *flavored* vodka. The Amaretto Sour had been hanging with that crowd, which put it in line for a healthy scoff by the people repopularizing the Old Fashioned.

That never sat right with Morgenthaler. Why not apply the tools of the Renaissance to make the drink well instead? It's not as though amaretto is a bad spirit—there are many very high-quality expressions. To realize this drink's full potential, Morgenthaler eschews sour mix in favor of fresh juice, beefs up the recipe with cask-strength bourbon, and softens the whole with an egg white.

Remember, the Morgenthaler Amaretto Sour is supposed to be mind-breaking, something that is recognizably an Amaretto Sour but also unlike any the drinker has had before. Morgenthaler's advice when serving it is to "grin like an idiot as your friends freak out." Think about what would inspire such a reaction. A hint: make it frothy!

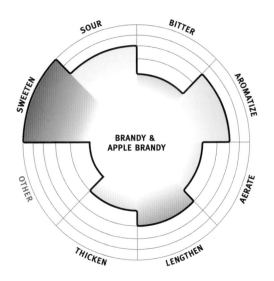

**If there is** a Saunders palate, it is one that skews toward gin, mint, citrus, and traditional ingredients. Most of the best known recipes she has devised can be thought of either as modern takes on the old-school backbar or neoclassical reinterpretations of popular contemporary drinks. The Tantris Sidecar is no different, a cocktail that contains all the elements of a Sidecar and even drinks like one, but that could not have found its way into wide circulation before the Cocktail Renaissance. There are two reasons for this.

The first, and the reason the Tantris Sidecar appears so late in this seminar and this book, is that it is a product of Saunders's famously rigorous recipe development process. Toby Maloney, who worked under Saunders at Pegu Club, estimated that they might make twenty-five iterations of a recipe. It would never be the last variation that got onto the menu—but often the third-to-last one.

This is a good lesson to remember when developing original cocktails. You may hit on a good construction early on, but that does not mean you have found the best one possible. Even if you have, you can't know that without trying more. It is unlikely enough that your first draft will be perfect that you should always assume it is not, and satisfy yourself by further investigation that no improvements can be made.

# Tantris Sidecar

1¼ oz. brandy

½ oz. apple brandy

½ oz. orange liqueur

½ oz. lemon juice

½ oz. simple syrup

¼ oz. pineapple juice

¼ oz. Green Chartreuse

Shake with ice. Strain into a chilled cocktail glass with a half-sugared rim. Express a lemon peel over the glass and discard.

*Adapted from a recipe by Audrey Saunders, Pegu Club, New York*

Look at this recipe. Seven ingredients, and three that use a quarter-ounce measure. It does not take much to imagine the painstaking process that went into its creation. Something like the Tantris Sidecar could have existed many years ago, but it would not have been subjected to the same exacting iterative experimentation and would therefore not have been likely to achieve the same level of success.

The second reason is that it's clearly post-tiki. Cocktails don't casually end up with an ingredients list like this; only after the greater excesses of tiki have raised the bar for "too much" is that possible. Had the Tantris Sidecar been invented in the 1940s, it might even have *been* a tiki drink, flash blended with extra Chartreuse and pineapple juice.

Saunders's recipe presents as simple and stirred, a Sidecar with layers within each ingredient—using tiki tools for a non-tiki result. It fuses into a single accessible flavor, but investigation reveals a fractalized palate, each detected aroma drawing attention to two or three others. The ingredients are hard to tease apart. Even so, it is accessible despite its complexity—as attested by its half-sugared rim, a reliable indicator of a drink safe for consumption. Sugared rims and citrus wedge garnishes are like sauce on an entrée: we include an amount that we are confident will work well with the recipe however much or little of it is consumed.

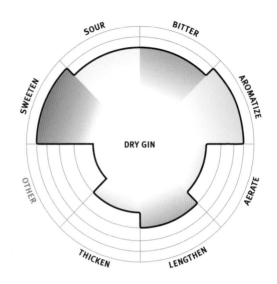

**5.26**

SOUR
BITTER
SWEETEN
AROMATIZE
DRY GIN
OTHER
AERATE
THICKEN
LENGTHEN

**I introduced** the regal shake several seminars ago, and since then we have used it in all manner of applications except the one for which it was originally intended: extracting oil from a citrus peel during the shake, an intermediate step between expressing it over the glass and muddling it or dropping it in. It is time at long last that we did so.

The number one recommendation from its modern progenitor Theo Lieberman is to add a grapefruit peel to the tin for a Daiquiri, and it is one I heartily endorse. But this is still in cocktail hacks territory. What about a recipe that is designed around the technique from the start?

Enter Rene Hidalgo's That's My Word. Another of the modern Last Word riffs, its name is a hip-hop-inflected allusion to its inspiration. Hidalgo opts for lower-octane Yellow Chartreuse and elderflower liqueur to replace the original's most assertive ingredients. Like the Corpse Reviver No. 2, That's My Word is an equal-parts-*ish* drink, with four ingredients in equal measure plus a highly unequal aromatic addition.

Here, the aromatic fifth player is even subtler, drawing out the brightness of the elderflower and the sweet citrus of the gin and Chartreuse,

# That's My Word

¾ oz. London dry gin

¾ oz. Yellow Chartreuse

¾ oz. elderflower liqueur

¾ oz. lime juice

grapefruit peel

Shake with ice. Strain into a chilled cocktail glass and garnish with a maraschino or brandied cherry.

*Recipe by Rene Hidalgo, Beloved, Brooklyn*

its peel oils contributing just a hint of bitterness to hold down the sugars in the liqueurs. By now, you should recognize the commonalities that help the other four ingredients fit together without my assistance.

It should be noted that the idea of a "Last Word riff" has a certain fluidity to it. Not all modern equal-parts drinks are thought of as Last Word riffs by their creator, while some that are considered as such have nothing in common with the Last Word except their proportions.

**FURTHER READING**

Another option worth exploring is the Cosmopolitan, a proto-Renaissance creation that has been both fairly and unfairly maligned over the years. Made well, there is nothing wrong with it. I recommend a recipe of 2 oz. of citrus vodka with 1 oz. each of triple sec, lime juice, and cranberry juice cocktail—shake, strain, serve up, and express a lemon peel over the top. If, however, you do not care to pick up a bottle of flavored vodka, use a regular vodka and regal shake with a lemon peel. The citrus oil element is important, and you want more than the expressed peel will give you on its own.

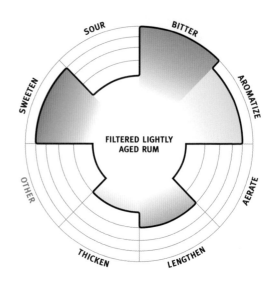

**5.27**

SOUR

BITTER

AROMATIZE

SWEETEN

FILTERED LIGHTLY
AGED RUM

OTHER

AERATE

THICKEN

LENGTHEN

**Kyle Davidson** first compounded the Art of Choke at The Violet Hour. His boss, Toby Maloney—who had been Petraske's first hire at Milk & Honey and Saunders's first head bartender at Pegu Club—would later say that it "ran against everything [he] taught him." But its disregard for the rules never stopped anyone from ordering it and a berth in *beta cocktails* ensured that it made it past The Violet Hour's hidden door on Damen Avenue and into the wider world.

Its base component should remind us of the Maximilian Affair, a split between a spirit and a liqueur—albeit a bitter one in this case. That is already unusual, and things get weirder from there. We have not tried Cynar with rum yet, and our most famous rum-amaro cocktail, the Jungle Bird, is one I have previously described as an outlier in its region of the canon. Plus, the Art of Choke is made with a less flavorful rum, something that will have a harder time standing up to a loud partner than the Bird's funky Jamaican rum will.

And everything besides the rum and Cynar is in such small proportions! The quarter ounce of Chartreuse seems generous when compared to the ¾ tsp. of lime and demerara syrup.* If you do not have

* As promised, the Penicillin does not have this book's most persnickety measurements!

# Art of Choke

1 oz. filtered lightly aged rum

1 oz. Cynar

¾ tsp. lime juice

¾ tsp. rich demerara syrup

¼ oz. Green Chartreuse

Stir with ice. Strain into a rocks glass with ice. Garnish with a mint sprig.

*Adapted from a recipe by Kyle Davidson, The Violet Hour, Chicago*

access to a ¼ or ¾ tsp. measure, this is a convenient time to make a double. Remember, 1½ tsp. is just ¼ oz., which tends to be much easier to measure in practice!

The mint is critical as an aromatic garnish. It blends quite well with the alpine herbs of the Chartreuse and the artichoke flavor of the Cynar. Note also that this is a stirred drink despite its citrus, and like the Fallback it's served on the rocks despite being stirred.

Maloney wasn't kidding. Nevertheless, the drink is another feather in the cap for his bar, and its name nigh-impossible to forget.†

**FURTHER READING**

A more obviously tiki preparation of Cynar is the Artichoke Hold, which combines ½ oz. each of orgeat and elderflower liqueur with ¾ oz. each of lime juice, Cynar, and Smith & Cross (or the house rum blend we substituted for it in the Red Maple Swizzle). These are given a short shake, strained over crushed ice in a rocks glass, and garnished once again with a big, fragrant sprig of mint.

---

† It's punning on the word *artichoke*. There may be a pattern of this in carciofo drinks.

# 5.28

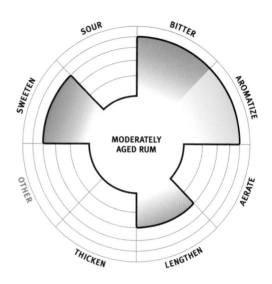

SOUR · BITTER · AROMATIZE · AERATE · LENGTHEN · THICKEN · OTHER · SWEETEN

**MODERATELY AGED RUM**

**The Bywater** may be less obviously extravagant than some of the other recipes at this end of the book, but it has three fairly advanced elements that justify its late placement. Let's take them in order.

The first and most obvious is its casual use of Amer Picon, an ingredient we haven't seen since I asked you to spend a period of weeks or months making it back in seminar three. It is a gutsy move for a modern recipe to include something that still hasn't been revived all the way.*

This is not the only third-millennium recipe to make good use of the defunct French spirit and its reconstructions, but it is the best I have personally encountered. It also represents an innovative use of falernum in a subtropical context, weaving it together with herbaceous elements typical of the New Orleans palate and the lost Amer. This is its second advanced technique, a successful blending of components from seemingly disparate mixological traditions and flavor profiles to make something that is not only good to drink but somehow also very New Orleans in flavor. It suggests that while the geist animating the

* If you have polished off your Amer Picon from seminar three, Hannah recommends replacing it with Averna amaro, adding two dashes of orange bitters, and expressing an orange peel over the finished cocktail.

# Bywater

1¾ oz. moderately aged rum

¾ oz. Amer Picon

½ oz. Green Chartreuse

¼ oz. falernum

2 dashes Peychaud's Bitters

Stir with ice for 20 seconds and strain into a chilled cocktail glass. Garnish with a maraschino or brandied cherry.

*Adapted from a recipe by Chris Hannah, Arnaud's French 75, New Orleans*

Sazerac and its cohort might be represented by or reflected in the set of ingredients that commonly appear in the cocktails of the Crescent City, it is not reducible to them. There is something more there: a meeting of ease and sophistication, a taste for complexity amidst celebration, sorrow and joy and stormy skies and maybe a whiff of aniseed all gathered together in a glass. It takes more than the right ingredients to make a New Orleans cocktail.

In a more technical sense, the third noteworthy feature of the Bywater is its explicit instruction to stir for 20 seconds. This is roughly double the norm, and when I first read the recipe, I assumed it was an error. Then I made the cocktail and saw the difference.

I should not have been surprised, and neither should you. We have seen short and long shakes, and we have seen shaken drinks we would have expected to be stirred. Why not a **long stir**? We have some bold flavors here, as well as the highly spiritous Green Chartreuse to temper. That little extra bit of water helps everything fall into place, without introducing the turbulence of the shaker. The drink stays placid, unaerated, and visually pristine, while getting just enough dilution. This is a rare technique, but it is worth having in your back pocket when your latest stirred recipe is running a bit too hot.

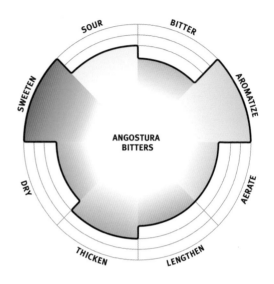

## 5.29

Chart labels: SOUR, BITTER, SWEETEN, AROMATIZE, DRY, AERATE, THICKEN, LENGTHEN, ANGOSTURA BITTERS

**That is not** a typographical error. This is a drink made with a full ounce of Angostura bitters—or put another way, a cocktail with Angostura as the base spirit.

It is hard to match the Trinidad Sour for sheer baroqueness. It uses a high-proof rye as a mixer. Its base is an alcoholic product that's sold in grocery stores because it is supposed to be too unpleasant to drink on its own. Strictly speaking, it is not "on its own" here, but it makes up a plurality of the volume—an honor we have never bestowed on absinthe, Chartreuse, Campari, or single-malt Scotch.

Giuseppe Gonzalez's creation is the Renaissance firing on all cylinders: none of its components are new, but the combination is very much so. That something this odd on paper has girdled the world says as much about the state of mixology during the High Renaissance as it does about Gonzalez's skill.*

Like most bitters, Angostura has an alcohol base. It clocks in at 44.7% ABV, on par with other base spirits. While it has a highly concentrated

---

* As Gonzalez tells it, he first concocted the drink while he was Reiner's head bartender at Clover Club, but it was when John Gertsen brought it to Drink that its star really began to rise. Once again, if you want a cocktail to become canonical, get it onto menus in two cities at once.

# Trinidad Sour

1 oz. Angostura bitters

1 oz. orgeat

½ oz. bonded or other high-proof rye whiskey

¾ oz. lemon juice

Shake with ice. Strain into a chilled cocktail glass.

*Adapted from a recipe by Giuseppe Gonzalez, Clover Club, Brooklyn*

flavor, it isn't texturally heavy, and it's less bitter in that quantity than its name suggests. It is somewhat akin to using a spiced rum as the base for a cocktail. The consumption of straight or nearly straight bitters is also amply precedented, hearkening back to their origins as patent medicines, good for whatever might ail one. While that is still a bit much for most palates, the Trinidad Sour squares the Angostura off with a similarly outlandish dollop of orgeat, bringing some fat to the middle of the sip and countering the bitterness of the bitters with its sweetness. The rye accounts for any overcorrection, and the lemon provides a third apex to the triangle of balance. This is all well and good for our structural understanding of the drink, but it is amusing that a high-proof rye is the smoothing and harmonizing agent here, as rum, honey, and orange have been in previous recipes.

Note that this is *not* an egg white drink. A curious overcorrection has arisen, in which all sours are assumed to be egg white sours—to the point that the egged variety somewhere acquired the moniker of "traditional sours." This is poppycock. Plenty of sours never had eggs in them, and we should feel no obligation to "restore" what was not there in the first place. (This goes double for a drink invented in the last twelve years!) There are enough almond proteins in orgeat that the drink should foam up a bit, like our honey and pineapple cocktails do; it just won't have the downy white blanket of a Boston Sour.

# 5.30

*In this final project, you will prepare a fat-washed spirit for use in the Fat-Washed Old Fashioned. The recipe for fat-washing a spirit is listed here, while the recipe for the cocktail is on the following pages.*

In *Liquid Intelligence,* Dave Arnold calls for 4 oz. of strongly flavored fat to wash a 750 mL bottle of spirit or 8 oz. of a more mildly flavored fat; my ratios are scaled-down versions of his. To wash a roughly single-drink volume:

■ For most fats, use ½ oz. of fat and 3 oz. and 1 tsp. of spirit.

■ For a mildly-flavored fat like butter, use 1 oz. of fat instead.

**The capstone** project for this chapter—and in a way, your senior thesis for this course—will be to make the Old Fashioned new again. Doing so will give you the chance to experiment with fat-washing spirits, an iconic technique of modern experimental mixology.

The core of fat washing is mixing something fatty with a distilled spirit, allowing them to sit for an extended period, and then separating them again. The spirit will retain some of the flavor of the fat and will generally come away with a richer body. The spirit's bite may also be softened by washing, particularly if your fat contains some tannin-stripping proteins as well.

The archetypal fat wash works as follows: Combine your spirit with liquid fat (melt it first if necessary) and stir or shake until well combined. Allow to sit, covered, for an hour or so, agitating periodically. It should start to separate. Transfer the container to the freezer and leave it there for three to four hours. A reasonably solid layer of fat should form at the top. Poke a hole in it and pour out the spirit. Strain it through a coffee filter before use or bottling, and be sure to keep it refrigerated if you're saving it for later.

# FINAL PROJECT: PART 1
# Fat-Washed Spirit

*Enfleurage* may require a higher fat proportion, so if you're working with something like a nut butter, use 2 oz. of it per 3⅙ oz. of spirit.

According to the *PDT Cocktail Book*, Don Lee's recipe for the Benton's Old Fashioned uses 1½ oz. of Benton's bacon fat per bottle. He knows bacon fat better than I do, so I'd listen to him—his proportions work out to about ¼ oz. of fat for 4¼ oz. of spirit. A similarly conservative approach may be beneficial for other extra-flavorful animal fats, like duck.

If your fatty ingredient also has lots of other solids, a better alternative is an old perfumer's technique called *enfleurage*. Get a large baking pan—one with a lip, so the liquor doesn't run off it—and spread your fat over it, ideally in a fairly even thin layer. Now pour your spirit on top. Cover it to protect against evaporation, and let it sit at room temperature at least overnight—it wouldn't hurt to give it twenty-four hours. When it's finished resting, carefully pour the liquor off into another container, leaving as much of the fat behind as possible to make straining easier. Then run the spirit through a coffee filter and proceed as above.

You can also wash spirits with oils, but doing so may require additional equipment. Olive oil, for example, will separate like other fats do, but it won't solidify in your freezer. The easiest way to solve this is to do your fat washing in a vessel with a spigot at the bottom, so you can pour off the heavier spirit without getting the oil. Chemists use a separatory funnel, a glass vessel that tapers to a spigot at its bottom; a gravy separator or any transparent vessel that allows you to pour from the bottom will also work.

# 5.30

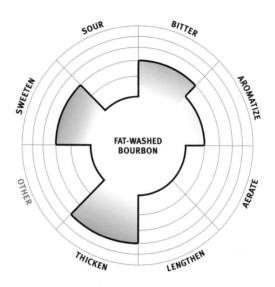

SOUR · BITTER · AROMATIZE · SWEETEN · AERATE · OTHER · THICKEN · LENGTHEN

**FAT-WASHED BOURBON**

**Fat washing** was first cultivated at New York's WD-50 by Eben Freeman, Tona Palomino, and Sam Mason. It would become famous at PDT, where Don Lee used it for the Benton's Old Fashioned, a much-imitated modern classic made with hickory-smoked artisanal Tennessee bacon; it remains the bar's hottest seller.*

Most instructions for this technique usually assume that you're doing a whole 750 mL bottle at once—which is a lot of fat-washed liquor. Remember, this technique was developed for restaurant use; the home bartender would be well advised to scale it down. Once you have proportions you like, you can try for a whole bottle.

There is no secret sauce to this assessment. I can't make your fat wash for you, and I am as powerless to guide you through the idiosyncrasies of your own kitchen and larder as I was when we made the Pearl Diver Punch.

There is also no one correct answer. I have recommended a maple-sweetened Old Fashioned made with fat-washed bourbon, and I think

---

* I considered making this assessment the Benton's Old Fashioned itself, but I know bacon is a nonstarter for many people for a variety of dietary and religious reasons. Besides, this approach requires more creativity on your part.

# FINAL PROJECT: PART 2
# Fat-Washed
# Old Fashioned

2 oz. fat-washed bourbon

½ oz. maple syrup

2 dashes Angostura bitters

Combine ingredients with ice in a rocks glass and stir. Garnish with an orange peel.

*Adapted from a recipe by Don Lee, PDT, New York*

bacon, butter, and peanut butter are all good choices for that cocktail. But just as you'll have to figure out for yourself *how* to fat-wash spirits effectively, it's also up to you to decide which ones you'll give that treatment and what you'll do with them afterward.

If you want to make a Benton's Old Fashioned exactly the way Lee does, go for it. If you want to try washing tequila with avocado oil, gin with tahini, or brandy with pistachio butter, give it a shot. Make an apple pie in a glass with lard-washed applejack and cinnamon simple syrup. Fat wash your way to a homemade coconut rum.

From here on out, the choices are yours. You have a fuller, deeper, and above all *richer* understanding of the cocktail than most people could have dreamed of when the Renaissance began. Your home bar is equipped to make just about anything. The time has come to experiment on your own, to chase after expertise in the areas that most interest you, to tumble down mixological rabbit holes just to find out where they lead—in sum, to partake in the dynamic vibrancy of the cocktail, no longer as a student but as a practitioner. Good luck to you. You have my confidence.

# INDEPENDENT STUDIES

## Additional Cocktail Recipes

Many cocktails exist besides those we have covered. As you continue to pursue a deeper understanding of this field, I invite you to experiment with these and see what makes them tick.

### Ampersand
*Waldorf-Astoria*

1 oz. Old Tom gin

1 oz. brandy

1 oz. sweet vermouth

2 dashes orange bitters

1 tsp. curaçao (rinse)

Stir first four ingredients with ice. Strain into a chilled cocktail glass rinsed with curaçao.

### Artist's Special
*Harry Craddock,*
**The Savoy Cocktail Book**

1 oz. whiskey (Irish single pot still recommended)

1 oz. oloroso sherry

½ oz. lemon juice

½ oz. raspberry or groseille syrup

Shake with ice. Strain into a chilled cocktail glass.

### Cuzco
*Julie Reiner*

2 oz. pisco

¾ oz. Aperol

½ oz. lemon juice

½ oz. grapefruit juice

¾ oz. simple syrup

1 tsp. kirschwasser (rinse)

Shake first five ingredients with ice. Strain into a chilled cocktail glass rinsed with kirschwasser. Express a grapefruit peel over the glass and discard.

### Dixie
*Tom Bullock,*
**The Ideal Bartender**

2 oz. bourbon

2 tsp. sugar

2 tsp. water

1 tsp. curaçao

2 dashes Angostura bitters

6 drops crème de menthe

Combine ingredients in a rocks glass with ice. Express a lemon twist over the glass and drop it in.

## Hanseatic Fizz
### Brian D. Hoefling

2 oz. aquavit

¾ oz. Cherry Heering

½ oz. lemon juice

egg white

~ 3 oz. seltzer

Shake first four ingredients without ice, then again with ice. Strain into a highball glass and top with seltzer.

## Pimm's Cup
### Traditional

2 oz. Pimm's No. 1 Cup

½ oz. lemon juice

3–4 slices cucumber

4 oz. ginger ale or lemon soda

In a highball glass, stack ice cubes and cucumber slices in alternating layers. Stir Pimm's and lemon juice without ice and pour over stack. Fill with ginger ale or lemon soda. Garnish with seasonal berries, mint, and/or more cucumber, as desired.

## Improved Culross
### Lee Edwards (Haus Alpenz)

¾ oz. rhum agricole or cachaça

¾ oz. apricot liqueur

¾ oz. Kina apéritif wine

¾ oz. lemon juice

Shake with ice and strain into a chilled cocktail glass. Express an orange peel over the glass and discard.

## Pisco Sour
### Traditional

1½ oz. pisco

½ oz. simple syrup

½ oz. lemon juice

egg white

Shake without ice, then again with ice. Strain into a chilled cocktail glass. Decorate with 3–5 drops of Amargo Chuncho Peruvian bitters.

## Nightglow
### Brian D. Hoefling

2 oz. brandy

½ oz. kirschwasser

½ oz. simple syrup

¼ oz. lemon juice

2 dashes Peychaud's Bitters

Shake with ice. Strain into a chilled cocktail glass.

## Vodka Espresso
### Dick Bradsell

1½ oz. vodka

1 oz. espresso

¾ oz. coffee liqueur

Shake with ice until foamy. Strain into a chilled cocktail glass and garnish with three coffee beans.

# RECIPES FOR HOMEMADE INGREDIENTS

### CINNAMON SYRUP

Combine equal parts sugar and water in a small pot, with three crushed cinnamon sticks per cup of water. Bring to a boil and stir until sugar dissolves. Reduce heat and simmer for two minutes. Then remove from heat and allow to stand for at least two hours. When ready, strain out cinnamon, bottle, and refrigerate. This recipe comes from Jeff Berry's book *Sippin' Safari*, and he estimates that it will keep for a month in the fridge. If you prefer to buy a bottled syrup, BG Reynolds makes a nice one.

### GINGER SYRUP, PLUS GINGER ALE/BEER

Jeffrey Morgenthaler is very good at finding and publicizing prep techniques that make a bartender's life much easier. He wrote up this very easy ginger syrup recipe after learning it from Jon Santer.

Roughly chop some ginger. Don't even bother peeling it, just chop it up. Measure the volume you have. Combine it in a blender with equal volumes of sugar (or honey) and boiling water. Puree until smooth. Strain out the solids with a cheesecloth or a fine mesh strainer. Then bottle and refrigerate until ready to use; Morgenthaler estimates that it will keep for a week.

Liber & Co. also has a nice ginger syrup—albeit also a very strong one! And various people, myself included, have published other ginger syrup recipes, but the Santer-Morgenthaler technique is the most straightforward by far.

To make homemade **ginger beer**, mix one part ginger syrup with three parts seltzer. For **ginger ale**, mix one part ginger syrup with one part simple syrup and six parts seltzer.

### GRENADINE

Combine equal parts of pomegranate juice and white sugar in a container. Shake briefly until sugar is dissolved. Refrigerate. Alternatively, combine ingredients in a pot, stir to combine, and gradually reduce the mixture until it reaches your desired viscosity. Some recipes also add orange flower water, fresh citrus juice, or a bit of liquor as a preservative. This recipe can also be used to make syrups from other fruit juices. If you do prefer to buy your grenadine, patronize a good-quality craft syrups company like BG Reynolds, Small Hand Foods, or Liber & Co.

### HONEY SYRUP

If your honey is too viscous to work with at room temperature, combine three parts of it with one part warm water and stir until well mixed. Bottle and refrigerate until ready to use.

Note that there are also less viscous varieties of honey that are easier to pour, like Atchafalaya honey from Louisiana.

### LIME CORDIAL

It is possible to make lime cordial at home, but it is much easier to get a bottled product. BG Reynolds and

El Guapo are the best I've had; avoid Rose's, which I have to think is a shadow of its former self.

This is the easiest way to approximate it at home: Peel some number of limes. Put the peels in a bowl and add between ¾ oz. and 1 oz. of white sugar for each lime. Mix very well and let sit for at least half an hour; the sugar should draw the lime oils out of the peels and the mixture should become wet. When ready, juice the peeled limes and strain the pulp out of the juice. Stir the juice into the bowl until the sugar is dissolved. Then strain out the peels, bottle, and refrigerate. This won't be as tart as a commercial lime cordial, so you may want to increase the proportion of it in your cocktails—or, take a tip from Morgenthaler and add ½ –⅔ oz. food grade citric acid per lime when making it. Some recipes further recommend reducing the mixture in a pot, adding lime leaves, etc.

## ORGEAT & OTHER SYRUPS

Making orgeat is a lengthy process that involves a lot of soaking and grinding almonds. You're welcome to try it, but I never have. I recommend buying a bottled version. Reputable products from BG Reynolds, Latitude 29, Liber & Co., and Small Hand Foods are all available online; an expertly crafted orgeat works wonders in cocktails.

My advice is similar for falernum, passion fruit syrup, and especially fassionola. There are online recipes for all three, but there's no need for most people to go down that rabbit hole. I've had good luck with BG Reynolds for passion fruit syrup, and with them and John D. Taylor for falernum. Jonathan English has the original fassionola, but if you have trouble tracking it down, there are great modern takes from BG Reynolds and Cocktail & Sons.

## RASPBERRY SYRUP

Take one part fresh or frozen raspberries and mash them. Add two parts white sugar and mix well. Allow to macerate for thirty minutes. Add one part warm (not hot or boiling) water and stir until sugar is dissolved. Pour through a fine mesh strainer to remove the seeds. Bottle and refrigerate. This recipe can also be used to make syrups from other berries. Commercial raspberry syrups are available, but this method is so easy and so rewarding that I haven't tried any of them.

## RICH DEMERARA SYRUP

Combine two parts demerara sugar and one part water in a small pot. Warm the mixture and stir until dissolved, then bottle and refrigerate.

Note that you can also make a rich simple syrup in this way, or a 1:1 demerara syrup using the simple syrup instructions below. I find that cocktails that benefit from the richer texture of 2:1 simple syrup also benefit from the richer flavor of demerara sugar.

## SIMPLE SYRUP

Combine equal parts of white sugar and water in a sealable container. Shake briefly until sugar is dissolved. Refrigerate. That's it!

# SUBSTITUTIONS

### BLACK RUM

If all you have is an unsweetened, decent-quality lightly or moderately aged rum, but you want to make a black rum recipe like the Jungle Bird, you can approximate the flavor and viscosity by adding a drizzle of molasses to the drink. Failing that, double down on rich demerara syrup or one of its substitutes. It won't be quite the same, but it'll be closer.

### CONDENSED MILK

If all you have is evaporated milk, use 1¼ oz. of it and 1½ oz. of sugar for every 2 oz. of condensed milk you would need (the Batida is a blender drink, so I assume you're making more than one at a time). Coconut milk is a reasonable alternative and a common Batida ingredient in Brazil.

### CREAM

Some of these recipes call for heavy cream, others for light cream or half-and-half. You can make something like half-and-half or light cream at home by combining heavy cream with whole milk in equal parts (or your preferred proportions). Directly substituting heavy for light cream or vice versa doesn't work quite as well, but it'll do in a pinch. Just add ½ oz. when switching from heavy cream to light, and take ½ oz. away when going in the other direction.

Coconut milk is another viable substitute for light cream, having a similar fat content. It would also be my first choice for a nondairy heavy cream substitute, with the understanding that the drink will be thinner than intended. In either case, bargain coconut milk can smell slightly off even if the drink tastes fine, so buy an upscale brand or be liberal with the aromatic garnishes.

### EGG WHITE

If you are unable to use egg whites in your cocktails, a reasonable alternative is **aquafaba**, or bean water. Cooking beans in water and then pouring the liquid off is one way to get it, but the far easier way is to open a can of beans and use the liquid in there. Chickpeas are a popular selection, because the water doesn't give off that strong of an aroma or have a color. It may, however, be salty or savory in a way egg whites are not. Pair with gin for best results.

One ounce of aquafaba should roughly replace an egg white. The consistency will be different, but it will be remarkably close all things considered.

### ELDERFLOWER LIQUEUR

Nonalcoholic elderflower cordials do well in cocktails, if a liqueur is unavailable, although you may need to adjust the proportions to accommodate their sweetness.

### FASSIONOLA

A mixture of passion fruit syrup and your preferred red fruit syrup (grenadine, raspberry syrup, etc.) will give you something that, while not really fassionola, should work in recipes that call for fassionola until you can get a bottle of the real stuff.

## GRENADINE VS. RASPBERRY SYRUP VS. OTHER RED FRUITS

Raspberry preserves are sometimes used in place of raspberry syrup in cocktails. You can also use them to make an ad hoc syrup by mixing them with water (and sugar to taste, if necessary). Grenadine and raspberry syrup can likewise be used in place of one another, and historically this has been a common substitution.

## HIGH-PROOF SPIRITS

To substitute a spirit of about 40% ABV for one of about 50% ABV, use ¼ oz. more of the spirit than the recipe calls for. To do the opposite, use ¼ oz. less. This isn't a perfect solution—and it may not always be necessary—but if your drink doesn't seem quite balanced, give it a try.

## HONEY VS. HONEY SYRUP

I find that ¾ oz. of syrup is roughly equivalent to ½ oz. of plain honey and vice versa. The difference between the two diminishes at smaller volumes.

## LEMONS & LIMES

Although one shouldn't get in the habit of it, lemon and lime juice can often be substituted for one another in cocktails without doing too much harm. Orange and grapefruit juice normally cannot.

## MAPLE VS. RICH SYRUP

Moscovado and turbinado sugar will give you similar flavor and texture to demerara in a simple syrup. Brown sugar will not work as well, but it'll be closer than white sugar. Alternatively, you can use maple syrup in place of rich demerara syrup; the sugar content will be about the same, and the flavor will be similar (if a bit more mapley).

## PUNT E MES

Two parts of sweet vermouth and one part of your favorite amaro (Campari, Cynar, etc.) will approximate the flavor of Punt e Mes.

# GLOSSARY

## Distilled Spirits

### ABSINTHE

A very high-proof (120°–150°) spirit traditionally flavored with wormwood, anise, and fennel. It is meant to be substantially diluted before drinking, giving the spirit a hazy appearance as dissolved hydrophobic flavor chemicals clump together. Mostly used in small doses in cocktails. Falsely charged with being a hallucinogen and banned for many years.

### APPLE BRANDY

A spirit distilled from apples, normally aged in oak. Often called **applejack** in the U.S., after a colonial-era product distilled from cider by freezing. **Calvados**, a French variety, is specified in some older cocktail guides. All these can be substituted for one another—just be sure you're using an actual apple brandy and not an apple-*flavored* grape brandy.

### BRANDY

A spirit distilled from fruits, especially grapes. The fruit is generally specified, e.g., apple brandy, peach brandy, plum brandy; if none is given, grape brandy is meant. Aged brandy is assumed in cocktails unless otherwise specified.

**Cognac** is produced in the French region of the same name, usually made from ugni blanc grapes and aged in French oak barrels. It is an ideal base for brandy cocktails and is often called for by name in old recipe books. "Cognac" is a contraction of *Cognac brandy* and should be capitalized.

**Pisco** is produced in Peru and Chile and is the national spirit of both. Peruvian pisco may not be aged in oak, while Chilean pisco can be but isn't necessarily; unaged pisco should be assumed unless otherwise specified.

### GIN

A spirit distilled like vodka and additionally flavored with juniper and other complementary botanicals, either by infusion or by vapor extraction during distillation. A similar spirit made in Scandinavia and flavored with caraway and dill instead of juniper is called **aquavit**.

**London dry gin** is the most common type of gin for cocktail use. It is heavy on juniper and citrus; no flavors may be added after distillation. Interestingly, it can be made anywhere in the world. **Plymouth gin** is a closely related style and a reliable alternative. Contemporary gins that use nontraditional botanicals—often at the juniper's expense—are sometimes grouped under the heading **New Western dry gin**.

All three of these styles are considered dry gins, in contrast to **Old Tom gin**. Popular in the nineteenth century and revived in the first decade of this one, it has a higher viscosity due to added sugar, barrel aging, or both.

## KIRSCHWASSER

An unaged cherry distillate traditionally produced in central Europe. Strongly flavored, it is used as an accent in cocktails, and appears as a base spirit only rarely. Often shortened to **kirsch**.

## MEZCAL

A spirit distilled from agave in certain regions of Mexico, especially Oaxaca. Its production process involves exposure to smoke over several days, which often imparts flavor to the finished spirit. Because the majority of mezcal is **joven**, or unaged, it is generally distinguished by the agave varietal used, **Espadin** being the most common. Mezcal can be made from any type of agave, including blue agave (although this is uncommon).

## RUM

A distilled spirit made from sugarcane and its derivatives, including cane juice, sugar, and molasses. Rums are classified by age, proof, country of origin, whether they're made from fresh cane juice or molasses, and whether any color has been added or removed. The common terms of light, white, silver, amber, gold, and dark are poor descriptors of rum; I avoid using them and encourage you to do the same.

The simplest categories in this book are **lightly aged rum**, which has spent 1–4 years aging in oak barrels, and **moderately aged rum**, which has spent 5–12 years aging in them. Lightly aged rum that has been filtered after aging to strip out the color imparted by the barrel is a specialty of Cuba and Puerto Rico, and is referred to in these pages as **filtered lightly aged rum**. Invariably some flavor is

also removed, so this is the lightest common variety of rum there is.

Many rums also have color *added*, and some are additionally sweetened. A rum that is ink-dark has almost certainly had both done; barrel aging turns spirits golden-brown, not black. There are valid uses for such products, and I have borrowed Martin Cate's term **black rum** to describe them.

**Jamaican rum** is known for an explosive density of aromatic esters, conveying fruity and rummy scents with a hint of wild fermentation. **Demerara rum** comes from a region of Guyana by that name and is known for its distinctively earthy, smoky, burntsugar taste. Demerara rums are often sweetened or colored at least a little. A very high-proof expression is also common, which I've called for here as **151-proof Demerara rum**.

**Cane rum** or **cane juice rum**, which in certain areas is called **rhum agricole**, is distilled from fresh sugarcane juice rather than from molasses. These rums tend to have green, grassy, or even savory flavors, particularly the lauded **Martinique rhum agricole**. The Brazilian spirit **cachaça** (kuh–SHAH–suh) is also distilled from cane juice; it can often be substituted for a rhum agricole or cane juice rum of similar age (and vice versa). Cachaça available in the U.S. is usually unaged, but much of it spends at least a year in barrels made from oak or native Brazilian woods.

## TEQUILA

A spirit distilled from blue agave in one of five regions of Mexico, especially Jalisco. Tequila is further classified by how long it's aged in oak:

not at all for **blanco,** 2–12 months for **reposado,** and 1–3 years for **añejo. Mixto tequila** is a blend of 51% tequila with 49% neutral grain spirit; it's the kind that gave you terrible hangovers in college and is called for nowhere in this book.

## VODKA

A spirit distilled from *anything,* generally until it is as close to pure ethanol as Nature allows, then blended with water until it reaches a potable strength. Known as **grain alcohol** or **neutral grain spirit(s)** if the dilution step is skipped. Contrary to what you may have heard, vodka is neither forbidden nor required to be made from potatoes.

## WHISKEY

A class of distilled spirit made from cereal grains, most commonly barley, corn, and rye. Typically aged in oak barrels after distillation. Spelled "whisky" for products from Scotland, Japan, and Canada.

There are two major types of American whiskey. **Rye,** or **rye whiskey,** is distilled from at least 51% rye grain and aged in oak barrels. **Bourbon** is distilled from at least 51% corn and aged in new American oak barrels which have been charred on the inside. Most bourbon comes from Kentucky, but it can be made anywhere in the U.S. American **blended whiskey** is a bottled mixture of whiskey and neutral grain spirit, intended to have some whiskey flavor but a lighter body and lower production costs. It should be avoided.

**Scotch,** or **Scotch whisky,** is made in Scotland and generally exposed to peat smoke during its production, which may give an earthy, smoky taste to the finished spirit. Particular flavors are associated with the whiskies from certain Scottish regions, including the especially smoky and peaty **Islay whisky.** A **single malt Scotch** is distilled from 100% malted barley at a single distillery; a **blended Scotch** combines a single malt with other Scottish whiskies, whether single malts from other distilleries or whiskies distilled from other grains. Blended Scotch is assumed in cocktails unless otherwise specified. "Scotch" is a contraction of *Scotch whisky,* and should be capitalized.

**Irish whiskey** is made in Ireland, generally either distilled from barley or made by blending barley whiskey with a whiskey distilled from other grains. It usually lacks the peat-smoke flavor of Scotch. Single malt Irish whiskies do exist, but the most traditional style is known today as **single pot still Irish whiskey** and made from a combination of grains that includes at least 30% malted barley and 30% unmalted barley.

# Wine

An alcoholic beverage made by fermenting grapes. Most of the wines we encounter have additionally been fortified, aromatized, or both. A **fortified wine is one** to which distilled spirits have been added, while an **aromatized wine** has been flavored with herbs and spices.

Both are generally sweeter than ordinary wine. **Port** and **sherry** are fortified wines, while **vermouth** and **quinquina** are both fortified and aromatized.

## KINA APÉRITIF WINE

Not a standard industry term, but used in this book to refer to any fortified and aromatized wine considered an acceptable substitute for the discontinued product Kina Lillet. Its modern descendant, Lillet Blanc, makes a lackluster replacement in its recipes.

Historically, Kina Lillet was a **quinquina**, a type of fortified and aromatized wine flavored with quinine and other spices. Other prominent quinquinas like Dubonnet and Byrrh make poor substitutes for it and for one another.

The best replacements are certain recently released quinquinas which include "Kina" in the brand name to telegraph their purpose, and **Cocchi Americano**, which is confusingly both a quinquina *and* an americano, a type of fortified wine flavored and bittered with gentian root.

Americano is considered a subtype of quinquina by some sources and a wholly separate category by others; the truth is that the two *can* overlap, but don't necessarily.

## PORT

A fortified wine originating in Portugal. The fortification occurs before fermentation is finished, leaving some of the natural sugars behind and making port particularly sweet. Comes in two varieties: the younger, sweeter **ruby port** and the drier, aged **tawny port.** Also called **port wine.**

## SHERRY

A Spanish fortified wine, aged using a *solera* system whereby new wine is added to existing aging stock in a barrel as some of the old mixture is drawn off. The major varieties, from dry to sweet, are **fino, manzanilla, amontillado, palo cortado**, and **oloroso. Cream sherries** have been sweetened, usually by blending with sweet wines. All sherry recipes in this book are tailored to amontillado, which is a good middle-of-the-road option for cocktails. For recipes where something richer is desired, oloroso makes a good alternative.

## SPARKLING WINE

A wine which has been carbonated through either fermentation or the direct addition of carbon dioxide gas. In cocktails, a dry sparkling white wine should be assumed. The gold standard is **Champagne**, made according to traditional methods in that region of France; American sparkling wines, as well as Spanish **cava** and Italian **prosecco**, can also work well in cocktails and are frequently less expensive.

## VERMOUTH

A fortified and aromatized wine, traditionally flavored and bittered with wormwood and other spices. Open bottles of vermouth should always be refrigerated.

**Dry vermouth**, also known as **French vermouth** or **Marseilles dry vermouth,** is pale in color and contains up to 40 grams of sugar per liter. **Sweet vermouth**, also known as **Italian vermouth**, is red and contains up to 150 grams of sugar per liter. These are the two most important types for cocktail use, but there is also **blanc** or **bianco vermouth**, which is as sweet as Italian vermouth but has a different botanical blend and no color.

**Punt e Mes** is an Italian product combining two parts sweet vermouth and one part amaro. This style of vermouth is sometimes called **vermouth con bitter**.

# Liqueurs

A product made by sweetening a distilled spirit and flavoring it, generally with fruits, spices, or both. Often but not always bottled at less than 40% ABV, with the 15%–30% ABV range sometimes called **liqueur strength**. The base is usually a neutral distillate, but it is not uncommon for it to be brandy, and other spirits are used from time to time. **Apricot liqueur** and **elderflower liqueur** appear in this book, in addition to the following special varieties.

### ALLSPICE DRAM

A traditional Jamaican liqueur, made with a rum base and flavored with allspice. Also called **pimento dram**.

### BÉNÉDICTINE

A traditional French liqueur with a flavor of honey and baking spice.

### CHARTREUSE (SHAR–TROOZE)

A brandy-based liqueur made by French monks according to a secret recipe with over one hundred ingredients. Comes in two varieties: the milder, 80-proof **Yellow Chartreuse**, and the bolder, 110-proof **Green Chartreuse**.

### CHERRY HEERING

A Danish spiced cherry liqueur aged in oak barrels, produced since 1818. Properly called **Heering Cherry Liqueur** and occasionally called **Peter Heering**, but Cherry Heering is the most common term.

### CRÈME DE [X]

A type of liqueur that contains at least 250 grams of sugar per liter (or 400 grams in the case of **crème de cassis**), which increases the viscosity and the perceived textural creaminess of the drink. It is generally mixed or used in cooking rather than consumed on its own. "[X]" is the French name for the principal flavor; this book includes **crème de menthe**, **crème de cacao**, **crème de mûre**, and **crème de violette**, which refer respectively to mint-, chocolate-, blackberry-, and violet-flavored liqueurs.

### CURAÇAO (KER–UH–SOW) & TRIPLE SEC

Traditionally, a liqueur flavored with the peels of the *laraha* fruit, a bitter orange native to the Caribbean island of **Curaçao**, often made with a rum or brandy base and additional spices. Sometimes spelled "curacao" or "curacoa" in old cocktail books.

**Triple sec** is a similar product, usually with a more neutral spirit base than curaçao has. Both are now commonly used to refer to any sort of orange liqueur regardless of origin or production process.

### FALERNUM

A low-proof Caribbean liqueur with a rum base, traditionally flavored with ginger and baking spices, and often with accents of nuts and lime. Sometimes available as a nonalcoholic syrup.

### MARASCHINO

A liqueur made by sweetening a distillate of marasca cherries, traditionally produced on the Dalmatian coast.

# Bitters

An infusion of herbs and spices in alcohol (or, occasionally, glycerin). *Nonpotable* bitters is considered by the U.S. government to be too unpleasant to drink on its own, and is therefore regulated as a grocery product rather than beverage alcohol. *Potable bitters* is similarly produced but is considered beverage alcohol under U.S. law.

### AMARI

A general term for bitter digestif liqueurs from Italy, increasingly also used to refer to similar products regardless of origin (such a spirit might otherwise be called a *bitter*). The plural is *amari*. Noteworthy examples include **Campari**, described below, as well as the earthy **Amaro Nonino** and the artichoke-based **Cynar**.

### CAMPARI & APEROL

**Campari** is a brilliantly red Italian amaro with a pronounced citrus note. Bracing, intense, and somewhat heavy. Many competing products are now available, giving rise to a category sometimes called **red bitter** or **Italian red bitter.**

**Aperol** is a lower-proof and lighterbodied product with a color and flavor that are otherwise similar to Campari. Products intended to compete with Aperol will usually be promoted as *aperitivi*.

### COCKTAIL BITTERS

A type of nonpotable bitters that chiefly uses drops or dashes at a time to aromatize cocktails. The most common example is **Angostura bitters**, a Trinidadian product with a pronounced spice flavor; products

designed to compete with it are generally labeled **aromatic bitters.**

The traditional New Orleans bitters is a proprietary product called **Peychaud's**, with flavors of stonefruit and anise. The third major category is **orange bitters**, which many companies produce.

Other bitters flavors exist. In this book, we specifically encounter **peach bitters**, which is self-explanatory, and **Boker's bitters**, a modern reconstruction of a popular nineteenth-century style that had a woodsy aroma with notes of cardamom and coffee.

### CARCIOFO

A style of amaro flavored with artichoke (*carciofo* is the Italian word for "artichoke"). The best-known example is **Cynar** (chee–NARR). Many cocktail guides call for it by brand name rather than by category, because other carciofi are scarce in most markets.

# Nonalcoholic

### AGAVE

A genus of succulents native to Mexico and nearby regions, from species of which mezcal and tequila are made (the reason they are sometimes collectively termed **agave spirits**). The juice of agave plants may also be refined into a sweetener known as **agave syrup**.

### CONDENSED MILK

Milk that has had a portion of its water removed, and ordinarily to which sugar has also been added. Both modifications are intended to preserve the milk.

**Evaporated milk** is an unsweetened version of this product, available in some markets as **unsweetened condensed milk.**

## CREAM

A dairy product made by separating fresh milk and concentrating its fat. Under U.S. regulations, **heavy cream** has a fat content of at least 36%, while **light cream** has a fat content between 18% and 30%. **Half-and-half** is a mixture of milk and cream with a total milk fat percentage between 10½% and 18%. (Milk, for reference, is about 3½% fat.)

## DEMERARA SUGAR

A less processed form of sugar which retains more of the flavor and characteristics of molasses than white sugar does. Useful for adding richness to cocktails. **Brown sugar** is refined white sugar which has had some molasses added back in.

## FASSIONOLA

A fruit syrup with a passion fruit base. Comes in red, gold, and green varieties, each with its own flavor; the fruit punch flavored red type should be assumed in cocktail recipes unless otherwise specified. Known as *passionola* until the mid-twentieth century.

## FLOWER WATER

A type of **hydrosol**, that is, a mixture of water and water-soluble aromatic chemicals extracted from a flower. Used in perfumes and confections, and occasionally in cocktails. **Orange flower water**, which is made from orange blossoms, and **rose water** appear in this book.

## GINGER ALE

A sweet soda with a mild ginger flavor. A more robustly flavored or alcoholic version is generally called **ginger beer**.

## GRENADINE

A syrup made from pomegranate juice and sugar, occasionally with distilled spirits or citrus accents added. In the United States, the term is commonly used for red-flavored corn syrup, but the word comes from the French for pomegranate (*grenade*), and this is the essential flavor in cocktails that call for grenadine.

## LIME CORDIAL

Preserved sweetened lime juice, developed as an antiscorbutic for use by the Royal Navy. The most flavorful ones incorporate lime oils from the peels or leaves in addition to the juice and sugar.

## ORGEAT

A traditional French syrup made from almonds, generally accented with orange flower water or other floral or citrus components. Pronunciation of this word is agreed upon by no one. Personally, I favor "or–ZHAH."

## SELTZER

Carbonated water to which nothing else has been added. **Club soda** is carbonated water with mineral salts added to imitate the flavor and texture of naturally occurring (and often naturally carbonated) **mineral water**. **Soda water** or **sparkling water** can refer to any of these. While distinct in flavor, other carbonated waters are usually satisfactory replacements for seltzer in cocktails.

# General Terminology

## AGED

Describes a spirit that has spent some time in a wooden barrel, usually one made of oak. The substances within the spirit react with one another and chemicals from the barrel walls so that its flavor profile evolves over time. Aging usually only refers to time spent in the barrel; any time spent in a nonreactive container, such as a stainless steel tank, may be considered **resting** instead, and is not normally counted toward the spirit's age.

## APERITIF

Any beverage intended to open or wake up the palate before other things are consumed. Generally dry, light in body and alcohol, and mildly bitter, sour, or saline.

## COLLINS

A category of drink that is prepared in a tall glass with ice—rather than being shaken or stirred in a separate vessel—and then filled with seltzer. Intended to be drunk slowly as the ice melts and chills it, rather than quickly like a **fizz**.

## DIGESTIF

Any beverage meant to seal off the palate after a meal and, traditionally, to aid in digestion. Usually strongly flavored, higher proof than an aperitif, and noticeably bitter and sweet.

## DOWN

A mixed drink served in a stemless glass without ice.

## DRY

In describing an alcoholic beverage, the opposite of sweet. May imply spirituousness or astringency.

## DUO

As defined by Gary Regan, a cocktail comprising a spirit and a liqueur. If a cream element is also included, it becomes a **trio**.

## FIX

A preparation from the nineteenth century akin to an individual punch or a fancy sour; also sometimes used to refer to shaken cocktails served on the rocks, in the absence of a more precise name for such drinks.

## FIZZ

A category of drink that is shaken to chill and then topped with seltzer without the addition of ice. Intended to be drunk quickly, like a shorter cocktail; rather than lingered over, like a **Collins**.

## FLIP

A category of drink that is shaken with a whole egg. Generally served cold and dusted with nutmeg.

## MARTINI

A cocktail consisting of gin (or vodka, if specified) with dry vermouth, a lemon twist or cocktail olive, and optionally orange bitters, and not one other godforsaken thing.

## NEAT

A straight spirit or other unmixed drink, served in a stemless glass without ice.

## [ON THE] ROCKS

A drink, mixed or otherwise, served in a stemless glass with ice.

## PIQUANT

A substance that induces a mild irritation of the trigeminal nerve, particularly one that creates a false burning sensation. **Pungent** is the scientific term for this phenomenon as a whole, with **piquant** reserved for less intense cases—like the ones in this book.

## PROOF

A measurement that corresponds to twice the percentage of ethanol in a spirit, which may be indicated using the degree sign (º)—e.g., a 45% ABV spirit could be described as ninety proof or 90º, both vocalized the same way. In this book, a **standard-proof spirit** is in the ballpark of 80º, a **high-proof spirit** is in the ballpark of 100º, and an **overproof spirit** is appreciably higher, in the 130º–150º range. Recipes should be assumed to call for standard-proof spirits unless otherwise specified.

## SLING

A spirit to which sugar and water have been added.

## SMASH

A category of drink in which herbs and citrus fruits are added to the shaker, their oils mechanically expressed by jostling with the ice and other ingredients.

## SOUR

A general term for mixed drinks with significant acidity, normally derived from citrus fruits.

## UP

A mixed drink served in a stemmed glass.

# TOPICS FOR CONTINUING EDUCATION

Further study of cocktails requires delving into more specific topics. Here are some recommended reading lists for such subject-specific graduate work:

**Cocktail Science:** *Liquid Intelligence* by Dave Arnold; *On Food and Cooking* by Harold McGee; *Craft Cocktails at Home* by Kevin Liu; *Proof* by Adam Rogers; *Distilled Knowledge* by Brian D. Hoefling

**Mixological Theory:** *The Fine Art of Mixing Drinks* by David Embury; *The Joy of Mixology* by Gary Regan; *Cocktail Codex* by Alex Day, David Kaplan, and Nick Fauchald; *Regarding Cocktails* by Sasha Petraske, with Georgette Moger-Petraske

**How to be a Bartender:** *Meehan's Bartender Manual* by Jim Meehan; *The Ideal Bartender* by Tom Bullock; *Harry Johnson's Bartenders Manual* by Harry Johnson; *The Joy of Mixology*

**Cocktail History (Primary Sources):** *How to Mix Drinks; or, The Bon-Vivant's Companion* by Jerry Thomas; *Harry Johnson's Bartenders Manual*; *The Savoy Cocktail Book* by Harry Craddock; *Harry of Ciro's ABC of Mixing Cocktails* and *Barflies and Cocktails* by Harry MacElhone; *The Old Waldorf-Astoria Bar Book* by Albert Stevens Crockett; *Recipes for Mixed Drinks* by Hugo Ensslin; *The Gentleman's Companion*, vol. 2, by Charles H. Baker Jr.

**Cocktail History (Secondary Sources):** *Imbibe!* and *Punch* by David Wondrich; *Vintage Spirits and Forgotten Cocktails* by Ted Haigh; *And a Bottle of Rum* by Wayne Curtis; *A Proper Drink* by Robert Simonson

**Tiki Cocktails & History:** *Smuggler's Cove* by Martin Cate, with Rebecca Cate; *Beachbum Berry Remixed* and *Sippin' Safari* by Jeff "Beachbum" Berry; *Minimalist Tiki* by Matt Pietrek and Carrie Smith; and, if you can find a copy, *Trader Vic's Bartender's Guide*

**Boston Cocktails & History:** *Drink and Tell* and *Drunk and Told* by Fred Yarm; *Drinking Boston* by Stephanie Schorow; "Periodista Tales" by Devin Hahn (digital source)

**Contemporary Mixology:** *The Craft of the Cocktail* by Dale Degroff; *The PDT Cocktail Book* by Jim Meehan; *Speakeasy* by Jason Kosmas and Dushan Zaric; *Death & Co: Modern Classic Cocktails* by Alex Day, David Kaplan, and Nick Fauchald; *The Bar Book* by Jeffrey Morgenthaler; *beta cocktails* by Kirk Estopinal and Maksym Pazuniak; *Drinking Like Ladies* by Kitty Amann and Misty Kalkofen; *Regarding Cocktails*; *Liquid Intelligence*

# SELECTED BIBLIOGRAPHY

These are the most important sources for understanding the development of cocktails and the mixological principles set forth.

Arnold, Dave. *Liquid Intelligence*. New York: W. W. Norton, 2014.

Arthur, Stany Clisby. *Famous New Orleans Drinks and How to Mix 'em*. New Orleans, LA: Harmanson, 1938.

Baiocchi, Talia. *Sherry*. Berkeley, CA: Ten Speed Press, 2014.

Baker, Charles H., Jr. *The Gentleman's Companion*, vol. 2. New York: The Derrydale Press, 1939.

Berry, Jeff. *Beachbum Berry Remixed*. San Jose, CA: SLG Publishing, 2010.

———. *Beachbum Berry's Total Tiki*. V. 1.2.7. Doudoroff LLC, 2014. iOS 10.0 or later.

———. *Sippin' Safari*. New York: Cocktail Kingdom, 2017.

Boudreau, Jamie. "Amer Picon." *spiritsandcocktails.com* (blog), Sept. 9, 2007. https://spiritsandcocktails.wordpress.com/2007/09/09/amer-picon/.

Brown, Derek, with Robert Yule. *Spirits Sugar Water Bitters*. New York: Rizzoli, 2018.

Bruni, Frank. "Smitten With a Cocktail Called Frisco." *New York Times* online, Oct. 28, 2010. https://www.nytimes.com/2010/10/29/dining/29tipsy.html.

Bullock, Tom. *The Ideal Bartender*. St. Louis, MO: Buxton & Skinner, 1917.

Cate, Martin, with Rebecca Cate. *Smuggler's Cove*. Berkeley, CA: Ten Speed Press, 2016.

Choong, Kim. "Jungle Bird—The True Facts." ThirstMag.com, Feb. 25, 2020. https://thirstmag.com/drinks/The-truth-about-Jungle-Bird-classic-cocktail.

Clarke, Paul. *The Cocktail Chronicles*. Nashville, TN: Spring House Press, 2015.

Cotton, Leo. *Mr. Boston Official Bartender's Guide: 75th Anniversary Edition*. Edited by Jonathan Pogash with Rick Rodgers. Hoboken, NJ: John Wiley & Sons, Inc., 2012.

Craddock, Harry. *The Savoy Cocktail Book*. London: Pavilion Books, 2011.

Crockett, Albert Stevens. *The Old Waldorf-Astoria Bar Book*. New York: A. S. Crockett, 1935.

Dagan-Wiener, A., Nissim, I., Ben Abu, N., et al. "Bitter or Not? BitterPredict, a Tool for Predicting Taste from Chemical Structure." *Scientific Reports* 7 (2017). https://doi.org/10.1038/s41598-017-12359-7.

Day, Alex, Nick Fauchald, and David Kaplan. *Death & Co*. New York: Ten Speed Press, 2014.

Day, Alex, Nick Fauchald, and David Kaplan, with Devon Tarby. *Cocktail Codex*. New York: Ten Speed Press, 2018.

Degroff, Dale. *The New Craft of the Cocktail*. New York: Clarkson Potter, 2020.

Difford, Simon. "French 75 Cocktail – Recipes and History." *Difford's Guide*. https://www.diffordsguide.com/encyclopedia/1267/cocktails/french-75-cocktail-recipes-and-history.

———. "Future Classic Cocktails." *Difford's Guide*, Sept. 6, 2019. https://www.diffordsguide.com/encyclopedia/1758/cocktails/future-classic-cocktails.

Embury, David. *The Fine Art of Mixing Drinks*. New York: Mud Puddle Books, 2009.

English, Camper. "The Complicated Aging Process for Cognac, as Seen at Cognac Hardy." *Alcademics* (blog), Feb. 25, 2015. https://www.alcademics.com/2015/02/the-complicated-aging-process-for-cognac-as-seen-at-cognac-hardy.html.

———. "The History of Grenadine Use in Cocktails: Literature Review." *Alcademics* (blog), Dec. 18, 2012. https://www.alcademics.com/2012/12/the-history-of-grenadine-use-in-cocktails.html.

———. "What's the Difference Between Orange Curacao and Triple Sec?" *Alcademics* (blog), Feb. 21, 2011. https://www.alcademics.com/2011/02/whats-the-difference-between-orange-curacao-and-triple-sec-.html.

Ensslin, Hugo R. *Recipes for Mixed Drinks*, 2nd ed. Self-published, 1917.

"Falernum Files: A Q&A with Richard Seale." *The Sugarcane Press* (blog), Nov. 11, 2018. http://www.thesugarcanepress.com/falernum-files-a-qa-with-richard-seale/.

Fleming, Ian. *Casino Royale*. London: Penguin Books, 2002.

Ford, Doug. "The Diamondback Cocktail." *Cold Glass* (blog), Mar. 7, 2015. https://cold-glass.com/2015/03/07/the-diamondback-cocktail/.

Gillman, Gary. "How Irish Whiskey Became Blended (Part I)." *Beer Et Seq* (blog), Oct. 24, 2019. https://www.beeretseq.com/how-irish-whiskey-became-blended-part-i/.

Greene, Philip. *To Have and Have Another*. New York: Perigee Books, 2012.

Hahn, Devin. "Periodista Tales." *DevinHahnFilms.com* (blog), 2010–11. https://www.devinhahnfilms.com/2010/08/01/periodista-tales-the-monteleone/.

Haigh, Ted. *Vintage Spirits and Forgotten Cocktails Deluxe Edition*. Beverly, MA: Quarry Books, 2009.

Harwell, Richard Barksdale. *The Mint Julep*. Charlottesville, VA: University of Virginia Press, 2005.

Judge Jr. *Here's How!* New York: Leslie-Judge Company, 1927.

Kappeler, George J. *Modern American Drinks*. Akron, OH: Saalfield Publishing Co., 1906.

Kirkmeyer, Sarah V., and Beverly J. Tepper. "Understanding Creaminess Perception of Dairy Products Using Free-Choice Profiling and Genetic Responsivity to 6-n-Propylthiouracil." *Chemical Senses* 28, no. 6 (July 2003): 527–36.

Kosmas, Jason, and Dushan Zaric. *Speakeasy*. Berkeley, CA: Ten Speed Press, 2010.

Lancashire, Robert J. "The Chemistry of Passion Fruit." Feb. 18, 2014. http://wwwchem.uwimona.edu.jm/lectures/psnfruit.html

Liu, Kevin. *Craft Cocktails at Home*. Self-published, 2013.

MacElhone, Harry. *Barflies and Cocktails*. Paris: Lecram Press, 1927.

———. *Harry of Ciro's ABC of Mixing Cocktails*. London: Christopher & Co., 1923.

McGee, Harold. *On Food and Cooking*. New York: Scribner, 2004.

Meehan, Jim. *Meehan's Bartender Manual*. New York: Ten Speed Press, 2017.

———. *The PDT Cocktail Book*. New York: Sterling Epicure, 2011.

Mennies, Leah. "Can Boston's Only Classic Cocktail Make a Comeback?" *Punch*, Nov. 25, 2015. https://punchdrink.com/articles/boston-classic-cocktail-ward-eight-cocktail-recipe-and-history/.

Morgenthaler, Jeffrey. "How to Make Ginger Syrup Without a Mess, While Avoiding Shredded Knuckles." Food Republic, Jan. 22, 2015. https://jeffreymorgenthaler.com/how-to-make-ginger-syrup-without-a-mess-while-avoiding-shredded-knuckles/.

——."How to Make Your Own Lime Cordial (Rose's Lime Juice)." Jeffrey Morgenthaler, Aug. 8, 2018. https://jeffreymorgenthaler.com/lime-cordial/.

——. "I Make the Best Amaretto Sour in the World." Jeffrey Morgenthaler, Feb. 9, 2012. https://jeffreymorgenthaler.com/i-make-the-best-amaretto-sour-in-the-world/.

Moss, Robert F. "Tale of Two Derbies (Brown Ones)." *Robert F. Moss* (blog), Aug. 20, 2017.

Mustipher, Shannon. *Tiki*. New York: Rizzoli, 2019.

Newman, Kara. "Hack Your Drink: The 'Regal Shake' Technique." *Punch*, Mar. 2, 2018. https://punchdrink.com/articles/hack-your-drink-regal-shake-cocktail-recipe-technique/.

North, Sterling, and Carl Kroch, eds. *So Red the Nose, or, Breath in the Afternoon*. New York: Farrar & Rinehart, 1935.

Peters, Nathaniel. "The Virtues of the Speakeasy." *First Things* online, Mar. 30, 2012. https://www.firstthings.com/web-exclusives/2012/03/the-virtues-of-the-speakeasy.

Petraske, Sasha, with Georgette Moger-Petraske. *Regarding Cocktails*. New York: Phaidon, 2016.

Pietrek, Matt. "Days of Dunder." *Cocktail Wonk* (blog), Mar. 11, 2016. https://cocktailwonk.com/2016/03/days-of-dunder-setting-the-record-straight-on-jamaican-rums-mystery-ingredient.html.

Pietrek, Matt, and Carrie Smith. *Minimalist Tiki*. WonkPress, 2019.

Regan, Gary. *The Joy of Mixology, Revised and Updated Edition*. New York: Clarkson Potter, 2018.

Schorow, Stephanie. *Drinking Boston*. Boston: Union Park Press, 2012.

Simonson, Robert. *The Martini Cocktail*. New York: Ten Speed Press, 2019.

——. *A Proper Drink*. Berkeley, CA: Ten Speed Press, 2016.

——. "The Rise and Fall of the Aviation Cocktail." *Punch*, Dec. 7, 2017. https://punchdrink.com/articles/aviation-cocktail-recipe-history-rise-and-fall/.

Steinbeck, John. *Sweet Thursday*. New York: Penguin, 2008.

Sullivan, Jere. *The Drinks of Yesteryear*. New Haven, CT: Self-published, 1930.

Sutcliffe, Theodora. "Ngiam Tong Boon." *Difford's Guide*. https://www.diffordsguide.com/people/51771/ngiam-tong-boon.

Tarling, W. J. *Café Royal Cocktail Book*. London: Publications from Pall Mall Ltd., 1937.

Thomas, Jerry. *The Bar-Tenders' Guide*. New York: Dick & Fitzgerald, 1862.

Trader Vic. *Trader Vic's Bartender's Guide*. Garden City, NY: Doubleday & Company, 1972.

Wondrich, David. "The Birth, Death & Rebirth of Irish Single Pot-Still Whiskey." *Daily Beast*, Oct. 27, 2018. https://www.thedailybeast.com/the-birth-death-and-rebirth-of-irish-single-pot-still-whiskey.

——. *Imbibe!* New York: Penguin, 2015.

——. "Please Leave My Classic Cocktail Alone." *Daily Beast*, Apr. 13, 2017. https://www.thedailybeast.com/please-leave-my-classic-cocktail-alone.

Yarm, Fred. *Boston Cocktails*. Self-published, Cocktail Virgin Industries, 2017.

——. *Drink & Tell*. Self-published, Cocktail Virgin Industries, 2012.

Zimmerman, Armin. "Quaker's Cocktail" (German). Bar Vademecum, Mar. 18, 2018. https://bar-vademecum.de/quakers-cocktail/.

# ACKNOWLEDGMENTS

It is always the case, in something so long in the works as this book, that more people have in some way had an impact upon it than the author can recall when the time comes to acknowledge them in print. I am grateful to scores of people for their encouragement and insight over the years, and to the following for their particular contributions to *The Cocktail Seminars*:

First, and most useful to future authors reading this, is the Exposition Universelle des Vins et Spiritueux, for maintaining a free online library of vintage cocktail books, without which my and others' historical research would have been immensely more difficult.

Many people assisted with the recipe testing process for this book (and for *Classic Cocktails*, which I drew on substantially in writing this one). Thank you to Jason Adams, Denise Alfonso, Ozair Ali, Emma Alles, Nick Andersen, Alyssa Bilinski, Alan Bishop, Luke Bradford, John Brewer, Steve Corman, Christopher Ell, Caroline Fenn, Anna Flores-Amper and her entire family, Jessica Leigh Graves, Carlos M. Greaves, Nick Groh, Allison Hadley, Derek Johnston, Brian Lagoda, Oren Lurie, Luke Massa, Sam Meyer, Angela Michaud, Michael Mitchell, Reed Morgan, Ayesha Nishtar, Rachel Orol, Liz Palazzolo, Keith Parker, Will Rasky, Katie Renshaw, Cristina Ruiz, Leah Libresco Sargeant, Maria Schwarz, Ritchie J. Suffling, Josh Terrill, and Steffi Weinraub, for helping ensure that the recipes in this book would be of the highest possible quality and have the broadest possible appeal.

I am also grateful to those who have helped me with other research, including Kelli Billstein, Jackson Cannon, Martin Cate, Lauren Clark, Lee Edwards, Camper English, Eric Felten, Lee Morgan, Jake Parrott, Jared Sadoian, Bob Sennett, Ezra Star, Jon Theris, and Fred Yarm. Thanks are particularly due to Matt Pietrek, for helping me work out this book's rum categorization system; and to Jeff Berry, Dan Huntley, and Martin Lindsay, for sharing unpublished information about fassionola's history in cocktails.

To Sandra Azzalina, David and James Querusio, and Molly Jarvis, thank you for the cocktail books you gave me early on, without which none of this would have happened. To George Donnelly, Matthew Schmitz, and Tristyn Wade, thank you for those early writing opportunities which began my career. To Shannon Fabricant, you were responsible for the existence of my first book, and of all the others by extension; I can never thank you enough. And to my parents, thank you for your supportive indulgence of the quixotic way in which I spend my life.

I am grateful to the whole team at Abbeville Press for their dedication and their customarily excellent work, in particular to copy editor Ashley Benning and designer Misha Beletsky for getting this book ready for prime time.

To my editor, Lauren Bucca, thank you for deftly shepherding this process past every obstacle, and for everything you did to help the abstract notions in my head be realized on the page. To David Fabricant, thank you for inviting me back and giving me the opportunity to write something I'd been wanting to for a very long time. It has been an honor and a pleasure to work with both of you again.

Special thanks are due to Alexander Michaud, Andrea Zurita, and in particular Elizabeth Aslinger, who in our quarantined times served as my core brain trust for testing recipes that were new to this book and offering extramural feedback on my writing. This book would not be what it is without you.

Finally, my sincerest and most heartfelt thanks to the participants in Mixology 110b, the original cocktail seminar from which this book ultimately derives. No one, least of all me, could have foreseen this at the time. To Nadia Danford, John Karpinski, and Ben Schenkel, thank you for being a part of this; to Master Pitti, thank you for allowing it to happen; to Chelsea Cole, Scarlett Lee, Danae Sossidis, and Kyle Torres, thank you for concocting the idea for the class with me in the first place; and to Clare Sachsse and my eventual co-instructor Jon Rubin, thank you both for your involvement in the original cocktail seminar and in the writing process for this book. I am grateful to all of you, and I hope that this unlikely epilogue to our senior year of college brings as much joy to you as it does to me.

# INDEX OF COCKTAILS BY NAME

# INDEX OF COCKTAILS BY BASE

## PHOTOGRAPHY CREDITS

# CONVERSIONS

1 tsp. = ⅙ oz.

1½ tsp. = ¼ oz.

32 oz. = 4 cups = 2 pints = 1 quart

750 mL is a little more than 25 oz.

juice of ½ lime ≈ ½ oz.

juice of ½ lemon ≈ ¾ oz.

juice of 1 lime ≈ 1 oz.

juice of 1 lemon ≈ 1½ oz.

1 sugar cube ≈ 1 tsp. sugar

1 tsp. of sugar or 2:1 simple syrup ≈ ¼ oz. of 1:1 simple syrup

## A NOTE ON THE DASH

According to cocktail scientist Don Lee, there are about forty-one dashes of Angostura to the ounce, and thirty dashes of Peychaud's or Regan's orange bitters. He has not, to my knowledge, tested any version of Boker's, but this gives us a reasonable benchmark of ~ 5–7 dashes to the teaspoon. Just remember that any time an ingredient is measured in dashes, it is expected to admit some variation each time a drink is made—"a dash is whatever squirts out of the top of the bottle," as David Wondrich puts it—while greater precision is intended when something is listed in teaspoons.

Project Editors: Lauren Bucca and David Fabricant
Copy Editor: Ashley Benning
Design: David Fabricant and Misha Beletsky
Production Manager: Louise Kurtz

First edition
10  9  8  7  6  5  4  3  2  1

*Library of Congress Cataloging-in-Publication Data*
Names: Hoefling, Brian D., author.
Title: The cocktail seminars / Brian D. Hoefling.
Description: First edition. | New York : Abbeville Press Publishers, [2021]
  | Includes bibliographical references and index. | Summary: "A thorough
  mixological education for all cocktail enthusiasts, with colorful
  infographics"—Provided by the publisher.
Identifiers: LCCN 2021005930 | ISBN 9780789214003 (hardcover)
Subjects: LCSH: Cocktails. | LCGFT: Cookbooks.
Classification: LCC TX951 .H5854 2021 | DDC 641.87/4—dc23
LC record available at https://lccn.loc.gov/2021005930

For bulk and premium sales and for text adoption procedures, write to Customer Service Manager, Abbeville Press, 655 Third Avenue, New York, NY 10017, or call 1-800-ARTBOOK.

Visit Abbeville Press online at www.abbeville.com.